MW01119617

Humber College Library
3199 Lakeshore Blvd. West
Toronto, ON   M8V 1K8

REIMAGINING
Shakespeare's
PLAYHOUSE

EARLY MODERN
STAGING CONVENTIONS
IN THE
TWENTIETH CENTURY

Numerous attempts have been made in the modern and postmodern era to recreate the staging conventions of Shakespeare's theatre, by directors from William Poel and Harley Granville Barker to Tyrone Guthrie, and, most recently, the founders of the New Globe. The work of these directors is examined within this volume, analyzing their practical successes and failures; it also engages with the ideological critiques of early modern staging advanced by scholars such as W. B. Worthen and Ric Knowles. The author argues that rather than indulging in archaism for its own sake, the movement looked backward in a progressive attempt to address the challenges of the twentieth century. Such staging therefore provides, as George Bernard Shaw noted in connection to the work of William Poel over a century ago, a "picture of the past" which is "really a picture of the future." A conclusion to the book discusses the ongoing potential of early modern staging in the new millennium.

DR JOE FALOCCO is Lecturer in English, Communication and Integrative Arts, Penn State Erie, The Behrend College.

REIMAGINING
Shakespeare's
PLAYHOUSE

EARLY MODERN
STAGING CONVENTIONS
IN THE
TWENTIETH CENTURY

Joe Falocco

D. S. BREWER

HUMBER LIBRARIES LAKESHORE CAMPUS
3199 Lakeshore Blvd West
TORONTO, ON.   M8V 1K8

© Joe Falocco 2010

All Rights Reserved. Except as permitted under current legislation
no part of this work may be photocopied, stored in a retrieval system,
published, performed in public, adapted, broadcast, transmitted,
recorded or reproduced in any form or by any means,
without the prior permission of the copyright owner

The right of Joe Falocco to be identified as the author of this work
has been asserted in accordance with sections 77 and 78 of
the Copyright, Designs and Patents Act 1988

First published 2010
D. S. Brewer, Cambridge

ISBN 978-1-84384-241-5

D. S. Brewer is an imprint of Boydell & Brewer Ltd
PO Box 9, Woodbridge, Suffolk IP12 3DF, UK
and of Boydell & Brewer Inc.
668 Mount Hope Ave, Rochester, NY 14620, USA
website: www.boydellandbrewer.com

A CIP catalogue record for this book is available from the British Library

The publisher has no responsibility for the continued existence
or accuracy of URLs for external or third-party internet websites
referred to in this book, and does not guarantee that any content
on such websites is, or will remain, accurate or appropriate.

This publication is printed on acid-free paper

Designed and typeset in Adobe Arno Pro by
David Roberts, Pershore, Worcestershire

Printed in Great Britain by
CPI Antony Rowe, Chippenham and Eastbourne

Contents

Illustrations

The author and publishers are grateful to all the institutions and individuals listed for permission to reproduce the materials in which they hold copyright. Every effort has been made to trace the copyright holders; apologies are offered for any omission, and the publishers will be pleased to add any necessary acknowledgement in subsequent editions.

A Note on Terminology

THIS book deals with twentieth-century attempts to emulate some of the performance conditions under which Shakespeare's plays were originally produced. The early incarnations of this phenomenon were known as the "Elizabethan revival." I adopt this usage when referring to the work of William Poel and his contemporaries and, throughout this study, I frequently use "Elizabethan" to refer to all such efforts at theatrical reconstruction in the modern and postmodern eras. I employ this locution in such formulations as "Elizabethan staging," "The Elizabethan Movement," "Elizabethanism," and "Elizabethanist(s)." These are terms of convenience that are not always strictly accurate. Attempts at the reconstructed Blackfriars Playhouse in Virginia to emulate the work of Shakespeare's company after 1608, for instance, are technically "Jacobean" in inspiration. I believe this imprecision is acceptable, however, as my primary goal throughout this volume is to analyze the work of twentieth-century practitioners and not their sixteenth- and seventeenth-century antecedents. In this broader sense, "Elizabethan" accurately describes the approaches of these more recent people of the theater. In the interest of stylistic variety, I have often alternated "early modern" with "Elizabethan" in phrases such as "Elizabethan practices" and "early modern staging." The sole goal of this usage is semantic variation. I do not attempt to signal with my use of "early modern" that the practices thus modified bridge the Elizabethan and Jacobean eras. In an effort to avoid confusion, I have also restricted my use of the term "original practices" to refer specifically to new Globe productions identified under this banner by their creators, and have consistently surrounded this phrase with quotation marks.

Introduction

SINCE the late nineteenth century, theater practitioners have frequently sought to recreate the staging conditions of early modern England. Despite the wide variety of approaches employed by William Poel, Nugent Monck, Tyrone Guthrie, and the founders of the new Globe, I perceive a common philosophical underpinning to their endeavors. Rather than indulging in archaism for its own sake, they looked backward in a progressive attempt to address the challenges of the twentieth century. "The theatrical past" served for them as "a crack in the present through which one could grab at a future" (Womack 81).

The original nemesis of William Poel was the extravagantly picturesque style epitomized by Herbert Beerbohm Tree's 1900 *A Midsummer Night's Dream*, in which live rabbits scampered through an onstage forest. This mode of production was doomed with or without the influence of the Elizabethanists. Inflation, as Poel noted, was "a serious tax on the managerial purse" of theatrical producers (*Monthly Letters* 82). The cost of staging Shakespeare in this traditional mode soon became prohibitive, and Tree, who had originally scoffed at Poel's methods, began to cautiously adopt a similar approach. Lavishly pictorial Shakespeare was no longer a profit-making endeavor and by mid-century it survived only in heavily subsidized theaters.

Along with rising costs, an emerging rival medium contributed to the demise of this elaborate production style. Tyrone Guthrie notes that within a few years of Tree's triumphant *Midsummer* "D. W. Griffith had made *Birth of a Nation*." The movies were a catastrophe for traditional producers, and the development of motion pictures with sound further wounded the stage. In 1932 Guthrie concluded, "No detached observer can seriously suppose that the big spectacular play has the slightest chance of survival against the big spectacular film" (*Theatre Prospect* 18). From that point onward, the prime objective of the Elizabethan movement was to provide a theatrical experience that film could not duplicate and thereby preserve a relevant place for live performance in the cinematic age.

Recent scholarship has positioned theater "as an implicit and explicit rival" of film and other electronic means of performance within a critique of globalization. Because theater is not "strictly reproducible," it resists, in this view, the commodification on which late capitalism thrives (Burnett 13). The response of Elizabethanists to cinema can be read as an early instance of this resistance to globalization. Their quest mirrored the approach of avant-garde practitioners like Jerzy Grotowski, who defined his efforts largely in reaction to the challenge from electronic media. Rather than pursuing what he considered "the wrong solution" to the problem of cinema's technological dominance by making theater "more technical" (41), Grotowski sought to emphasize the "one element of which film and television cannot rob the theatre: the closeness of the living organism" (42). A similar rationale informed the architectural solutions proposed by Nugent Monck's Maddermarket Theatre,

Tyrone Guthrie's Stratford Festival Stage, and the new Globe. The success of these endeavors has been, to some extent, a victory over cinema. "It shows," says Rory Edwards who played Orleans in the Globe's 1997 production of *Henry V*, that "we haven't completely succumbed to the mechanistic world of film and technology" (quoted in Kiernan 139).

In the twenty-first century, Elizabethan staging's potential for audience involvement allows it to take advantage of a current paradigm shift in performance media. Philip Auslander suggests that "televisual" modes which came to dominance in the twentieth century (including cinema) are currently being "absorbed" by a new digital discourse that offers greater potential for interactivity (196). The "defining quality" of this new paradigm for Auslander is "feedback" (197). As Christie Carson was the first to note ("Democratising" 120–1), early modern conventions encourage a high degree of spectator participation that accommodates this postmodern need. The new Globe and similar theater spaces may therefore continue to thrive in the new millennium while traditional cinema goes the way of Beerbohm Tree's bunnies.

Elizabethanism has consistently defined itself as forward-looking in its engagement with modernity, but many critics have interpreted the movement as artistically and politically regressive. For some scholars early modern staging represents an attempt to avoid contact with the material circumstances of contemporary culture. Productions employing Elizabethan conventions, in this view, use the cultural authority of a universal Shakespeare, frozen in time, to forestall societal change and preserve the interests of ruling elites. More particularly, the charge of abetting colonialism has been leveled at Elizabethanists from both sides of the Atlantic. North American scholars accuse Tyrone Guthrie of following an "imperialist British model" (Knowles, "Nationalist to Multinational" 20) in founding the Stratford Festival, thereby preventing "postcolonial actors" in Canada from achieving an indigenous theatrical identity (Salter 114). Some British critics similarly see the new Globe, a project spearheaded by the American actor Sam Wanamaker, as an act of "cultural imperialism" (Drakakis 39) which constitutes "the continuation of American foreign policy by other means" (Hawkes 153). While it is impossible to know what latent urges might have motivated Guthrie or Wanamaker, they did not consciously pursue an agenda of cultural hegemony. Instead, Guthrie's stated goal of helping Canadians develop a "distinctive national style, whether of acting, producing, writing or criticizing plays" ("First Shakespeare" 28) stressed local empowerment rather than an imperial paradigm, an ethos echoed by Wanamaker's populist agenda for urban renewal in the new Globe's Bankside neighborhood.

Other critics are less damning in their interpretation of the movement's political significance, but see it as advancing an artistically conservative agenda. For W. B. Worthen Elizabethanism is complicit in a broader critical project which, while claiming to value Shakespeare's plays in performance, actually endorses a fidelity to the text that serves to "disqualify the processes that produce meaning in the theatre as legitimate objects for our attention and scrutiny" ("Deeper" 452). Because early modern staging severely limits set and light design, it places a greater emphasis on the received words of the playwright. For Worthen, this privileging of the literary text over other aspects of performance limits theater to an interpretative function and denies it the opportunity to independently create artistic meaning. Elizabethanism thus advances "an understanding of dramatic performance as the embodiment of a textualized past" (*Force* 28), and the new Globe stands as a "monument to a writerly understanding of theatre" (25). The comments of some scholarly advocates of the Elizabethan movement (such as Muriel St Clare Byrne and Alan Dessen) support Worthen's reading, but the actual activity of its practitioners does not. While Elizabethan stagings often place more emphasis on a play's language than do more heavily designed productions, this linguistic sensitivity is not (as Worthen asserts) inherently connected to chimerical notions of authorial intent or of an authoritative, originary text (*Authority* 64). William Poel, Nugent Monck, and Tyrone Guthrie never showed much concern for the sanctity of Shakespeare's intentions. They all freely edited the plays for performance and Guthrie in particular was notorious for his extra-textual interpolations. Productions at the new Globe, particularly those of the "free-hand" variety, continue to demonstrate that early modern staging is not necessarily constrained by a notion of textual fidelity.

The wide divergence between the intents of Elizabethanism and its reception by scholarly opponents is partly explained by the contradictions the movement inherited as the twentieth-century heir of Pre-Raphaelitism. This "Brotherhood" was formed in the mid-nineteenth century by three students at the Royal Academy of Art: John Everett Millais, Gabriel Charles Dante (later Dante Gabriel) Rossetti, and William Holman Hunt. William Gaunt describes the Pre-Raphaelites as "Knights of Art, born out of their time, who went a-roaming through the spacious but prosaic reign of Queen Victoria, like so many don Quixotes." These "baffled idealists in a material age" battled what they perceived as artless modernity. "They tilted not at windmills but at factories; they fought against dragons which were not the lizards of fable but railway trains, the steel-clad, steam-snorting dragons of the industrial age" (9). While the Pre-Raphaelites sought to escape into a romantic past, they were also reformers of contemporary social conditions. This political activism became more pronounced during the "second wave" of Pre-Raphaelitism when William Morris, a disciple of Rossetti, sought to "extract socialism from the fourteenth century" (21) by transforming society according to an idealized vision of that pre-industrial age. While Morris advocated overturning the existing social order, he also "loved all things old and hated all things new" and therefore championed "a revolution that looked backwards" (20). This later Pre-Raphaelitism passed on to the Elizabethan revival a seemingly contradictory mixture of nostalgia and progressivism.

William Poel's exposure to Pre-Raphaelite influence began when he posed as a child for a portrait by William Holman Hunt. At age twenty-one, Poel became a stage manager for F. R. (Frank) Benson, a follower of William Morris, and was deeply impressed by Benson's philosophy. The early Elizabethan revival incorporated both the aesthetic and the political aims of the Brotherhood. "Following the lead of the Pre-Raphaelites," Robert Shaughnessy writes, "Poel promoted a medievalized, vibrantly colorful, stylized-realist art as a way of restoring a lost wholeness of life to an increasingly mechanized industrial society" (*Shakespeare* 36). Nugent Monck also acknowledged the direct influence of Pre-Raphaelitism, as did George Bernard Shaw, who was an ardent supporter of Poel and Monck. While he did not expressly align himself with the Brotherhood, Tyrone Guthrie shared many ideals with William Morris. Morris encouraged the continuation of traditional crafts as a way for the rural population to avoid moving to the "great cities," which he considered "heaps of filth" (Morris 286). Guthrie similarly spent much time and money during the last years of his life promoting the traditional production of jam near his Irish home in County Monaghan as a means to keep the local population from emigrating. In his youth Guthrie was heavily involved in the "Folk Art revival" which, like Pre-Raphaelitism before it, "aimed to keep alive simple and ancient expressions, in danger of disappearing with the change-over from a predominantly agricultural to a predominantly urban and industrial society" (Guthrie, *Life* 43).

Morris lamented in 1883 that "for centuries, the working-class have scarcely been partakers in art of any kind" (285). The Elizabethanists have shared this view, as witnessed by Poel's early involvement with the Old Vic and Nugent Monck's efforts at theatrical outreach in provincial Norwich. Guthrie likewise believed that art should be for everyone and sought with his far-flung theatrical peregrinations to reach a geographically and economically diverse audience. Sam Wanamaker, founder of the new Globe, similarly eschewed elitism. He regretted that, since the Restoration, theater had become "the prerogative of the bourgeoisie" and hoped that his Bankside playhouse would make performance accessible to the proletariat (quoted in Holderness, "Interview" 21). Theo Crosby, Wanamaker's lead architect, denounced "the concentration on ever higher returns" (85) of industrial capitalism and shared Pre-Raphaelitism's interest in preserving the architecture of earlier eras. Crosby considered pre-industrial buildings to be "reminders of our better selves, our communal responsibilities and of our present slavery to the requirements of the production process" (85), a process which he symbolized as "the machine" (9).

While it shares Pre-Raphaelitism's revolutionary passion, the Elizabethan movement also partakes of the Brotherhood's escapist nostalgia. Frank Benson, the Socialist disciple of William Morris, acted as "Herald" for a re-enacted chivalric tournament at 1912's "Shakespeare's England" exhibition. This event, as Marion O'Connor convincingly demonstrates, served the agenda of the participating ruling class ("Theatre of Empire" 93–4). Benson's case therefore illustrates how fascination with the past can sometimes overshadow the responsibilities of the present. At times Elizabethanism has fallen into this trap. William Poel's inclusion of an authentically costumed audience on the stage of his 1893 *Measure for Measure*; Tyrone Guthrie's insistence on hand-made period shoes for his 1953 *Richard III*; and the costumers of the current Globe's "strange obsession with urine, onionskins and original underwear" (Schalkwyk 44) – these all display a solipsistic concern with antiquity that has alienated potential supporters.

This occasional self-indulgent archaism, however, should not obscure the movement's real achievements. Franklin J. Hildy observes that

Elizabethanism "has taught us that when we are dissatisfied with the status quo, we are not limited to our own resources to begin new approaches." Instead, Hildy suggests, "we can look back" and learn from the examples of previous eras ("Why Elizabethan" 116). Politically, the concerns which motivated William Poel one hundred years ago have not diminished in importance. In 1966, William Gaunt expressed the enduring dilemma confronted by the Pre-Raphaelites: "Is society to be one vast soulless machine? Is the production of machinery, ever more powerful, ever more intricate, the end of living? Or are we the victims of a system which we have ourselves created?" (21). Four decades later, these queries are even more appropriate. The Elizabethan movement, which offers a local and participatory alternative to the passive and commodified paradigm of globalization, may point a way forward from our current dilemma.

This study examines some of the major figures involved in the rediscovery of early modern staging, but it is not comprehensive. Time and space have not allowed me to address the important contributions of George Pierce Baker at Harvard University or Angus Bowmer at the Oregon Shakespeare Festival, and I only briefly discuss the work of Thomas Wood Stevens and Ben Iden Payne. I am also obliged to omit consideration of significant Elizabethanists like Bernard Miles and George Murcell.

My history begins with a chapter on William Poel in which I urge a re-examination of the conventional view of Poel as an antiquarian crank. He actually cared more about what his work said to a contemporary audience than about how well it imitated Elizabethan practices. Poel's methods offered an ideological alternative to the capital-intensive industrial paradigm of Herbert Beerbohm Tree and a political response to the totalitarian avant-garde of Edward Gordon Craig. I explore how Poel used his writings and his theatrical practice to advocate socio-political change and conclude with an analysis of Poel's identification with the role of Peter Keegan in *John Bull's Other Island*.

I then devote chapters to Harley Granville Barker and Nugent Monck, both of whom began their careers with Poel. I challenge the assumption of Muriel St Clare Byrne and others that Barker's Savoy stagings reflected the ideals of the Elizabethan movement. While Poel's efforts and those of his disciple Monck embraced the minimalist aesthetic of what Grotowski later termed a "Poor Theatre," Barker relied heavily on expensive visual spectacle. Barker's scenography was also more representational than his supporters have acknowledged, and his major contribution to Elizabethanism was the dubious achievement of establishing the movement's reputation as an essentially literary phenomenon in which the creativity of practitioners is sublimated to the dominion of the text. Nugent Monck, on the other hand, took the first tentative steps toward an architectural reimagining of twentieth-century performance spaces, an advance which led to later triumphs in early modern staging. Monck also pursued a populist strategy that mitigates criticism of Elizabethanism as an elitist endeavor.

In examining Tyrone Guthrie's career, I trace the sporadic and irregular development of his commitment to early modern staging. My chapter examines Guthrie's use of an Elizabethan-style permanent set at the Old Vic and his accidental discovery of the thrust configuration and universal lighting in a hotel ballroom at Elsinore. I then review Guthrie's use of early modern conventions at the Edinburgh Festival and the British Stratford, and scrutinize his achievements in Ontario. I also discuss some Canadian critics' charges of cultural imperialism and suggest that these scholars have largely misconstrued the ideological content of Guthrie's work.

My final chapter reviews the various conclusions that scholars of different eras have drawn from the scant historical record regarding early modern playhouse design and examines how these theories influenced construction of the new Globe. I contend that the planners of the current Bankside amphitheater did not consider strongly enough its ultimate function as a living theater and therefore made design choices which have negatively impacted the playhouse's viability as a performance venue. This chapter also analyzes ideological objections to the new Globe and asserts that, while cultural materialists are rightly suspicious of a nostalgic "Shakespeare industry" that sometimes serves sinister ideological ends, this distrust has often blinded critics to the genuinely populist potential of early modern staging.

This work concludes with a discussion of the efforts of contemporary Elizabethanists, like those of the American Shakespeare Center, to offer participatory theatrical engagement as an alternative to the soporific alienation of the "televisual." I propose ways in which professionals and amateurs can incorporate the three principal features of early modern staging – a permanent architectural set, universal lighting, and placement of the audience in a deep-thrust configuration – into their productions of Shakespeare's plays. My hope throughout this study is that, by illustrating the imperfect but significant achievements of the Elizabethan movement in the twentieth century, I might encourage scholars and practitioners to continue exploring early modern practices in the new millennium.

1 *William Poel*

IN recent decades, scholars have implicated William Poel in a phenomenon termed "Shakespeare as Fetish" (Garber 242), in which Elizabethan productions are perceived as endorsing the hegemonic status quo. In this scheme an essential, authentic Shakespeare, frozen in time by the use of early modern staging conventions, serves to "naturalize a monolithic and monumental past as a means of governing the representation of the present" (Worthen, *Authority* 186). These critics see Poel as complicit in an effort to neutralize Shakespeare's potential impact by packaging and marketing his plays as banal nostalgia. This process is sometimes linked to the later "Disneyfication" of postmodern culture, in which any attempt at historical reconstruction assumes the ideological baggage of theme parks. The new Globe is thus seen as the "1990s fulfillment of Poel's aspirations in the 1890s," in which drama is reduced "to a museum piece and performances to a tourist attraction" (Innes 119).

In contrast to this postmodern interpretation of the Elizabethan movement, Poel did not actually advocate a "monolithic" set of theatrical conventions to govern all kinds of performances. His non-Shakespearean productions, and indeed his later Shakespearean ones, demonstrate that Poel willingly experimented with a wide variety of theatrical forms. Rather than employing an artistically conservative set of unchanging practices to subtly endorse a regressive agenda, Poel's work represented his own Radical political philosophy. He believed that artistic and political institutions were not sacred, but instead needed to constantly justify themselves and change with the needs of the times. Through the active political engagement of his efforts, Poel sought not to reinforce the existing power structure, but to transform it. His productions strove not merely to reconstruct a distant past but also to instruct a modern audience.

Refuting the Conventional Wisdom

THE problem with reading Poel as an antiquarian is that it obscures his other virtues. George Bernard Shaw understood this when he wrote that despite Poel's significant contribution to theatrical art he "received little acknowledgement except of the quainter aspects of his Elizabethanism" (review of *The Spanish Gypsy* 521). Unlike Shaw, many of Poel's contemporaries viewed him as an archaist. The standard critique of "museum Shakespeare" was articulated by the *Times Literary Supplement* in 1905. Poel was "a 'hard-shell' antiquary" who "would stop the clock" and "isolate Shakespeare in the Elizabethan playhouse from the ever-changing life of the world outside" ("Shakespeare as the Sleeping Beauty" 178). Postmodern critics have largely inherited this view. W. B. Worthen, for instance, cites Poel's "antiquarian impulses" (*Authority* 157), and Christopher Innes equates Poel's approach with "ugly pedantry" (38).

A careful analysis of Poel's theory and practice reveals, however, that historical reconstruction was not his main objective. Rinda Frye Lundstrom, one of few critics to consider the broader implications of Poel's œuvre, writes that he never indulged in "archaism for its own sake" (159) but was instead "always more interested in the content than in the form of his productions" (155). Poel was more concerned with his work's impact on contemporary audiences than with how well his productions reproduced early modern practices. He stated this overtly in 1913: "Some people have called me an archeologist, but I am not. I am really a modernist. My original aim was just to find out some means of acting Shakespeare naturally and appealingly from the full text as in a modern drama" (quoted in Speaight, *William Poel* 90). Although he speaks of his "original aim," this quotation comes from the middle of Poel's career. It therefore conforms to a shift from greater emphasis on historical accuracy in some of his early work to a later period in which Poel embraced the functional necessities of Elizabethan staging – continuous action, the thrust configuration, and the absence of scenery within a sparsely functional set – without regard for antiquarian decoration.

Some of Poel's productions before 1905 partially justify accusations of pedantry. The most notoriously archaist of Poel's efforts was his 1893 *Measure for Measure* at the Royalty Theatre, in which costumed extras on stage smoked antique clay pipes and otherwise played the role of an Elizabethan audience. J. L. Styan likens this arrangement to "a charade" (*Shakespeare Revolution* 57). Edward M. Moore condemns it as an exercise in "cultivated anachronism rather than an attempt at the most effective way to perform Shakespeare." Because the audience was asked "to watch not *Measure for Measure* but a simulated audience watching *Measure for Measure*," Poel's production became merely "a by-product of the historical-accuracy school" instead of a legitimate artistic endeavor ("William Poel" 26). This critique overlooks the fact that, besides indulging in antiquarian masquerade, the onstage spectators at the Royalty enforced Poel's notion that "in the Elizabethan playhouse audience and actors were one" (Speaight, *William Poel* 83). He believed that this early modern precedent might offer the solution to a contemporary theatrical problem.

The use of alternative spatial arrangements for audience members was characteristic of most modern attempts to challenge the traditional proscenium format. Poel's placement of pseudo-spectators within the playing area of his 1893 *Measure for Measure* therefore relates, however clumsily, to the quest of continental avant-garde practitioners like Antonin Artaud and, later, Ariane Mnouchkine to redefine the relationship between public and performers. "The common goal" of these efforts was "to favor a more active, engaged, and creative reception by audience members" (De Marinis 105). Later Elizabethanists like Tyrone Guthrie explicitly articulated this same objective, and it informed Poel's efforts at the Royalty. Poel believed passionately in the thrust stage, which he deemed the "most notable feature of the Elizabethan playhouse." In most of his productions, Poel was forced to work in variously modified proscenium spaces, but he always looked to "a space on three sides" to "accommodate the spectators" as an ideal (*Playhouse*

9). Thrust, in semiotic terms, produces "open performances" which "leave plenty of interpretive freedom to the audience" (De Marinis 103). Spectators occupying different places see, in effect, different performances. This contrasts with the "singleness of purpose" of proscenium staging and cinema, which "ruthlessly" controls an audience's point of view (Taylor, Gary 274). Critics have not generally recognized the ideological implications of Poel's endorsement of the thrust configuration. In the same article in which she rejects the potential experimental value of Poel's productions, for instance, Marion O'Connor notes that he valued the forward thrust, or "projection," increasingly as his career progressed ("Useful" 18). Poel's 1910 stage for *Two Gentlemen of Verona* extended far more into the audience than had his earlier configurations, and his productions after 1920 came even closer to the three-quarter ideal. In one of Poel's last efforts, a 1927 production of William Rowley's *When You See Me You Know Me* at the Holborn Empire, he finally succeeded in distributing the audience equally on three sides of the stage. This completed Poel's journey toward a new theatrical paradigm, which had begun with his placement of mock spectators on stage in his 1893 *Measure for Measure*. While his experiment would have been more valid if he had actually sold tickets for the seats on stage rather than filling them with supernumeraries, one can nevertheless see in this practice a theoretical inquiry beyond the goal of historical reconstruction.

Poel is normally judged by the standards of his Elizabethan Stage Society, an organization founded "with the object of reviving the masterpieces of the Elizabethan drama upon the stage for which they were written, so as to represent them as nearly as possible under the conditions existing at the time of their first production" (Poel, *Shakespeare* 203). Many of the Society's offerings were staged on Poel's "Fortune fit-up," a portable structure designed to recreate some characteristics of an early modern theater. While taking its name from the Fortune playhouse contract, Poel's simulacrum primarily reflected the influence of the de Witt sketch of the Swan Theatre. This sixteenth-century illustration was discovered in 1888 and had a tremendous impact on late Victorian scholars. The fit-up contained a *frons scenae* consisting of a balcony above with doors right and left below, as in the Swan drawing. It also, however, contained a central entrance closed by oak doors and covered with tapestry curtains, a feature which has no analog in the de Witt sketch. Although the Fortune fit-up was built for indoor use, and particularly for the stage of the Royalty, it included a roof or "heavens." This covering extended out from the *frons scenae* half-way down the stage, where it was supported by two 18-foot pillars.

A description of the fit-up published at the time of its 1905 auction explains the function of the heavens and stage posts in an indoor theater. This document states that the mid-stage columns were complemented by "a pair of reproduction curtains, each 18 feet high by 9 feet, suspended on brass rods between the pillars, with ropes, pullies, etc." (quoted in O'Connor, *William Poel* 28). Poel used a "traverse" curtain hung between these posts to enable the "alternation theory" of Elizabethan staging. In this method, one scene was played upstage of the pillars with the drapery open, followed by a scene downstage with the traverse closed. This eliminated time for set changes, as it allowed props and furniture to be placed behind the curtain while another scene played in front. Poel actually used very little furniture, and the alternation theory seems primarily to have provided a level of psychological comfort for an audience accustomed to the picture-frame stage. As Peter Womack writes, Poel "could not quite bring himself to confront his public with the bare open platform" (76).

Poel's adherence to the alternation theory (then prevalent among scholars) prevented Stage Society productions from being "authentically" Elizabethan in a twenty-first-century sense. Stagings in early modern halls, such as that of *The Comedy of Errors* at Gray's Inn in 1895, "afforded conditions which were as close as Poel would ever get to those for which Shakespeare had written his plays" (O'Connor, *William Poel* 37). Yet Poel sometimes used his Fortune fit-up even in such settings. In 1897 he staged *Twelfth Night* in Middle Temple Hall, where the existing architectural configuration (a wall with doors topped by a gallery) provided the structural features required for Elizabethan staging. Poel nevertheless mounted his "tawdry lathe and canvas fit-up" in front of this authentic early modern backdrop, so that he could divide the stage with his pillars and traverse curtain in observance of the alternation theory (51).

Costuming was one area in which Poel normally achieved a high degree of historical accuracy. During the early years of the Society, when he was comparatively flush with cash, Poel spent large sums to have costumes custom-made in imitation of early modern paintings and illustrated books. Sometimes, however, he violated historical accuracy in order to achieve theatrical effect. The Mephistopheles in his 1896 production of *Doctor Faustus* wore a hood which "concealed an incandescent light." O'Connor finds this anachronistic "installation of electricity in the hood of a costume for an Elizabethan play" to be an "instructive" indication of the limits of Poel's archaism. "The memorable pictorial aids in Poel's production of *Doctor Faustus*," she writes, "were not so much those which demonstrably were copied from Elizabethan models as those which exhibit the theatrical imagination of the producer" (45).

The Elizabethan Stage Society existed from 1895 to 1905, despite sporadic attempts to revive it in later years. Poel's career as a producer/director, on the other hand, spanned over fifty years from his First Quarto *Hamlet* in 1881 to 1932's *David and Bethsabe* (a 1931 *Coriolanus* was Poel's final Shakespeare). Poel's enthusiasm for historical accuracy changed over time. In 1881 he was, according to Moore, not "concerned with attempting to simulate Elizabethan stage conventions at all" ("William Poel" 22). This is indicated, among other evidence, by Poel's use of seven curtains to define scene shifts and intervals during his production of the Q1 *Hamlet*. Poel then passed through a period of comparative antiquarian fidelity with the Elizabethan Stage Society. Jan MacDonald claims, on the basis of correspondence related to Poel's 1912 collaboration with Martin Harvey, that by this point in his career Poel was "becoming less antiquarian in methods of staging" (308). Lundstrom writes that by the 1920s Poel had undergone "a shift toward a conventional, stylized approach to staging and away from archaism" (136). Poel's later productions, especially his notoriously modern 1920 *All's Well That Ends Well*, confirm this view.

Poel's antiquarianism therefore flourished primarily during the decade of the Elizabethan Stage Society. Yet even then he rejected pedantry. "A modern Shakespearian representation," Poel wrote in 1898, "can hardly have anything Elizabethan about it." He observed of the Society that "had we persisted in retaining all the original conditions, our representations could have been little more than costume recitals" (*Account* 7) and cited the group's desire to "keep the past in touch with the present" (12). Their archaism was perhaps largely in the eye of the beholder. George Bernard Shaw and William Archer, for instance, disagreed about the meaning of the Society's efforts. Their respective reviews of Poel's 1896 *Doctor Faustus* illustrate this difference. Archer called the production "a very pleasant and memorable orgie [*sic*] of antiquarianism" (review of *Doctor Faustus* 204–5), while Shaw felt that it provided instead "an artistic rather than a literal presentation of Elizabethan conditions" (review of *Doctor Faustus* 37). Archer was interested in theatrical archeology, and valued the Society only to the extent that it could aid in historical reconstruction. "These performances," he wrote, "lose all their interest when they cease to attempt the reproduction, by diligent study and cautious conjecture, of primitive Elizabethan methods" (review of *Doctor Faustus* 208). Shaw, on the other hand, saw the group's work as pointing the way toward a new paradigm for modern theater:

> The more I see of these performances of the Elizabethan Stage Society, the more I am convinced that their method of presenting an Elizabethan play is not only the right method for that particular sort of play, but that any play performed on a platform amidst the audience gets closer home to its hearers than when it is presented as a picture framed by a proscenium. (review of *Doctor Faustus* 36)

These contrasting views of theatrical practice suggest a deeper philosophical divide. Archer was amused by antiquarianism, but his positivist mindset could not accept that "primitive Elizabethan methods" might hold lessons for the modern era. For him, the only value in looking backward was to see how far the world had come. Shaw, conversely, was more sympathetic to the Pre-Raphaelite viewpoint, which looked upon technological and industrial developments with deep suspicion. The Elizabethan revival, in its rejection of modern methods, represented for Shaw a viable alternative to the status quo: a "picture of the past," he wrote, which "was really a picture of the future" (37).

By judging Poel as an antiquarian, critics have doomed him to failure, owing to the impossibility of absolute historical accuracy. The *Times* noted of his 1893 *Measure for Measure* that there was "a striving after accuracy in various small points of detail, while striking anachronisms obtrude themselves unchecked" ("Shakespeare under Shakespearean Conditions" 4). Beyond these inevitable lapses lay a greater problem recognized by the *Times Literary Supplement* in 1905:

The attempt to restore Elizabethan methods of stage-production has failed because it was necessarily partial; its proper complement was the restoration of the Elizabethan environment, the Elizabethan frame of mind in the spectator. With all the enthusiasm in the world, Mr. Poel could not accomplish that miracle. ("Shakespeare as the Sleeping Beauty" 178)

Almost a century later, W. B. Worthen framed a similar objection. "It is hard to imagine," he observed, "that we can inhabit the body in ways even approximating those of Shakespeare's era; although sight, pain, cold have probably not changed, our ways both of understanding the body and of mapping it into the signifying web of our culture are radically altered" ("Staging" 23). While Worthen's language reflects the influence of postmodern theory, the substance of his observation differs little from that of his Edwardian predecessor.

These critiques would indeed be damning if Poel's primary goal had been antiquarian reconstruction. One can sense instead annoyance with such a pedantic approach in Poel's rejection of William Archer's archeological endeavors. Archer had written a lengthy and well-researched article examining some controversies regarding the early modern stage, including the position of the "traverse curtain" (Archer, "The Elizabethan Stage" 459). Poel responded in the *Daily Chronicle*, "When Mr. Archer has discovered the exact position for the traverse, the place for the doors, the height of the gallery, and the depth of the recesses, we shall still be as far removed from a perfect representation of one of Shakespeare's plays as we were before." Such archeological detail was insignificant because "Shakespeare's play lives and pleases by reason of its own inherent vitality." It was therefore "a matter of small importance where the traverse is placed or how the doors open" (Poel, "Reply" 8). My intent is not, of course, to justify sloppy, impatient or tendentious scholarship on Poel's part. Rather I wish to suggest that, while as a "revival" his movement was inherently engaged with the past, Poel was concerned primarily with the theatrical effect of his productions, and not their archaist veracity. Elizabethan staging was a means to an end, and never an end in itself.

In addition to being an antiquarian, Poel has often been misperceived as elitist. Among his contemporaries, Edward Garnett wrote approvingly that Poel could "accept no stultifying compromise" and therefore "made his appeal to the intelligent elite" ("Mr. Poel" 590). Less sympathetically, Archer claimed that Poel's was "a form of representation which appeals only to the dilettante and the enthusiast" ("Elizabethan Stage Society" 221). As in the case of Poel's alleged archaism, late twentieth-century critics largely accepted this interpretation. For Cary M. Mazer, the Elizabethan revival was "a coterie movement with strictly limited impact" (*Refashioned* 84), which "was as elitist as the membership of the private societies which supported it" (83). These charges are not entirely unjustified, as witnessed by Ivor Brown's 1927 exhortation: "Let one of the many millionaires who read the *Saturday Review* give Mr. Poel a theatre for his birthday" ("Salute to William Poel" 91). Yet Poel's writings also appeal repeatedly to a sense of democratic populism. He longs nostalgically for "Shakespeare's day," when "the nobility and ground-lings together resorted to the playhouse" ("Responsibilities" 112), and boasts that "English drama sprang from the entertainments of the people, and not from those of the court" (*Playhouse* 6). Poel managed the Old Vic for Emma Cons during its early days. Cons had founded this institution to bring art to the underprivileged, and Poel wrote in the *Daily Chronicle* of his experience at the Vic, "It came home to me, the frightful contrast, the awful difference between the lives of the rich and the lives of the poor." Ever since that time, Poel claimed, he had "striven to change the dramatic world" in an effort to ameliorate these conditions (quoted in Shaughnessy, *Shakespeare* 35). Robert Shaughnessy sees in this quotation "a motivating agenda for Poel's revivalism" (*Shakespeare* 35).

Poel's connection to Modernism may explain this paradoxical attitude toward elitism. He may have intended his 1913 declaration that he was "really a modernist" more generally, and not to align himself with Pound and Eliot. Michael Bristol and Kathleen McLuskie, however, place Poel among "the first generation of theatrical modernists" (18). Poel apprenticed as a young man in a firm of building contractors at a time when, as Robert Speaight describes, "London was being transformed (from one of the most beautiful cities in Europe to one of the ugliest) before his eyes" (*William Poel* 17). The Pre-Raphaelite anguish at the alienation endemic to industrial society which Poel developed during this apprenticeship echoes a concern voiced by Modernist texts like *The Waste Land*.

On the one hand, Modernism meant "real literature," aimed at "a cultural elite" (Taylor, Gary 245). It sought to protect high culture from a proliferation of new popular forms, such as sound recording and film, made possible by technological advances. At the same time, some Modernists proposed a "culture of 'the people'" as an alternative to the mass-produced insipidness of commercial entertainment (Bristol 9). Shakespeare became "the elusive point of coherence which might unite 'the people' against the dangerous and narcotizing seduction of endlessly proliferating modes of commercial and technological cultural pleasures" (19). Simon Shepherd and Peter Womack argue that this conflict between elitism and populism marks most approaches to Shakespeare in the Modern era. It has created "the contradiction which stalks the subsidized classical theater," in which "Shakespeare always should, and never can, be given back to the groundlings" (Shepherd and Womack 118). Poel largely fits into this subset of theatrical Modernism, but he was not typical of the movement in every way. In *No Man's Land*, Sandra M. Gilbert and Susan Gubar argue convincingly that Modernism was "a men's club," which sought to exclude women from participation in the artistic process (156). Poel, conversely, sought to include women in his theatrical endeavors and frequently cast them in men's roles, a procedure which "quite lacked Elizabethan precedent" (Speaight, *William Poel* 130). In his desire to aid women in their quest for emancipation and equality, Poel stands apart from the latent misogyny of doctrinaire Modernism as defined by Gilbert and Gubar.

The charges of antiquarianism and elitism leveled at Poel have two things in common. They have been made consistently from the Edwardian era forward, and they have some factual basis in Poel's theatrical practice. The notion that he was a textual purist shares neither of these qualities. Poel frequently wrote of the need to edit early modern texts in performance, noting for instance that "it was often found, in these revivals of old plays, not merely that omissions were necessary, but also some re-construction of the play" (*Account* 9). He never hesitated to cut, or indeed to rewrite, Shakespeare's plays for production. Marion O'Connor writes that "Poel's textual interventions – not just excisions but also transpositions" were "worthy of Shakespearean adapters from Nahum Tate to Charles Marowitz" ("Useful" 24). Contemporary critics recognized this, as exemplified by John Palmer, who wrote in 1914 that "Mr. Poel's *Hamlet*, in a word, is not Shakespeare's *Hamlet*" (review of *Hamlet* 139). Scholars in the decades following Poel's death did not consider him excessively faithful to the plays' literary form. Robert Speaight wrote in 1954 that "Poel had no scruples about discarding as 'superfluous conversation' the most subtle or sublime poetry on the grounds that no one would listen to it" (*William Poel* 173). By 1963, however, Muriel St Clare Byrne claimed that Poel "sought nothing less than the authentic Shakespeare, to be found, hitherto, only in the study" (Foreword xi). Byrne's comments come in her writings about Harley Granville Barker and reflect an attempt to read Barker's philosophy backward onto Poel rather than a direct analysis of this earlier practitioner's efforts. As Rinda Frye Lundstrom notes, "textual purity" was "an idea embraced by his pupil, Harley Granville-Barker, but not by Poel" (7). While Poel's writings do contain some pleas for presenting Shakespeare's plays "in their authentic form" (*Shakespeare in the Theatre* 44), these passages inevitably relate not to cutting the texts per se but rather to the Victorian practice of staging scenes out of sequence in order to facilitate set changes. Poel was therefore less concerned with presenting Shakespeare's texts uncut than he was afraid of having his actors upstaged by elaborate scenography. Alignment with an agenda of literary hegemony has nevertheless provided a central justification for those postmodern critics who perceive Poel as artistically and politically regressive.

The ideological goal of Poel and the Elizabethanists, according to W. B. Worthen, mirrored the desire of literary scholars to identify a single, authoritative text directly transmitted by the playwright himself (*Force* 83). In this view, early modern staging seeks to "disclose the original practice of Shakespeare's theatre and so the original meanings of Shakespeare's plays" (*Authority* 64), thereby "turning away from the question of how our acts of representation are implicated in the dynamics of contemporary culture," and "effacing the dynamic of cultural change behind the mask of performance" ("Staging" 25). This denial of contemporary material circumstances is accomplished through a fetishistic reverence for the plays as Shakespeare supposedly wrote them. Worthen claims that "the strength and simplicity of Renaissance staging arises from the openly rhetorical gesture of fidelity to the text" (*Authority* 64), which is linked to "a cognate urge to restore an authentic Shakespeare, one who inhabits the texts of the plays" (33). This appeal to "the author" implicates Poel in the phenomenon J. L. Styan calls "The Shakespeare Revolution." For Worthen, this is "no revolution at all" (*Authority* 159), but instead "really a covert operation, a restoration in disguise" (158). Elizabethanists have therefore been (perhaps unconsciously) co-opted into a mode of interpretation that unduly privileges Shakespeare's authorial intent. Worthen chides theater artists and scholars for refusing "to move in a direction charted by Roland Barthes some time ago" ("Staging" 17). Yet William Poel, the driving force behind the Elizabethan revival, moved in just such a direction.

In 1881, Poel staged the First Quarto *Hamlet*. The provenance of this text is notoriously disputed, but what matters to my argument is how Poel understood it. He described the Q1 *Hamlet* as "a deliberate tampered version of the Globe Playhouse copy" that had been "reconstructed and compressed" by "the skill of the actor or stage manager, and not that of the poet or dramatist" (quoted in Lundstrom 54). Poel's decision to stage this play, which he elsewhere identified as "an Elizabethan actor's cut-down version ... printed from an imperfect text" ("Shakespeare's 'Prompt Copies'" 75), suggests that Poel did not seek to "restore an authentic Shakespeare, one who inhabits the texts of the plays," but rather chose to stage productions that deliberately challenged this notion of proprietary authorship. In 1924, Poel staged *Fratricide Punished*, an obscure German adaptation of *Hamlet*, which has even less connection to Shakespeare's "original text" than does the First Quarto version. These examples from different decades show that Poel willingly accepted the collaborative participation of actors and others in the process of early modern authorship. He embraced, in short, the very "death of the author" which Worthen accuses performance critics and Elizabethanist practitioners of refusing to acknowledge.

Poel Versus the Theatrical Status Quo

WILLIAM Poel's conflict with the theatrical establishment represented a deep ideological divide between "the traditions of enlightened Victorian liberalism and the new radicalism" (Mazer, *Refashioned* 54). Mainstream theater practitioners like Herbert Beerbohm Tree and critics like William Archer and Max Beerbohm embraced a Liberal, positivist ideology, which saw all technological and scientific advancement as inherently good. Poel, on the other hand, was a Radical and a Pre-Raphaelite. As such, he rejected the notion of inexorable evolutionary progress toward a better world. Poel's introduction to Pre-Raphaelite thought came in 1884, when he worked as a stage manager for F. R. Benson, whom Poel described as "a disciple of William Morris ... that apostle of radicalism" (quoted in Speaight, *William Poel* 60). Benson and his troop lived outdoors while on tour, recreating the premodern existence of traveling players. This experience had a profound impact, and Poel frequently quoted Morris in his pleas for theatrical reform.

Poel's Pre-Raphaelite ideals, like Tyrone Guthrie's later connection to the Folk Art revival, were politically ambiguous. Industrialism and mass production, for all their faults, did raise the material standard of living for a large segment of the population. To dismiss them is therefore, on one level, elitist. It smacks of paternalism for upper-class men like Morris, Poel, and Guthrie to preach rejection of technology to the poor masses, who would use it to improve their lives. Poel appears insensitive, for instance, in his objection to "the decision of the Charity Commissioners to disturb the peace of Stratford-upon-Avon by the sound of a factory bell," which would "cause discomfort and sorrow to those who travel there in order to worship at the shrine of genius" (Poel, *What's Wrong* 17). That the factory bell might be necessary for the citizens of Stratford to earn their livelihood apparently did not concern him. Whatever its ultimate moral and political value, however, Poel's position challenged the current socioeconomic system. As a consequence, the theatrical powers that be had little use for him.

While he would adopt some Elizabethan practices late in his career, Herbert Beerbohm Tree's attitude toward Poel was initially dismissive. Tree felt that Poel was "an absolute crank – and an unsuccessful crank to boot" (quoted in Glick 16). Without mentioning Poel by name, Tree outlined the difference between his own methods and those of the Elizabethan revival in a 1900 article for the *Fortnightly Review*. In this piece, Tree condemned "those who contend that, in order to appreciate [Shakespeare's] works, they must only be decked out with the threadbare wardrobe of a bygone time." These plays must instead "be presented with all the resources of our time," making full use of "those adjuncts which in these days science and art place at the manager's right hand" (53). Tree's repeated use of the word "science" in this article suggests a positivist tendency and links his theatrical position to a broader philosophical agenda. "Every man should avail himself of the aids which his generation affords him," Tree writes. "It is only the weakling who harks back to the methods of a by-gone generation" (59). This characterization of Elizabethanists as "weakling[s]" supports Lundstrom's assertion that a "theatrical form of 'cultural Darwinism' " informed the accusations of pedantry and antiquarianism leveled at Poel by his positivist opponents (83).

Tree's appeal to the staging practices of early modern masques may subconsciously betray his politics. He claims that "Shakespeare intended to leave as little to the imagination as possible, and to put upon the stage as gorgeous and as complete a picture as the resources of the theatre could supply." Tree cites the "mounting, scenery, costume, and music" employed in royal "masques and interludes" as evidence of what was possible on stage during the English Renaissance (61). Stephen Orgel in *The Illusion of Power* and Barbara Lewalski in "Milton's *Comus* and the Politics of Masquing" have interpreted the political significance of these masques as bulwarks of royal prerogative. Only the monarch could afford to stage such elaborate ceremonies, and these performances therefore served to celebrate the royal monopoly on wealth and power. A similar concentration of capital was required to produce the elaborate Shakespearean spectacles of Tree and his contemporaries. Rather than supporting the monarchy, however, these modern productions reinforced the dominant status of industrialism. The interpretation of the early modern masque advanced by Lewalski and Orgel is by no means definitive. Martin Butler, for instance, asserts that these spectacles did not merely "function as political propaganda and information management" (2) but instead served more complexly to "affir[m] the two-way tie between monarch and subjects" (7). Nor does a view that reads elaborate staging as inherently endorsing the status quo suggest that either Tree or Inigo Jones were consciously propagandists for the dominant ideologies of their respective eras. Tree was an artist and a businessman, not a philosopher or political activist. The secondary title of his *Fortnightly Review* article, "A Defense of Public Taste," indicates that he was more concerned with the practical consequences of Shakespearean staging in the theatrical marketplace than with ideology. Nevertheless, it cannot be denied that elites in every age tend to support art that they find philosophically compatible and to marginalize artists like Poel whose work represents a threat to established authority.

Poel responded to Tree in the same issue of the *Fortnightly Review*. He contested the use of the royal masque as a paradigm for English Renaissance stagecraft and took Ben Jonson's side in the quarrel with Inigo Jones, arguing for the primacy of language over spectacle. Poel claimed that scenery was redundant because "Shakespeare was his own scene-painter" ("Staging of Shakespeare" 355) and cited Jonson's disparagement of Jones's elaborate designs, which for this playwright belonged to a "money-got mechanic age" (from Jonson's "An Expostulation with Inigo Jones"; quoted in Poel, "Staging of Shakespeare" 356). Elsewhere, Poel developed his own theory of the ideological function of early modern theater, which focused, like the later readings of Orgel and Lewalski, on elaborate staging as an expression of royal power. According to Poel, Elizabeth "looked with suspicion on Shakespeare's writings" (*What's Wrong* 5). She established the lavishly produced children's company at Blackfriars to divert attention from the politically conscious historical dramas being staged by the Lord Chamberlain's Men, whom Poel saw as partisans of the Earl of Essex. He writes that Elizabeth "succeeded in her object in substituting the 'show' for the reality, and Shakespeare might well break his magic wand in 1611" and withdraw to Stratford (*Monthly Letters* 80–1). Poel's timeline with regard to the Essex rebellion and Shakespeare's retirement does not make much sense. What interests me, however, is his theory that the elaborate staging of the children's company served to support the political authority of the monarch against a revolutionary threat from the bare stage of the Globe. This anticipates the postmodern, ideological interpretation of the Stuart masques advanced by Orgel and Lewalski, and suggests a parallel in the early twentieth century. Tree's elaborate scenography endorsed the status quo, as had that of Inigo Jones, while Poel looked to the minimalist aesthetic of the Elizabethan revival as a challenge to that dominant power structure.

Positivist critics attacked Poel with arguments similar to those employed by Tree in the *Fortnightly Review*. Max Beerbohm wrote, "If Shakespeare could come to life again he would give Mr. Poel a wide berth" (*More Theatres* 222). Beerbohm's frequent references to "the science of scenic production" imply a fetishistic reverence of technology, as does his assertion that the Elizabethan Stage Society "finds in the darkness of the dark ages its natural element." In contrast to the crepuscular nature of Poel and his followers, Beerbohm assures his readers that "we are the children of light" (*Around Theatres* 258). Beerbohm displays in the following passage what Mazer considers a typical "progressive fallacy" (*Refashioned* 68):

Good modern scenery would be distracting (at first) to a resur-
rected Elizabethan, because he never would have seen anything like
it. Hansom cabs and bicycles would also puzzle him. But it does not
follow that, because modes of locomotion were few and primitive in
his day, hansoms and bicycles ought to be abolished. They save us a
great deal of time and trouble. Nor have they produced decay in our
faculty of walking ... Even so the developments in modern scenery,
which are but a means of quickening dramatic illusion, do not signify
that the imagination of the race has been decaying. (Beerbohm, *More
Theatres* 232)

A century after Beerbohm expressed these sentiments, he has been proven
at least partly wrong. Bicycles have done no harm, but later developments
in transportation have indeed "produced decay in our faculty of walking"
along with other, more serious, unintended consequences. Meanwhile, film
and television, the visual descendants of Beerbohm's "modern scenery," have
almost certainly contributed to decay in the "imagination of the race."

Poel, in contrast, was keenly aware that an excessive emphasis on the visual
"threatens the adult with paralysis of the imagination" by urging people to
"turn to pictures for the realisation of what they themselves hesitate to visual-
ize" ("Picture Pedantry" 60). He predicted in an article for the *Manchester
Playgoer* that this ocular addiction would develop a tolerance which increasingly sensational technologies would attempt to satisfy. "Humanity, however,
can grow impatient of counterfeits, and a picture is not alive," Poel warned.
"Then comes the cinematograph" (60). He ends his examination of the tyranny of the eye in modern culture with a question that, a hundred years later,
seems eerily prophetic. "Is it man's destiny to regard life as if it were a vast
Kaleidoscope, existing for the sole purpose of being looked at, until his brain,
wearied by watching the ever revolving machine, becomes incapable of concentrated and continuous thought?" (62). The connections recently drawn
by Mark Bauerlein in *The Dumbest Generation* and Susan Jacoby in *The Age
of American Unreason* between the dominance of visually based electronic
technologies in the twenty-first century and a corresponding decline in the
mental faculties of young people suggest an affirmative response to Poel's
query.

William Archer's attitude toward Poel was more complex than that of
Tree or Beerbohm. He agreed that "Shakespeare is horribly maltreated
on the modern commercial stage" ("Elizabethan Stage Society" 222) but
rejected Poel's approach as merely academic. Archer could not accept that
early modern staging might offer a meaningful alternative to current theatrical practice. While he was intrigued by the archaist aspects of the Society's
endeavors, Archer believed that "an Elizabethan Playhouse can never be
[a] popular institution" (225). "It is because," he professed in 1895, "I think
they are diverting valuable energy into a mistaken channel that I take up an
almost hostile attitude toward experiments which, in themselves, are harm-
less and interesting." Archer then offers a curious and oddly gendered metaphor. "Bare-back riding is excellent, perhaps indispensable, practice," he

writes, "but it is in the saddle that the accomplished rider 'witches the world with noble horsemanship.' " (226). Archer may perhaps have been referring to the enthusiastic but amateurish acting of Poel's company and to the need to constrain these performers within the "saddle" of theatrical discipline. But his antithesis of "Bare-back" and "in the saddle" more likely refers to the need for Poel and his company to accept the positivist paradigm of the theatrical status quo: to take the bit of science and industry into the mouth of their artistic endeavor (if one is willing to extend the equestrian metaphor) in order to be taken seriously as professionals.

In 1900, an anonymous reviewer from the *Era* was less patient with Poel, and more typical of the critical consensus. "We do Shakespeare a disservice," he wrote, "when we refuse to avail ourselves of the means which modern invention has supplied for presenting his works as beautifully and elaborately as possible." The critic asserted that if Shakespeare "could come to life we are confident that he would choose to be canvassed and appareled in the manner employed at our artistic London theatres rather than in the style of his own time," and concluded that there was "no good end served by reverting to the primitive practices of the early Shakespearian stage" (review of *Hamlet* 7). Here one sees what Lundstrom identifies as the "assumption that Elizabethan stage practice was naturally inferior to modern because it belonged to the past" (7), and what Mazer calls the concern "with forward progress of the theatre as a cultural institution; and [the] belief that culture and society can and must progress inexorably forward" (*Refashioned* 55). Unfortunately, society in the twentieth century did not move "inexorably forward." Instead it experienced a breakdown that almost led to its destruction. The stagecraft of Edward Gordon Craig charted and facilitated this near collapse, and the humanist aesthetics of William Poel proposed, and continue to offer today, a healthful alternative.

Poel and Gordon Craig

Many narratives describe William Poel and Edward Gordon Craig as members of the same theatrical school. This movement is the eponymous *Shakespeare Revolution* of J. L. Styan, who describes Craig's "provocative ideas" as having "tallied exactly with the new thinking about Shakespeare" represented by the Elizabethan movement (81). Both Poel and Craig would have rejected this linkage. Mazer has rightly critiqued Styan's "great creation myth" in which a movement toward non-representational productions of Shakespeare progresses seamlessly from William Poel to Peter Brook ("Historicizing" 151). W. B. Worthen similarly objects to lumping so many disparate practitioners into a common definition (*Authority* 159). Yet neither critic specifically addresses the injustice done to both Poel and Craig by attributing them a common philosophy. These two theatrical rebels scorned each other's methods. Craig wrote dismissively of the Elizabethan revival, "This love of the antique has come into the theatre now and then; it entered into England with William Poel and his Elizabethan Stage Society." He mocked what he perceived as the archaist sales pitch of the Elizabethanists, " 'Lo, the ruins of the sixteenth century! Tickets sixpence; plan and excavations, two pence extra'" (*Theatre – Advancing* 107). Poel for his part disparaged Craig's reliance on elaborate scenography. He described Craig's logic as "the more of Gordon Craig's scenery the better, because Shakespeare and his actors are very little good without it" (*Shakespeare* 226).

Craig's lack of interest in verisimilitude has led scholars like Styan to ally him with the Elizabethan movement, which was also non-illusionary. This interpretation overlooks the critical fact that Craig was as dependent on spectacle, and on the scientific and economic resources required to produce it, as was Beerbohm Tree. The difference is that Tree used the technological and financial powers at his disposal in the pursuit of realism. For example, Tree's *Tempest* featured a "fully-rigged" ship for Prospero's return to Milan at the play's conclusion, which somehow vanished "over the horizon's rim" on His Majesty's stage (Speaight, *Shakespeare* 126). Craig employed similar means toward abstract ends. Christopher Innes describes Craig's staging of Hamlet's first soliloquy in a 1908 collaboration with Konstantin Stanislavski at the Moscow Art Theater:

> A light black tulle curtain, or gauze, was stretched directly behind him and cut him off sharply from these [other characters in the preceding scene], giving them a misty effect. On Claudius's line, "Come away," this gauze was slowly loosened so that, although the figures remained in place, their outlines were gradually blotted out as if they receded from Hamlet's thoughts rather than moved off the stage ... This was so impressive that the scene received an ovation. (152)

Craig's dependence on visual effects of this kind had more in common with the positivist theatrical status quo than with Elizabethanism. His vision epitomized a theater that ever more valued technology and stagecraft and simultaneously disparaged the human contributions of actors. As a logical conclusion to this process, Craig wrote that "the actor must go, and in his place comes the inanimate figure – the Über-marionette" (*Art of the Theatre* 81).

Craig's totalitarian political vision similarly exhorted the benefits of technology over the contributions of individuals. Gary Taylor has noted the connection between Craig's Über-marionette and the contemporary zeitgeist, describing the early twentieth century as "a world of mass production, mass transportation, mass war, mass unemployment, mass politics [and] mass media," in which "human beings looked like moving multitudes of puppets" (272). It was an easy leap from viewing people as faceless cogs in a socio-economic machine to denying them basic human dignity. Craig dismissed the value of individual liberty in words that recall the ideologues of fascism. "The whole nature of man tends towards freedom," he wrote, and therefore "as *material* for the theatre he is useless" (*Art of the Theatre* 56). His son Edward saw the connection between Craig's model for theater and his politics. "Mussolini had always appealed to him as a man of genius and a man of power combined," writes the younger Craig, "a man who controlled everything – rather as he imagined his 'stage director' would do in the theatre" (Craig,

Edward 337). Taylor reinforces this connection when he writes that Craig's "total theatre" bore "an uncomfortable resemblance to its contemporary, totalitarianism." For Taylor, "the architecture of light in Albert Speer's Nuremberg rallies realized the ambitions of Adolphe Appia and Edward Gordon Craig for a theatre composed of abstract planes of mass and light, wholly dwarfing the individual performers" (271). Not all advocates of the New Stagecraft endorsed such political extremism, but the authority of Craig's commanding "Artist of the Theatre" derived from mastery of the same technologies employed at Nuremberg. The acceptance of a mode of theatrical production in which performers must practice "willing and reliant obedience" (Craig, *Art of the Theatre* 172) to those who controlled these technical means facilitated the replication of this relationship in the political sphere.

Poel objected to Craig on both practical and philosophical grounds. "As an advocate of Elizabethan methods," he wrote, "I have every right to protest against scenery being thrust into Shakespeare's plays" ("Mr. Gordon Craig" 12). Poel warned that "Shakespeare has long since failed to hold his own against modern staging, and the possibility of bringing more taste, skill, and naturalness into the art of the scene painter does not remove the difficulty, but rather increases it" (*Shakespeare* 222). A few lines later, Poel merges this artistic critique of Craig's work with a deeper moral objection. "The central interest of drama is human," he writes, "and it is necessary that the figures on the stage should appear larger than the background" (223). The Elizabethan theater, for Poel, was one in which "attention was concentrated on the actor" (*Playhouse* 18). Craig offered instead, in the words of his partisan Innes, "a vision of theater so radical that it seemed to have no place for the actor at all" (3). Consequently, Poel lamented, "There is no room for man in Mr. Craig's world" (*Shakespeare* 223).

Given Poel's humanistic philosophy and Craig's unfortunate support of fascism, one is tempted to see the founder of the Elizabethan movement as a spotless champion of individual dignity and the creator of the Übermarionette as a heartless autocrat. The truth is more complicated. Although Poel rejected Craig's approach in theory, S. R. Littlewood's description of Poel's 1914 *Hamlet* as incorporating "Gordon Craig suggestions of vast rectangularities for the Elsinore battlements" (quoted in Speaight, *William Poel* 223) indicates that Poel sometimes emulated Craig's style in his later productions. There were also similarities in their directorial approaches. While Poel argued for the primacy of the actor, his dictatorial methods suggest that he aspired to the kind of control exerted by Craig's hypothetical "Artist of the Theatre."

Poel believed "that every speech has one particular 'tune' to which it must go, and no liberty of interpretation is possible" (David 82). He and his actors therefore spent countless rehearsal hours finding these "tunes" (or as Poel sometimes called them, "tones"). Robert Bruce Loper describes this process in agonizing detail:

Poel rode his hobby-horse of inflection unrelentingly ... the girl playing Osric in the old Hamlet play *Fratricide Punished* ... was compelled to recite over and over again the five words the character says when handing over the poisoned cup: "here is the warm beer." Poel would have no other reading than a rapid ascent of the scale on the first four words and a drop of "several semitones" on the word *beer*. In his production of *The Bacchae* in 1908 ... the chorus was required to read the lines, in Mrs. Ernest Thesiger's words, "bleating like goats, Me-e-e-ing on every word! If any one of us lapsed he stopped us and said "No! No! I must have my TREMULO." (195)

While he probably didn't realize it, Poel's parrot-like approach to actor training accurately reconstructed early modern rehearsal methods. Tiffany Stern writes that playwrights, master actors, and other "instructors" of the Renaissance theater would provide novice performers with "a complete performance of the pronunciation and gestures required by the part, to be imitated by the actor" (*Rehearsal* 69). This process "left actors little opportunity to contribute anything of their own to their parts" (70) and "was not a creative event, nor did it encourage textual exploration and discovery" (121).

However historically authentic his methods, Poel's people skills as a director left much to be desired. Yet his attempts at vocal micro-management nevertheless demonstrate that Poel believed the actor, and the actor's voice, to be the center of performance. Gordon Craig did not share this view. Instead, according to the *Saturday Review*, he preferred "to dwarf his players by presenting them as frail, drifting, remote figures moving against a lofty and spacious background." The anonymous critic observes that "in Mr. Craig's theatre the actor is a necessary evil." He then condemns Craig's approach, writing that "for Shakespeare Mr. Craig's methods are fatal" because "instead of hanging upon every word that Hamlet says, we are almost surprised that he should speak at all. We should not be much more greatly astonished if somebody in one of Mr. Augustus John's cartoons were suddenly to address us" (review of *Hamlet*, dir. Martin Harvey 4). Such negative response to Craig's efforts suggests that, for once, Poel was on the side of popular opinion in rejecting him. Craig may have been the only major theatrical figure of the period to experience less commercial success than Poel. His legacy, however, has been great. Craig was the prime mover behind what Ralph Berry called in 1985 "the rise of the designer," in which productions' technological achievements regularly steal focus from actors and directors ("Reviewer" 595). A quarter century after Berry's observation, the spiritual heirs of Gordon Craig continue to mount elaborately stylized and highly conceptual productions, against which the contemporary descendants of Poel's Elizabethan revival compete with theatrical offerings that instead emphasize the human contributions of actors. This is the battleground of the real "Shakespeare Revolution," and the outcome has yet to be decided.

Theater and Economic Reform

William Poel has a reputation as an elitist dilettante, but he was always deeply affected by the practical economics of theater. As a young man, Poel toured the provinces as an actor, hauling the troupe's props and costumes in a donkey cart. Born William Pole, he was literally baptized by the material circumstances of performance when "by a mistake in the programme Pole became Poel overnight" (Speaight, *William Poel* 30). The traveling company's finances were so precarious that Poel once had to pawn his trousers to pay for lodging on the road. Throughout his career, he had little success as a theatrical businessman. Ben Iden Payne sums up Poel's lack of pecuniary ambition with an anecdote from 1934. "Poel told me," Payne writes, "that he now saw the mistake he had made when producing Elizabethan plays other than Shakespeare's. The mistake had been in charging admission!" (184). "How much money does it draw?" Poel asked rhetorically. "Only four or five pounds. That's all you lose and if you make admission free, you are saved all the annoyance of bookkeeping" (quoted in Payne 184). Poel was always deeply suspicious of the commercial mind-set of his countrymen, and his early writings periodically condemn the for-profit basis of English theater. After the collapse of the Elizabethan Stage Society in 1905, these occasional critiques became an obsessive crusade. Poel's main effort from this time forward was toward what Rinda Frye Lundstrom calls "the reform of modern capitalistic theatre" (93).

Poel analyzed the problems facing his art in Marxist terms. "No social problem," he wrote in 1914, "can be solved until its economic conditions are understood" ("Trade in Drama" 210). According to Poel, the increasingly speculative nature of theatrical financing was ruining the stage. Producers no longer mounted plays in quest of artistic success, or even immediate financial gain. Instead, Poel describes a situation eerily reminiscent of Hollywood in the twenty-first century, where profits are made not through an initial box office release but instead by way of global, "after-market" distribution:

> Managers are out to produce revues, farces, and sensational melodramas, because these are the kind of plays which are marketable over the largest area of the world's surface. And the scramble among the theatrical capitalists is to secure London theatres, because the mediocre play when produced in them obtains a hallmark which increases in value the further away from the place of its original production the play is acted. (*What's Wrong* 10)

The process of script selection Poel describes likewise resembles the way projects are currently evaluated by motion picture studios. "The ultimate decision as to what play shall be put in rehearsal is determined, not, as it is on the continent, by men of the theatre, but by members of the Stock Exchange," Poel complained. Only if "the name of some actor or author popular on the Stock Exchange" was connected to the endeavor would financing be provided. The play under consideration was "never read" but "only discussed" (9) by the captains of industry who bankrolled theatrical production.

This "wild speculation" drove honest artists out of the theater. Rents rose to unaffordable levels due to the large number of financial opportunists seeking to produce an elusive hit. "The root of the evil, therefore," Poel wrote, "is economic" (*What's Wrong* 10), and he called for government intervention. Poel advocated legislation to outlaw short theatrical runs in an effort to remove "the inducement to gamble with plays." This seems counterintuitive today, when the long run has come to symbolize commercialism on Broadway and in the West End. Poel was concerned however with unscrupulous producers who mounted short runs of inferior plays just to claim that these works had played in London, so they could then market them to an unsuspecting public worldwide. He therefore advocated "legislation which would prevent the mere speculator from renting a theatre or engaging a company of actors for a shorter term than a year" (*Monthly Letters* 7). Instead of the current theatrical model, which served only "the purpose of encouraging stupidity" ("Truth" 567), Poel proposed "Theatres for the People" on the Berlin model ("Trade" 214), which would provide "an example of how the protest of the depressed proletariat could be ennobled – not stifled – by communion with the greatest minds" (Speaight, *William Poel* 208).

Poel's attitude toward the theater reflected his broader political views, and his agenda for societal reform was more revolutionary than scholars have generally acknowledged. Toward the end of *What's Wrong with the Stage*, Poel quotes the Socialist and Pre-Raphaelite William Morris. "Commercialism," Morris wrote, "has sown the wind recklessly, and must reap the whirlwind; it has created the proletariat for its own interest, and its creation will and must destroy it; there is no other force which can do so" (quoted in Poel, *What's Wrong* 37). Poel first heard these words when working for Morris's apostle, F. R. Benson, who saw Socialist ideals as an integral part of his theatrical message. Poel's citation implies a similar intent. As a Radical, Poel was a member of both an organized political movement and a more general protest phenomenon. Underpinning Radical philosophy was "a rankling hatred of the Establishment – the established church, its privileges, and the whole system of class privilege and social discrimination" (Wolfe 1). In this orientation, Radicals shared much of the Socialist platform. Poel was not as red as Shaw, whom William Wolfe describes as a "born communist" (113), but his advocacy of change extended beyond the boundaries of the stage. His anger at those who regarded art as "solely a business proposition" (quoted in Speaight, *William Poel* 253) reflected Poel's larger concern that commercialism was ruining not only the theater where he worked but also the nation where he lived.

Elizabethan History and Contemporary Politics

WILLIAM Poel's view of history profoundly impacted his work in the theater. He was greatly influenced by Sidney L. Lee's "The Topical Side of the Elizabethan Drama," read at the New Shakespeare Society in 1886 and published the following year. In his 1881 Q1 *Hamlet*, Poel did not greatly concern himself with either early modern theatrical conventions or the broader topical circumstances of Elizabethan England. It was only after being exposed to Lee's ideas that Poel developed an intense historical focus (Lundstrom 42). One hundred years before Stephen Greenblatt, Lee argued for a "conjoint study of Elizabethan history and literature" (Lee 4). He suggested that such an approach would yield "revelations of interest not only to professed antiquaries, but to all who devote attention to the humanities." This implies an objective beyond mere archaism and recalls a traditionally humanistic concern for the lessons of history. Poel, however, did not always hew to this broader application of Lee's approach. Ironically, the example Lee describes of the pitfalls of too narrowly reading Elizabethan plays within their topical context was one into which Poel would stumble. Lee cautions that students of his method "may be unable to prove any ingenious or partisan theory – may fail to show that Hamlet is identical with Essex" (5). Poel would attempt just such an identification in 1914. Yet while Poel sometimes too closely identified Shakespeare's plays with their historical context, he also interpreted the political messages of these works as parables for his own generation.

Lee was primarily concerned with identifying topical references in Elizabethan drama, among which were tributes to the Earl of Essex. He sparked Poel's interest when Lee wrote that "the tragedy of Essex's life had deeply impressed itself on every Londoner, and [Shakespeare] readily turned to account the sympathies of his audience" (18). Poel became obsessed with the Earl's role in the power struggle among Elizabeth's advisers toward the end of her reign. Two weeks before his 1914 *Hamlet*, Poel wrote an article for the *Saturday Review* to argue against many of the stage traditions associated with this play. Poel devotes much of this piece to describing the political circumstances that he believed shaped *Hamlet* and Shakespeare's other plays of the late Elizabethan period:

> Who was to replace the old Burleigh in the confidence of the Queen? Was it to be Essex? Or Raleigh? Or Burleigh's son – Robert Cecil? The bitter fight for supremacy led to Essex's death on the scaffold in 1601, and Raleigh's disgrace in 1603, thus leaving Robert Cecil in power. There was probably no more unscrupulous intrigue carried on during Elizabeth's reign, and few residents in London could have been ignorant of what was taking place. (Poel, "Hamlet Retold" 73)

Poel linked this political turmoil to early modern theater. He even used it to explain recondite texts like the *Parnassus* plays. "The approaching death of Elizabeth, and the question as to who should be her successor," Poel wrote of these student-written works, "so overshadowed all other matters among the ruling political classes and heads of colleges that young discontents were left free to have their say" (*Monthly Letters* 100).

Poel saw Essex as directly influencing Shakespeare's dramaturgy. The Earl, he wrote, "for political reasons, encouraged Burbage and Shakespeare in their presentation of the historical plays" (*Monthly Letters* 78). With the Lord Chamberlain's Men serving as his personal propaganda ministry, Essex initiated a struggle for royal favor, the influence of which could be seen throughout the canon:

> But in 1599 the Privy Council tried to prohibit the further representation of English historical plays because they were made use of for political purposes. In the previous year the death of Lord Burleigh had left the Queen without any equally great and disinterested counselor,

and all the country was watching the political chess-board with anxiety. ... Shakespeare must have watched that grim fight with the mind of a seer, and *Troilus and Cressida*, which appeared in 1598, *Henry IV part two*, *Henry V*, and *Hamlet*, are all plays containing disguised references to the times. Then, when the English histories are no longer countenanced, the poet-dramatist turns to Roman history and finds in *Julius Caesar* his opportunity for saying what he thinks about Essex's death. (Poel, "Hamlet Retold" 73)

Like much contextual scholarship before and since, Poel's interpretation is both speculative and reductive, and his dating of Shakespeare's plays is idiosyncratic. What interests me, however, is the ideological position he attributes to Shakespeare's works in response to the political circumstances of the Elizabethan era.

Poel saw Shakespeare as taking a stand with Essex against the political status quo. Many of his plays were therefore, for Poel, overtly oppositional. They "represented the revolutionist on the stage in a sympathetic light" (*Monthly Letters* 130), with the "revolutionist" understood as Essex. Poel staged many productions as allegories of the Earl's career and, by his 1931 *Coriolanus*, "reached the point where practically everyone was Essex" (Speaight, *William Poel* 255). The key question, with regard to my thesis, is whether Poel pursued these and other historical parallels merely as part of an archaist effort to recover the past, or instead sought to use this material to didactically instruct his contemporary audience. I believe that the "historical" settings of Poel's later productions reveal a program of contemporary advocacy that endorsed pacifism and the emancipation of women while at the same time rebelling against the hypocrisy and corruption that Poel perceived as plaguing his post-Victorian age. Such a moralistic use of history is consistent with Cary M. Mazer's claim, in connection to the Elizabethan revival, that "history was a mirror in which the Edwardians looked to see an image of themselves" (*Refashioned* 50).

Pacifism and Troilus and Cressida (1912)

William Poel clearly documented his commitment to pacifism. In a 1925 *Manchester Guardian* article, he wrote that "the truest definition of evil is that which represents it as something contrary to nature. The strongest objection that can be used against depriving a person of life is that it is an unnatural act and therefore an offence against the living" ("History in Drama" 5). Poel enlisted the posthumous assistance of Elizabethan dramatists in his pacifist crusade. In a letter to the *Times* he claimed that in *Caesar and Pompey* "Chapman denied the right of anyone to deprive another of his life," while reserving the option of suicide as a noble opposition to tyranny. Poel went on to assert, incongruently, that Shakespeare went even further in *Julius Caesar* because this play "did not defend suicide as being an heroic deed" ("The Right to Kill" 15). Poel even claimed that "today Macduff would be called a pacifist, since he refused to strike at Macbeth's conscripted men" (*Monthly Letters* 31).

The carnage of World War I affected Poel deeply. At the war's conclusion he advocated abandoning the Christian calendar and inaugurating 1918 as Year One. "It has become an absurdity," he wrote, "to talk about one man having died to save the world since five million men have laid down their lives for that purpose" (quoted in Speaight, *William Poel* 167). Poel saw the conflict as an expression of capitalist economic policies, which he increasingly opposed. The English were "a well-meaning race" who had been led into war by "those who think that nothing matters in the life of a nation but what is of gross and material advantage." Poel wrote of the 1918 victory celebration in London, ironically called a "peace pageant," that "it is significant that the poorer classes were not largely represented, and that labour men apparently absented themselves. On the other hand, shop-keepers and their wives and children were to be seen everywhere" (*Monthly Letters* 116). Here one can read Poel's sympathy for the primarily working-class victims of the war, along with his contempt for both the ruling classes which had caused the conflict and the bourgeoisie, the "shop-keepers and their wives," who had profited from it.

During the war, Poel rejected "the tub-thumping patriotism in vogue" (Speaight, *William Poel* 225). He refused to participate in anti-German hysteria and offended members of the Royal Society of Arts by praising Germany's "People's Theatre" at the height of hostilities in 1915 ("Germany and Shakespeare" 5). In December 1912, with Britain already preparing for an inevitable military clash, Poel chose to produce *Troilus and Cressida*. The very decision to mount this play was something of a political statement. It had been staged in England only once (excluding Dryden's adaptation) since Shakespeare's lifetime (Moore, "William Poel" 33). Besides this single London performance in 1907, the only modern stagings of *Troilus* were in Germany in 1898 and 1904 (Wright xx). While he nowhere mentions these Munich and Berlin productions, Poel was keenly aware of recent German theatrical history. He may have hoped to mitigate the rising militarism by presenting a play about the futility of war that had been rediscovered by Britain's current adversary. As Robert Speaight notes, the selection of this play for staging in 1912 reflected "that anti-militarism which was then blowing through the English intelligentsia" (*William Poel* 193).

The *Times* reported that *Troilus* was to "mark the close of the series of productions of a similar character that Mr. Poel has given for more than 30 years past" ("Dinner to Mr. William Poel" 11). In actuality, his career continued for another two decades. At a dinner prematurely scheduled to celebrate his retirement, Poel said of *Troilus and Cressida* that it was "the most ethical thing that Shakespeare ever wrote" (quoted in Speaight, *William Poel* 193). The critics of his 1912 production did not agree. The *Times* called it "a strange, uncanny, disquieting affair" and complained of "the ugliness of it ... The mincing, detestable Cressida! The moping, 'degenerate' Troilus!" (review of *Troilus and Cressida* 10). This was the general consensus of the newspapers, which "proved unusually cantankerous" (Speaight, *William Poel* 201). A clue to the source of this indignation can be found in Poel's writings on *Troilus and Cressida*. He emphasized its timeliness, claiming that "the play might have been written yesterday, while the treatment of the subject, in its modernity, is as far removed from *The Tempest* as it is from *Henry V*" (*Shakespeare* 114). The point of *Troilus*, for Poel, was "the false ethics underlying the Troy story, which Shakespeare meant to satirize" (113). These statements taken together indicate that Poel meant for his production to satirize the "false ethics" of his own modern age. Poel asserted that in *Troilus* Shakespeare "comes down from the clouds and says to his friends, 'Now I will tell you something about your fellow creatures as they are in Elizabethan London'" (quoted in Speaight, *William Poel* 193). As Speaight notes, "In Edwardian London they were not so different" (193). Conservative journal critics picked up on this parallel and resented it.

Some of Poel's interpretive choices emphasized this topical commentary. This *Troilus and Cressida* was costumed in an early modern manner, with the Greeks "dressed as Elizabethan soldiers, smoking the tobacco which Raleigh had just introduced from Virginia" (Speaight, *William Poel* 196). Yet the production was more modern in style than many of Poel's earlier efforts. The *Daily Chronicle* asserted that Poel's "lighting experiments" made the production "not Elizabethan" and complained that Poel's use of carpet and curtains amounted to "the whole thing [being] designed in the modernist of modern ways" (quoted in Garnett, *Troilus* 188). Poel was careful to point out that, in spite of the production's Elizabethan costumes, he did not see the play as a sixteenth-century allegory. "It is not presumed that Achilles is Essex," Poel wrote, "nor that Ajax is Raleigh, nor Agamemnon Elizabeth, or that Shakespeare's audience for a moment supposed that they were" (*Shakespeare* 111). Poel further de-emphasized the parallel with Essex by cutting those "passages which admit reference to the Earl" in the third act dialogue between Achilles and Ulysses (O'Connor, *William Poel* 98). Apparently, Poel did not intend his *Troilus* to serve as belated propaganda for one or another faction at Elizabeth's court. Instead, he used his production to mock the bellicose posturing of early modern courtiers, and by extension, similar braggadocio on the part of pre-war Londoners. Poel cut Troilus's angry speech at the end of the play, and concluded his production with the death of Achilles. Speaight sees in these cuts a "rooted distaste for invective" on Poel's part (*William Poel* 198) and senses in this moment and in the production overall "a plea for pacifism" (233). If so, then Poel's *Troilus and Cressida* was the first of many "anti-war" stagings of this play during the twentieth century. He did not write at length about the impact of his production, but Poel did note coyly that he was glad his *Troilus and Cressida* had "set people thinking" (quoted in Speaight, *William Poel* 199).

The Politics of Hamlet

In 1914, William Poel made his most overt attempt to connect a production to the Elizabethan political milieu. In that year's *Hamlet*, Gertrude was played as ancient, much older than Claudius. Poel intended her to represent Elizabeth in the final years of her reign. The male characters were made to resemble the various ministers and courtiers jockeying for power in her court. This was not lost on the critics. S. R. Littlewood wrote that "it all came upon one in a flash

... Queen Bess and old Polonius-Burleigh, and Raleigh and Essex, and all the throng of splendid youth who fought for a moment's favor at Elizabeth's own court" (quoted in Lundstrom 115). The *Times* noted that "if you make the Queen elderly you also remind us of Elizabeth, whose hold on affairs had weakened by the time the play was first acted, and emphasize its 'topical' element (review of *Hamlet*, 1914 9). Poel saw Hamlet as "a revolutionary" (quoted in Lundstrom 121), and referred to the play in program notes for his 1914 production as "the revolt of youth" (quoted in Lundstrom 113). In an article this same year for the *Saturday Review*, Poel teasingly hinted that "it would not be difficult to name one or two young noblemen at Elizabeth's Court who were distinctly of Hamlet's temperament" ("Hamlet Retold" 7), but the Elizabethan revolutionary whom he had in mind as a model for Hamlet was undoubtedly Essex. Poel "was by this time obsessed with the Essex business" (Moore, "William Poel" 33) and saw as key to his interpretation the fact that Hamlet "lost the companionship of a noble father to find himself, as the young Essex did, at the mercy of a sanctimonious schemer," referring to the Earl's guardianship under Burleigh (Poel, "The King in 'Hamlet' " 5).

Less obvious than the production's references to the Elizabethan political situation was what, if any, didactic message Poel intended this *Hamlet* to relay to his twentieth-century audience. While no critics at the time or since have seen a political agenda in Poel's 1914 *Hamlet* directly related to the current situation in England, a letter to the *Saturday Review* protesting the production suggests that it touched a very contemporary nerve. Attributed only to "An Actress," this missive announced, "If Queen Gertrude – the 'Beauteous Majesty'–was intended to suggest Queen Elizabeth in any way whatever, it was an exceedingly poor compliment to that august lady, and would certainly have landed the contemporary producer in a nasty damp dungeon, well deserved." The actress objected to the "elderly early Victorian rigidity of propriety" with which Gertrude was portrayed ("Protection for Dramatists" 236). The root of the writer's outrage can perhaps be seen in her use of the adjective "Victorian." While she may have intended her choice of phrase to refer more generally to a nineteenth-century cultural ideal, this usage also betrays a specific anxiety regarding the late queen. In 1914, the image of Gertrude as an elderly widowed monarch habitually marked by "rigidity of propriety," yet inappropriately engaging in romantic activity, would have sparked memories in much of the audience related to the contretemps surrounding "Mrs Brown" toward the end of Victoria's reign. The actress' exclamation that there was "no scandal about Queen Elizabeth, I hope!" hints at such a connection (236).

Poel described the setting of the play as "a Danish court in which a terrible crime has been committed, and over which an avenging angel is hovering," where "no one ... is worthy to rule" and "the kingdom must be taken away and given to a stranger" (*Shakespeare* 157). He felt that "a community that did not expel this 'canker' out of its system was bound to have its health-springs poisoned." Hamlet's life, Poel wrote for the *Pall Mall Gazette* in 1913, was not "a failure" because "catastrophe was better than corruption" ("The King in 'Hamlet' " 7). Poel expressed similarly apocalyptic ideas about modern England, which he described as "the saddest of all sights." He wrote that "to a country so misled there must come a day of awakening" (*Monthly Letters* 116). Poel's most extensive commentary on the evils of his own age was his 1920 pamphlet *What's Wrong with the Stage*. He closed both this piece and his 1913 article on *Hamlet* with the same quotation from *Macbeth*, "Things at the worst will cease, or else climb upward / To what they were before" (4. 2. 24–5). Poel believed that things were "at the worst" both in his own society and in the world of *Hamlet*.

Poel's 1914 production style "was not in the least Elizabethan" (Speaight, *William Poel* 223). S. R. Littlewood notes the "darkened auditorium" along with the "purple-carpeted, soft-trod stair and scene, with heavy velvet curtains," and even what he termed "Gordon Craig suggestions of vast rectangularities for the Elsinore battlements" (quoted in Speaight, *William Poel* 223). These design choices illustrate how little Poel's later productions conformed to the doctrine of early modern practices that he espoused during the years of the Elizabethan Stage Society. Many critics see this variance as evidence of unfortunate decline. "Poel," in this view, "became more eccentric as he grew older" (Hildy, *Shakespeare* 15). There is no doubt some truth in this, but the departure from early modern staging in Poel's later efforts also indicates that he was willing to experiment with a wide variety of theatrical forms in order to advance his vision of a particular play. He was not, therefore, the "hard-shell antiquarian" of theatrical legend. At this point in his career, Poel believed that the political and societal influences on a play's creation were more central to its meaning than were original staging conventions. He also saw a play's ideological message as transcending any particular set of theatrical practices. I believe that Poel was wrong about this. The medium of Elizabethan staging, in its rejection of expensive staging and technological effects, is its own message. As Poel himself suggested in his analysis of the ideological function of elaborate staging in the context of the early modern children's companies (*What's Wrong* 5; *Monthly Letters* 80–1), such staging serves to endorse the political power structure that enables it. By adopting Gordon Craig's methods in 1914, Poel (perhaps unknowingly) partly acquiesced to Craig's futuristic political vision. His Hamlet/Essex would have therefore been a better revolutionary if Poel had used less spectacle to stage the tragedy.

1914 was a time of great societal transformation. The remnants of the Victorian period were about to be swept away. Poel's *Hamlet* captured the essence of this moment by creating a parallel with the late Elizabethan age, when similar anxiety about social and political upheavals dominated the cultural landscape. One aspect of change in Poel's era related to traditional gender roles. As Gary Taylor notes, "the only victors in World War I were women" (259), who were able to move into new fields of endeavor owing to a shortage of manpower in the war's aftermath. Poel used his 1920 *All's Well That Ends Well* to investigate this phenomenon and to support women's efforts toward equal rights.

All's Well That Ends Well and the Emancipation of Women

As in the case of *Hamlet*, Poel believed that *All's Well That Ends Well* was inspired by topical events toward the end of Elizabeth's reign. Specifically, he thought that the play reflected the controversy surrounding the Earl of Southampton's secret marriage to Elizabeth Vernon in 1598 (Speaight, *William Poel* 233). For Poel's 1920 production, however, this Elizabethan context took a back seat to *All's Well*'s contemporary relevance. Design elements connected the production's setting to World War I. At least one scene was played in the dark, to create the effect of a military barracks after "lights out" (223). Poel abandoned his normal practice of Elizabethan costuming. Instead, characters were dressed in contemporary clothes. Most notably, the king of France was wheeled about the stage in a modern wheelchair by a nurse in a VAD uniform (Moore, "William Poel" 34). This organization, the Voluntary Aid Detachments, was comprised primarily of women who cared for wounded soldiers. As the war dragged on and casualties mounted, the VAD grew increasingly essential to the war effort. These female volunteers became symbols of the growing power of women in English society during and after the war. In *All's Well* the most powerful male figure is dependent on Helena for his well-being (she cures him of a fistula). By adding the wheelchair and the uniformed nurse Poel introduced a second female figure in a position of power. The king could literally not make a move without her. This increased the challenge to traditional gender roles already inherent in Shakespeare's play, and the contemporary dress highlighted the topical resonance of this theme. This radical departure from Poel's norm of Elizabethan costuming constituted an attempt to connect the situation of Helena to that of women in the audience, who had only recently been given the vote and who were, like Shakespeare's lady doctor, striving for acceptance.

Poel's 1920 *All's Well* expressed his long-standing interest in the emancipation of women. Throughout his career, Poel employed what today is called "non-traditional casting" by placing women performers in roles written for men. What Barry Jackson called Poel's "abnormalities" (89) in this regard have long puzzled critics. Robert Speaight considered this practice a "disconcerting perversit[y]" (*William Poel* 138), and Max Beerbohm complained that it was not "sound archeology" (*More Theatres* 146). Beerbohm also objected to a more famous instance of cross-gender casting, Sarah Bernhardt's Hamlet. "Sarah ought not to have supposed," Beerbohm wrote, "that Hamlet's weakness set him in any possible relationship to her own feminine mind and body" (*Around Theatres* 37). Beerbohm's identification of "weakness" with "feminine" is typical of the period, and Poel sought to reject such paradigms through his theatrical endeavors. For instance, Poel's casting of a woman as Thersites, the master satirist, in 1912 served to intensify this production's critique of traditional gender roles. This *Troilus and Cressida* was, for contemporary observer Edward Garnett, a "triumph" that "undermine[d] the overweighted moral verdicts of its masculine commentators" ("*Troilus*" 185).

Equity between the sexes was not Poel's only motivation for employing cross-gender casting. There was also a practical motive, as more women than

men were willing to rehearse long hours for little or no pay. Yet Poel sometimes linked his rationale to dissatisfaction with traditional gender roles as
defined by Edwardian society:

> On the English stage girls are needed to act the boy lovers; for here
> young men fail lamentably … In the Englishman the necessary qual-
> ity of voice is wanting to give physical expression to words of love. In
> real life his lovemaking is comic and hopelessly unromantic because
> unemotional. But there are no similar drawbacks in the Englishwoman,
> whose voice is capable of expressing delicate feeling, while at the same
> time it is flexible enough to delineate passion, and to indicate the mas-
> culine traits of emotion. (*Monthly Letters* 28–9)

Critics have been uncomfortable with this description. Edward M. Moore
wishes that Poel "had said that he found girls' voices easier to train and more
flexible and left it at that" ("William Poel" 32). This unease is partly due to the
passage's ideological significance. Poel's rejection here of what he perceives
as the unexpressive quality of typical English masculinity and his contention
that women were capable of embodying traits normally thought of as "masculine" imply that he shared with George Bernard Shaw the desire to define
new boundaries of acceptable behavior for both men and women.

If Poel did participate in the Shavian quest for a redefinition of gender
roles, his choice of *All's Well That Ends Well* to address this issue would have
pleased the Irish playwright. Shaw felt that this play represented an "experiment, repeated nearly three hundred years later in *A Doll's House*," in which
the "nobler nature" of a wife is contrasted with the venality of her husband
(*Shaw on Shakespeare* 7). He connected the play to contemporary struggles
for women's emancipation by noting that "the stock objection of the *Brix-
ton Family Shakespear* to *All's Well That Ends Well* –that the heroine is a lady
doctor" was "fortunately, getting harder to understand nowadays than it once
was" (*Shaw on Shakespeare* 8). Poel's own writings about *All's Well* complement those of Shaw. "Bertram," Poel wrote, "is no hero, and it is even questionable whether Helena does not compromise her self-respect in wishing to
marry him" (*Monthly Letters* 35). Only when Bertram "is degraded in the eyes
of his social equals" does he "realise how dependent he is on a woman's loving
heart to protect him from himself" (36).

By 1920 Shaw had ceased critiquing plays for the *Saturday Review* and he
did not comment extensively in print on Poel's production of *All's Well*. But
a cryptic observation from an unexpected source may illuminate the playwright's thoughts on this project. In a prefatory "Aside" to Lillah McCarthy's
1933 autobiography Shaw claimed that he had shaken "serious impostures,
including that of the whole rotten convention as to women's place and worth
in human society which had made the Victorian sham possible. But for that I
needed the vigorous artificiality of the executive art of the Elizabethan stage"
(Shaw, "Aside" 8). It was typical of Shaw to write primarily of himself in the
preface to someone else's autobiography. It was also not uncommon for him
to assume credit for the accomplishments of others. Plays like *Mrs Warren's
Profession* clearly challenged "the whole rotten convention as to women's

place and worth," but it is not clear how the playwright had ever used the "art of the Elizabethan stage" for this purpose. Shaw had, however, been invaluable in getting Poel's work noticed during his years as a journal critic. Besides writing favorable notices, Shaw had been a major fundraiser for the Elizabethan Stage Society, issuing appeals in print and often contributing from his own pocket (Shaw, *Letters to Granville Barker* 97). Shaw perhaps saw Poel's *All's Well* as the moment when "the Elizabethan Stage" was used to "shake" current assumptions about gender roles. If so, he may have felt justified, as one of Poel's major benefactors, in taking some of the credit.

Peter Keegan

WILLIAM Poel expressed his political and philosophical ideals through an identification with the character of Peter Keegan in George Bernard Shaw's *John Bull's Other Island*. Poel played Keegan in a 1906 production and in subsequent revivals in 1909 and 1912. Harley Granville Barker performed the role in the play's 1904 premiere but, according to Elmer Salenius, "did not succeed completely" (5). This may be because Barker was only twenty-seven years old in 1904, whereas Poel in 1906 was fifty-four and therefore more naturally suited to play a character Shaw describes as having "white hair and perhaps fifty years on his back" ("John Bull" 138). Poel played Keegan for over one hundred performances. It was an unusual thespian triumph for Poel, who was never much of an actor. He received good notices as Angelo in *Measure for Measure* and as Pandarus, but even sympathetic observers conceded that "Poel's genius lay in other areas than his acting" (Payne 91). Shaw and Barker were not sure that Poel would be up to the task of performing in *John Bull*. The playwright proposed a number of flexible casting options to cover their bets "if Poel proved impossible as Keegan" (*Letters to Granville Barker* 66). Yet Poel succeeded because he had been type-cast. Shaw wrote to Poel at the start of the rehearsal period, "Do not make any attempt to *act* Keegan." He added, "You need not make up; you need not wear a wig; you need not change your coat," because with Keegan, "You can be more really yourself than you can be in actual life" (*Collected Letters* 641–2). Poel later acknowledged his inherent affinity with the character. "I satisfied the management," he wrote, "because I was Keegan myself" ("Incompetent Actors" 8).

Peter Keegan is a saintly Irish mystic. A former priest, he is forced to leave the church because of his radical beliefs. Like Keegan, Poel rejected traditional religion for a broader spiritual path linked to an agenda of economic reform. "I am not interested," he wrote, "in any religion that ignores the ethical and economic conditions of life which create so much injustice and unhappiness in this world" (quoted in Speaight, *William Poel* 227). Keegan experiences an epiphany while administering extreme unction to an "elderly Hindoo." The "clear-eyed resignation" of this non-believer in the face of death demonstrated to the curate "the mystery of this world." Keegan came to see Earth as "very clearly a place of torment and penance, a place where the fool flourishes and the good and wise are hated and persecuted"(Shaw, "John Bull" 183). The function of life was "as the Indian revealed … to expiate crimes committed by us in a former existence" (184). Along with this Karmic philosophy, Keegan adopted a respect for all living things, including asses, grasshoppers, and pigs, whom he addresses as "brother" (199). Poel, a committed pacifist who often rehearsed his productions in a vegetarian restaurant, was similarly attuned to Eastern philosophy. He produced Kalidasa's *Sakuntala* in 1899 and 1913 and wrote "Hindu Drama on the English Stage," for the *Asiatic Quarterly Review* in the year of this second production. One can see in Poel's choice of this play and in his sympathetic treatment of Kalidasa in this article something of the fictional priest's admiration for Indian culture and philosophy.

Keegan's transcendental resignation, however, does not prevent him from speaking out against injustice. He recognizes and chastises the imperialistic greed behind the development scheme of the "conquering Englishman" Thomas Broadbent, who plans to swindle local farmers out of their land and enrich himself by spoiling the Irish countryside. Poel played Keegan shortly after the collapse of the Elizabethan Stage Society, at a time when his thought and artistic activity were becoming increasingly politicized. His critique of current theatrical business practices echoes the condemnation by Keegan of Broadbent's development scheme. The key similarity is that both systems were designed to *not* make money in the short term. Poel wrote of theatrical speculators, "What they consider carefully is the amount of capital needed to keep a play running at a London theatre, at a *loss*" until it gained notoriety ("Truth About the Stage" 564). Profit was then made through the international distribution of a play's acting rights. Little consideration was given to investors in the original production, because "although nine out of ten of these experiments are failures, there are still always fresh applicants waiting at the stage door" (*Monthly Letters* 6). Keegan similarly debunks Broadbent:

> When the hotel becomes insolvent your English business habits will secure the thorough efficiency of the liquidation. You will reorganize the scheme efficiently; you will liquidate its second bankruptcy efficiently; you will get rid of its original shareholders efficiently after efficiently ruining them; and you will finally profit very efficiently by getting that hotel for a few shillings on the pound. (Shaw, "John Bull" 200–1)

A "chicken or the egg" quality informs some of the similarities between William Poel and Peter Keegan. Poel did not write extensively about the commercial corruption he perceived in the theater until after he had performed in *John Bull*. But while Poel may have taken some of his talking points from the fictional Irishman, he and Keegan intuitively shared the "vigorous morality" which William Wolfe identifies as the "emotional core of Radicalism" (8).

While Poel and Keegan strongly resisted greed and venality and were quick to point out injustice, both ultimately resigned themselves to the impossibility of satisfactory change. They were men for whom, as Speaight writes of Poel, "battles are never won, because the victory that [they] strove for was absolute, never to be gained in an imperfect world" (*William Poel* 254). Keegan notes with melancholy before his final exit, "I only make the hearts of my countrymen harder when I preach to them: the gates of hell still

prevail against me" (Shaw, "John Bull" 203). Poel expressed a similar sentiment. "I was not born to live in a corrupt age," he confessed to his nephew,
"and when I see all those about me selling their immortal souls for the pure
love of silver, I suppose I cannot conceal my disgust and that makes me
unpopular" (quoted in Speaight, *William Poel* 239).

The Irish mystic and the eccentric theater artist each possessed an
unworldly, saint-like quality. When Keegan protests to Patsy Farrell, "Don't
kneel to me: I'm not a saint," the peasant responds ("with intense conviction"
as per the stage directions), "On in throth yar, sir" (Shaw, "John Bull" 141).
Similarly, Poel's acquaintances frequently describe him as holy and ethereal.
Ben Iden Payne suggests that Poel's "face was reminiscent of austere medieval saints" (86), and Speaight refers to him as "a *revenant* from some world
... whose mystery he wore like a cloak" (*William Poel* 183). Lillah McCarthy
suggests whose ghostly spirit Poel may have represented when she writes that
upon meeting him for the first time she "saw William Shakespeare," a connection that grew in McCarthy's mind throughout their working relationship.
"The more I came to know William Poel," she claims, "the more clearly I saw
in him Shakespeare come to life again" (28).

In 1932, a committee commissioned a portrait of Poel in commemoration
of his eightieth birthday. The *Times* announced that Professor Henry Tonks
had agreed to execute this work and solicited contributions to cover its cost.
Poel at first refused to have his portrait painted. He only consented when
Tonks agreed to portray him in the costume of Peter Keegan (Figure 1).

WILLIAM Poel wrote that Shakespeare lived "as an alien in a philistine
world" (*What's Wrong* 17). While there is little in the biography of
the self-made gentleman from Stratford to suggest such an identification, it
describes rather well Poel's own position. He was, as Payne wrote, "an ideal-
ist and quite indifferent to worldly success" (85). Poel's ascetic temperament
led him to reject the lavish pictorial realism of Herbert Beerbohm Tree and
the equally elaborate expressionism of Edward Gordon Craig in favor of the
minimalist aesthetic of the Elizabethan revival. While he looked to the past
for answers, Poel did not slavishly pursue antiquarian reconstruction. Instead,
he embraced the key elements of early modern staging in order to reject the
technologically complex and capital-intensive theatrical status quo. In Poel's
alternative paradigm, as John Gielgud noted, "all the hectic research for novelty – the atmospheric heights and depths and ingenuities of designers ...
all this would no longer be possible, nor even matter any more" (quoted in
Speaight, *William Poel* 275).

Poel's artistic agenda had a political aspect, as it challenged the positivist
mindset which underpinned industrial capitalism. The inherent humanism
of the actor-centered Elizabethan revival also protected Poel from the seduction of fascism to which many of his fellow Modernists succumbed. This
opposition to conservative and far-right ideologies belies the reactionary
status often attributed to Poel and the Elizabethan movement by postmodern

critics. Poel was deeply committed to understanding the influence of political and socio-economic factors on both early modern plays and their modern productions. This inquiry led him in turn to scrutinize the shortcomings of twentieth-century England. He strove passionately to reform the theater and society of his era, and his legacy should reflect this effort.

1 William Poel as Peter Keegan. Oil on canvas by Henry Tonks.

2   Harley Granville Barker

HARLEY Granville Barker and Nugent Monck were almost exact contemporaries. Barker was born on 25 November 1877, and Monck less than three months later on 4 February 1878. Their lives, however, ended very differently. Barker died on 31 August 1946. By this time, he had long retired from active work in the theater. According to his biographer C. B. Purdom, when Barker "deserted" the stage he "lost his vocation, and died as an artist" (285). At the end of his life, Barker suffered from delusions and was extremely unhappy. During his final days he reportedly exclaimed, "I feel my life is useless" (quoted in Purdom 277). Monck, on the other hand, survived until 21 October 1958. Shortly before, in June of that year, he staged *Elizabethan Patchwork*, a performance comprised of scenes from John Lyly's *Campapse* and Marlowe's *Doctor Faustus*. This was Monck's last production in a career that lasted fifty-eight years. Throughout this long span, he never lost faith in theater's ability to reach a broad audience through the simple staging of early modern plays. The forces that shaped the lives of Monck and Barker to such different ends also determined their distinct contributions to the Elizabethan movement.

William Poel directly influenced both Barker and Monck. Barker's performance as Richard II for The Elizabethan Stage Society in 1899 was his first major success as an actor. Nugent Monck played Fellowship in the Society's 1902 revival of *Everyman* and went on to stage manage many of Poel's productions including, probably, a 1903 *Edward II* in which Barker played the lead. In contrasting ways, these two younger practitioners advanced Poel's ideas during the first half of the twentieth century. Barker's Shakespeare productions at the Savoy between 1912 and 1914 were highly influential although, as I will argue, they had only a tangential relationship to the ideals of Elizabethanism. After his retirement from the stage, Barker advocated early modern staging practices in his *Prefaces to Shakespeare*. These writings, rather than Barker's practical example, helped inspire later Elizabethanists. Monck built a playhouse on a modified Elizabethan model in Norwich, with no proscenium and limited seating right and left of the stage. There he mounted all of Shakespeare's plays (the first modern producer/director to do so), along with hundreds of other classical and contemporary works. Monck was hampered by the faulty scholarship of his time regarding historical accuracy, but he nevertheless demonstrated that it was possible to successfully produce Shakespeare's plays without the elaborate scenic devices of the proscenium stage. It was at Monck's Maddermarket Theatre that Guthrie first saw Shakespeare presented in such a manner. Monck's practical example, along with Barker's theoretical arguments, motivated Guthrie's initial experiments in early modern staging.

Monck encouraged many other theater practitioners to explore alternative approaches to Shakespeare, yet his contribution has not been widely recognized by later scholars. Part of the problem is that, as Franklin J. Hildy notes, not all artists were "so frank in confessing their debt as Tyrone Guthrie," who freely acknowledged Monck as a mentor (*Shakespeare* 121). Harley Granville Barker inspired many of the same directors and, in most accounts, Barker's impact is viewed as predominant to the point of overshadowing and, indeed, obliterating that of Monck. J. L. Styan, for instance, lists as having "been touched" by Barker's vision the same people Hildy describes as disciples of Monck: Barry Jackson, W. Bridges-Adams, Robert Atkins, and Harcourt Williams (*Shakespeare Revolution* 106). Styan, however, makes no mention of Monck's parallel influence in his brief discussion of the Maddermarket (124–5). In a similar oversight, Elmer Salenius claims that Guthrie followed Barker's lead "in the elimination of realistic scenery and the use of a permanent 'structure,' with the actors close to the audience" (22), but does not mention that Guthrie, in his autobiography, cites Nugent Monck's 1930 production of *Love's Labour's Lost* as his immediate inspiration for adopting these practices (Guthrie, *Life* 84).

My point is not merely that Monck deserves more credit than he has received for promoting early modern staging practices. Rather, I wish to suggest that by emphasizing Barker's influence scholars have advanced a literary rather than a theatrical vision of Elizabethanism, justifying the ideological charges leveled against this movement by some postmodern critics. Barker saw Shakespeare's text as sacrosanct in performance, giving credence to W. B. Worthen's assertion that the "strength and simplicity of Renaissance Staging arises from the openly rhetorical gesture of fidelity to the text" (*Authority* 64). In his early career, Barker seemed obsessed with maintaining every word of what he took to be Shakespeare's original. In 1910, he chastised Max Reinhardt for cutting a German-language *Comedy of Errors* in Berlin. "Certainly it is not the play as Shakespeare wrote it," Barker lamented, apparently oblivious to the irony of this critique when applied to a production staged in translation ("Theatre in Berlin" 6). Similarly, rather than cut obscure jokes from *Love's Labour's Lost*, Barker in his 1927 *Preface* to this comedy proposes "a glossary in the program" and even suggests "a preliminary lecture" to precede each performance of the play (*Prefaces* 4: 1).

William Poel did not share Barker's excessive respect for the text, and later Elizabethanists followed Poel's lead in liberally adapting early modern plays to suit the needs of performance. Nugent Monck cut the entire first act of *Pericles* from two productions of the play and took such liberties with his 1946 *Cymbeline* that on the evening of its premiere Monck "thanked heaven that the author was well dead and so could not be waiting for him that night" (quoted in Hildy, "Reviving" 384). Tyrone Guthrie eliminated 45 percent of Marlowe's text in compressing the two parts of *Tamburlaine* into a single evening's performance (Maloon 8); updated the text of Jonson's *The Alchemist* with "references to Speedy Gonzalez, flick-knives, and the poofs" (review of *The Alchemist* 16); and interpolated original lines "in undistinguished but unpretentious blank verse" and an extended scene of non-textual comic business into several productions of *All's Well That Ends Well* (Guthrie, "Dominant" X1).

Barker wrote in the Introduction to his *Prefaces*, "The text of a play is a score waiting [*sic*] performance" (*Prefaces* 1: 5). This is typical of those kinds of performance criticism which, as Worthen describes, "avowedly locate performance" as "supplemental to the designs of the text" ("Deeper" 444), thereby valuing the authorial intent of a dead playwright above the creative contributions of living practitioners. In contrast to this author-centered model, Poel, Monck, and Guthrie highly valued the role of practitioners in creating theatrical meaning. Guthrie went furthest in rejecting Barker's musical metaphor. He asserted that "the actor has infinitely more technical latitude and a far more creative task than the orchestral player. This is because the script of a play reveals so much less of its author's intention than does the score of a symphony" (*Life* 137).

The written text, Guthrie insisted, was "only a *part* of the raw material of performance" because the "performance of a play is not merely the re-creation of an already fully realized idea" (17). Guthrie scoffed at the notion of authorial prerogative. "With regard to what the script is about," he wrote, "the last person who, in my opinion, should be consulted, even if he is alive or around, is the author" ("Audience" 246). "I would lay any money," Guthrie proclaimed, "that Shakespeare had only the vaguest idea of what he was about when he wrote *Hamlet*" (quoted in Forsyth 219).

Despite his unique position regarding textual fidelity, Barker's pronouncements have sometimes been read as representative of the Elizabethan movement as a whole. His literary prejudice earned the enthusiastic commendation of critics like Muriel St Clare Byrne, who boasted that "First and last ... Barker was absolute for the integrity of the text" (Foreword xxii). Byrne also attributed this anti-theatrical bias backward from Barker onto Poel. "We must thank Poel and Barker," she writes, "and their devotion to drama first and theatre afterwards" (xiv). Poel, concerned primarily with the life of plays on stage, would likely have rejected such thanks. Written in 1963, Byrne's comments are typical of what Cary M. Mazer perceives as a common attitude of that era. "For one brief period of time, in the mid-twentieth century," Mazer writes, "directors *did* define the script as a 'score' waiting to be 'realized'; no wonder that scholarly score-readers felt that they could finally communicate with them" ("Historicizing" 164).

The excitement felt by "scholarly score-readers" like Byrne at finding a kindred spirit helps explain why Barker's reputation as a director (or "producer" as the position was known during Barker's lifetime) is greater than his practical accomplishments warrant. Brian Pearce describes how "Barker champions" have exaggerated "the originality of his work" (397) and offers, in relation to the Savoy *Winter's Tale*, a theory as to the origins of this inordinate praise:

> How do we account for the enormous popularity which this production has enjoyed among scholars? Perhaps one answer might run like this: "The popularity of Barker's production of *The Winter's Tale* has more to do with the aesthetic prejudices of present day Shakespeare studies than with the actual originality of Barker's interpretation, which is one which happily conforms to the established values

of modern scholarship. Barker ... gave the text in its entirety, proving conclusively that it could be performed as it was written. It is the sort of production which leaves the scholar untroubled. He can return to the text with full confidence in its autonomy ... Barker's production was not really an interpretation at all, it was merely a filter for Shakespeare's text, for his genius, conclusive proof that scholars, with artistic leaning, can sometimes produce plays." (Pearce 407)

Pearce wrote this in 1996, and the consensus of "present day Shakespeare studies" may have shifted by that date beyond the conservative attitude he describes. Pearce's observation nevertheless supports my assertion that the adulation bestowed on Barker by mid-century critics like Byrne stemmed from Barker's refusal to cut the plays in performance and from his concomitant reverence for Shakespeare as a literary icon.

Postmodern critics (perhaps including Pearce himself) have rejected this text-driven paradigm and instead value the creative input of theater practitioners over the authority of the playwright. Scholars, however, have sometimes conflated Barker's personal agenda with that of Elizabethanism as a whole and have therefore wrongly associated the entire movement with an excessive fidelity to Shakespeare's authorial intent. When Byrne writes, "The Poel-Barker reforms had one aim: for the theatre they sought nothing less than the authentic Shakespeare, to be found, hitherto, only in the study" (Foreword xi), she is only half correct. This was Barker's aim, but never Poel's. My goal in this chapter is to disentangle Barker's unique contribution from the common philosophy of Poel, Monck, and Guthrie.

Biographical Context

BARKER'S theatrical colleagues lamented his decision to abandon the stage in 1915 for a life of literary study. Lewis Casson writes wistfully of how Barker "gave up the struggle, threw off the dust of battle and became a mere professor" ("Foreword" viii). "It was a profound pity," W. Bridges-Adams mourned in funereal terms of Barker's retirement, "He was not yet forty" (*Lost Leader* 13). Barker, however, had never been completely comfortable working for an audience. He was forced into show business at a young age by his mother, a variety performer who earned her living as "a reciter and bird-mimic" (Purdom 3). Mrs Barker dragged her reluctant son on stage in a sailor suit and forced him to recite poetry for his supper. While not as desperate as the early career of Edmund Kean, Barker's experiences as a child star left him permanently bitter about the need to please a fickle public. In 1937, decades after he last trod the boards, Barker complained that performing can "be very demoralizing." The demands of an unenlightened public inevitably force actors to "lower and lower their standards until the biggest idiot there cannot fail to appreciate what they are doing" (Barker, "Alas" 426). Barker confessed to Helen Huntington shortly before their marriage, "I do believe that my present loathing for the theatre is loathing for the audience. I have never loved them" (quoted in Salmon 123). These sentiments do not suggest the gregarious *joie de vivre* generally considered a prerequisite for a happy life on the stage.

Barker had, in his early years, a commitment to socialism and progressive reform. He joined the Fabian Society in 1901. As a member of the Court Theatre company, Barker worked in a hotbed of political activity where "the will to reform the theatre went hand-in-hand with a will to reform the lot of the actor in society and, indeed, society as a whole" (McDonald 80–1). This desire for social change merged with an artistic vision in which "every theatre" would be "a popular theatre, crowded with all sorts and conditions of people" (Barker, *Exemplary* 284). Barker's most ambitious attempt at popularizing classical drama was his 1915 American staging of two tragedies by Euripides, *Iphigenia in Taurus* and *The Trojan Women*, at a number of college football stadiums including the Yale Bowl. There was little opportunity for subtlety in such venues. "The choreography," Samuel L. Leiter writes, "had to be as striking as possible because of the dimensions involved. Similarly, as can be discerned from the available photographs, the gestures of the principal players had to be extremely expansive and nonrealistic merely in order to communicate across the vast spaces" (30). The stage included a huge *Skena* 100 feet wide and 40 feet high, in front of which lay a circular playing space 100 feet in diameter. The actors' task was made even harder by the poor acoustics of such a vast and unforgiving performance space. Athena as *dea ex machina*, appearing on top of the stage-house, had to use a megaphone to be heard.

This project was as ill-conceived at the time as it seems a century later. The attendance figures of 10,000 for the opening of *Iphigenia* at the Yale Bowl and of 60,000 total attendees for all eleven performances seem at first to indicate popular success. These audiences, however, consisted largely of public school pupils on organized visits. In New York, for instance, large numbers of high school students were required to attend. These adolescents did not particularly appreciate the epic wonder of Greek tragedy performed outdoors in a sports stadium. Lionel Braham, who played Thoas and Poseidon, was a particular target of abuse from the sophomoric crowd due to his "booming voice and outlandish appearance" (Kennedy, *Granville Barker* 184). Adults also had difficulty taking the proceedings seriously. Dennis Kennedy notes that "when the sun dropped below the rim of the Yale Bowl, hundreds of men rose to put on their overcoats, accompanied by multiple titters and jests about the seventh-inning stretch" (185).

Barker's effort to bring Greek tragedy to the American masses failed financially, a setback which helped convince him to abandon the theater. A greater motivation for his retirement, however, was his second marriage to the wealthy American Helen Huntington. She wanted Barker to give up the stage, and he willingly agreed. His new marriage also led him to renounce his leftist ideals. According to George Bernard Shaw, Helen quashed Barker's political activity because "to her all socialists were infamous guttersnipes" (quoted in Salenius 111). Shaw's statements on the matter cannot be completely trusted, as he deeply resented being cut off from Barker by his friend's second wife. Barker's self-interest as a new member of the moneyed class may more simply explain his desertion of the Left. He seems to have adjusted quickly to life as a member of the economic elite. Despite his early socialism Barker was really, Purdom writes, "a conservative at heart" (192).

Evidence of a reactionary tendency appears as early as 1919, when Barker suggested that the amateur dramatic movement should be encouraged as a means to stave off proletarian revolt. Without such an outlet, Barker warned, the "people" would be forced to express themselves "catastrophically, in strikes, [and] in revolution" ("Reconstruction in the Theatre" 11). By the end of his life, Barker had become rather crotchety in his conservatism. In his 1945 *The Use of the Drama* Barker displays an unsettling suspicion of "political democracy," which he claims cannot function "on a large scale, in a complex world" (24). He provides ammunition for those who see the study of English literature in general and Shakespeare in particular as a means of cultural imperialism when he describes the scholarly mission as "a fight for the future of Christian civilization." Most disturbingly for twenty-first-century readers, Barker likens himself and his academic colleagues to "a band of Christian Knights [who] would gather for such another eight hundred years' struggle as expelled the Moslem from Spain" (88).

Barker was also conservative regarding the representation of gender on the Shakespearean stage. His restrictive attitude toward women diverges sharply from the tolerant practices of William Poel, who sought to increase female representation by casting actresses in roles written for men. Barker favored instead a return to the Elizabethan model of all-male casting. He would only allow women performers to participate if they accepted the following stricture: "Let the usurping actress remember that her sex is a liability, not an asset" (*Prefaces* 1: 15). Barker believed that the best way for an actress to approach one of Shakespeare's female roles was "by imagining herself a boy" ("Shakespeare's Dramatic Art" 54). He appears at times preoccupied with constraining female behavior on stage, and this anxiety creeps into Barker's descriptions of Shakespeare's characters, as when he writes that "Cleopatra, spider-like, sits spinning a new web" into which Antony will fall (*Prefaces* 3: 10). This fear of women may be an expression of the typically modernist misogyny identified by Gilbert and Gubar, coupled with the particular unease that Barker felt in a position of economic dependence on his wealthy second wife. He seemed under siege when he wrote in 1926, "There were no women to act upon Shakespeare's stage. Was the artistic loss so great? One gallantly says 'Yes.' In these gynarchic days who dare say otherwise?" (Barker, "Stagecraft" 710).

The nature of Harley Granville Barker's sexuality is open to question. While he was very publicly married twice, Eric Salmon cites Norman Marshall's unpublished assertion that "Barker was not interested in women at all and that his natural leanings were homosexual." Salmon suggests that Marshall's "terms of personal friendliness" with Barker gave him valid grounds for this conclusion (235). In *Bernard Shaw: The Ascent of the Superman*, Sally Peters makes a case for the erotically charged, if perhaps unrequited, nature of Barker's relationship with George Bernard Shaw. If Barker was a closeted homosexual, this might help explain his odd stance regarding the portrayal of women's roles in Shakespeare. The fact that these parts were written for boys made the plays, Barker claimed, void of sexual passion. Shakespeare's "men and women encounter upon a plane ... which surpasses mere primitive lovemaking." Barker therefore oddly saw *Antony and Cleopatra* as "a tragedy of sex without one single scene of sexual appeal" (*Prefaces* 1: 15). Barker was somewhat obsessed with this topic and addressed it in most of his major writings. Never, however, does he explore the possibility that the presence of boy actors on the Elizabethan stage may have itself been erotically charged. Although Barker was writing at a time when such matters were not within the purview of mainstream scholarship, his unwillingness to explore the homo-erotic dimension of transvestite performance on the early modern stage combines with his vehement denial of heterosexual passion in Shakespeare's plays to suggest, perhaps, conflicted feelings about his own sexuality.

Like Nugent Monck and William Poel, Harley Granville Barker worried that the theater was being overwhelmed by technology and spectacle. In his theoretical writings, Barker often argued for scenic austerity. "The best basis for any production is a bare stage," he asserted in 1922 (*Exemplary* 214). "Far better four boards, creaky and unscrubbed as a stage for our passion than that it should be choked by a collection of bric-a-brac" (202). He wrote that "the most importance difference of all" was that "our stage is the stage of visual illusion" while "Shakespeare's appeal was primarily to the ear" ("Stagecraft" 707). Barker was particularly wary of mechanization. "Man and machine," he warned, "are false allies in the theatre, secretly at odds; and when man gets the worst of it, drama is impoverished" (*Prefaces* 1: 7). Barker collaborated in 1913 on a short play with Dion Clayton Calthrop, titled *The Harlequinade*. This piece expressed the futuristic vision of a theater destroyed by scientific indus-trialism, in which plays are produced by a "Factory of Automatic Dramaturgy" (Calthrop and Barker 75) and performed by gramophones without the use of live actors. Elmer Salenius wrote in 1982 that the "amount of truth in this fan-tastic prophecy" was "amazing," and that Barker and Calthrop were "uncom-fortably close to accuracy in their prediction" (74). Advances in computer graphics during the decades since Salenius's observation make *The Harlequi-nade* seem even more prescient. Yet in practice Barker often succumbed to the very evils he argued against in his theoretical writings. His Savoy productions sometimes resembled the high-concept offerings he derided in 1932 as "meg-alomaniac projects for vast stages, dotted with strange symbolic structures, weird lights flashing and weird music sounding, and a few actors crawling dejectedly around," in which "Shakespeare and his play" were reduced to "a mere peg on which to hang the whole pretentious trumpery" (*Associating* 27).

Barker's Shakespeare Productions

GRANVILLE Barker's first staging of Shakespeare was *The Two Gentlemen of Verona* at the Court Theatre in April 1904, in which he also played the role of Speed. This production was traditional in its realistic stagecraft. The *Era* noted on 16 April 1904, "The comedy is adequately staged, the sets representing Julia's garden and the terrace of the Duke's palace in Milan being especially worthy of note" (review of *Two Gentlemen* 12). By this point in his career Barker had acted in two revivals for William Poel that were staged in an Elizabethan manner, but chose not to take this approach at the Court. If he had wanted to employ such unconventional practices, Barker might have been hindered by the circumstances of the production, which was bankrolled by J. H. Leigh as a vehicle for his wife, Thyrza Norman. Barker accepted the engagement because Leigh allowed him to simultaneously stage matinees of Shaw's *Candida* (Salmon 99). Without full creative control, Barker apparently viewed *Two Gentleman* as a journeyman endeavor, which he conventionally staged in exchange for the opportunity to pursue more experimental work.

In contrast to this conservative effort at the Court, Barker adopted a radical approach that flouted realistic conventions in his three Shakespeare productions at the Savoy Theatre between 1912 and 1914. Early modern staging practices were not, however, his principal inspiration. In a published letter to *Play Pictorial* in November 1912, he wrote, "We shall not save our souls by being Elizabethan" (rpt. in *Granville Barker and his Correspondents* 530). Rather, since "realistic scenery won't do, if only because it swears against everything in the plays" (529), the task at hand was to "invent a new hieroglyphic language of scenery" (530). Barker's Savoy productions owed as much to the New Stagecraft of Gordon Craig, whom Barker's costume designer called the "greatest genius and inspiration the theatre has had in our time" (Rutherston 21), as to the Elizabethan revival of William Poel. W. Bridges-Adams notes "acknowledgments to Craig" in the Savoy *Winter's Tale*'s "setting of tall white pylons against a limitless expanse of white," and suggests that Barker's rejection of strict Elizabethanism was motivated by practical marketing concerns. "If Barker had set up an Elizabethan Stage at the Savoy," he writes, "there were not Poelites in London to keep him going for a week" (Bridges-Adams, *Lost Leader* 8).

Some scholars have nevertheless exaggerated the Elizabethanism of Barker's Savoy productions. The three-tiered stage structure he used is sometimes likened to an early modern platform stage. The upper level of this configuration, according to Dennis Kennedy, "created a raised acting area similar to the Elizabethan 'inner stage'" (*Granville Barker* 124), which formed a "discovery space" (*Looking* 73). Purdom similarly asserts that this level was "used as something like the inner stage of an Elizabethan theatre" (140), and Byrne claims that the upper stage "provided an acting area which could be used for set or furnished scenes in much the same way as the Elizabethan inner- or rear-stage" ("Fifty Years" 8). In fact, there is no meaningful similarity between the highest tier of Barker's Savoy configuration and the modest curtained alcove seen today in historically accurate reconstructions like the new Globe or the Blackfriars Playhouse in Staunton, Virginia.

In Elizabethan theaters, the "discovery space" is located under a balcony in the center of the *frons scenae*. The balustraded space above therefore becomes the spectator's focal point, and the curtained area beneath is relegated to a secondary, though still important, stage position. There was no balcony on stage at the Savoy, so Barker's upper level (four steps above the stage floor) drew greater focus than does the discovery space at the current Globe or Blackfriars. More importantly, Barker's upper tier was many times larger, and could therefore accommodate the kind of elaborate sets that have no place in Elizabethan staging. Cary M. Mazer describes Barker's upper level as delineated by a "false proscenium a few feet upstage of the real one" (*Refashioned* 136). Photographs reveal that this border came in only a few feet from the true proscenium at either side (Figures 2 and 3), making Barker's upper level far wider than even the most exaggerated contemporary estimates of what had constituted an Elizabethan "inner stage." The under-balcony of Monck's Maddermarket Theatre, for instance, was 13½ feet wide (Hildy, *Shakespeare* 45), less than half the breadth of the upper tier of Barker's structure. Rather than a discovery space designed to expose a specific image like the witches' cauldron in *Macbeth*, Barker's upper stage housed entire built sets including that of Olivia's garden in *Twelfth Night*. Barker himself apparently did not see his upper stage as an Elizabethan discovery space and instead placed a portable version of this small, curtained alcove downstage on the apron, in front of the proscenium, for the revelation of Hermione's statue in *The Winter's Tale*.

William Archer's approval of Barker's Savoy productions further indicates that these were not significantly Elizabethan. Archer was a harsh critic of Poel's efforts, which he dismissed as antiquarian, but he wrote to Barker regarding the Savoy *Midsummer*, "On the whole I was charmed: the spirit is right, the decoration right, 99 details out of 100 absolutely right" (*Granville Barker and his Correspondents* 59). The only aspect Archer objected to, "the soliloquies spoken at the audience," resulted from Barker's use of a downstage apron, the only truly Elizabethan feature of his Savoy configuration (60). Four steps below the upper level was a main stage that extended to the fixed proscenium arch. Two steps below this, Barker built "a curved apron out over the orchestra pit and into the stalls, wider than the arch, and twelve feet deep in the center," which "allowed at least some of the intimacy between actor and audience so important in Barker's view of Shakespearean performance" (Kennedy, *Granville Barker* 125). Mazer concurs that "the rapport between audience and actor on the platform stage, and the spatial difference in the actor's presence on the apron and the main stage" were elements of Elizabethan practice that Barker recreated in his Savoy productions (*Refashioned* 135).

Some contemporary critics appreciated Barker's intention and felt that the atmosphere created by the apron was the most significant feature of his Savoy staging. John Palmer found the delivery of asides on this Elizabethan forestage to be "gloriously effective," and wrote in his review of *The Winter's Tale* for the *Saturday Review*, "The value of Mr. Barker's revival – apart from the acting – rests almost wholly upon his production [or projection] of the stage into the auditorium" (391). Shaw said in an interview with the *Observer* that Barker's configuration "apparently trebled the spaciousness of the stage" and created a novel play-going experience. "To the imagination it looks as if he had invented a new heaven and a new earth," Shaw claimed. "Instead of the theatre being a huge auditorium, with a picture frame at one end of it, the theatre is now a stage with some unnoticed spectators around it" (quoted in Bartholomeusz 149). Yet even these favorable commentators admitted that

2 Photograph of the Palace for Barker's Savoy *Winter's Tale*

3 Photograph of the Garden for Barker's Savoy *Twelfth Night*

most observers overlooked the intimacy and perspective created by Barker's apron stage. Shaw lamented that most people "never noticed the change." He claimed this was because "it was so right that they took it as a matter of course" (quoted in Bartholomeusz 149), but Palmer was probably closer to the truth when he suggested that spectators were distracted by the outrageous visual effects. "Critics seem for the most part," Palmer wrote, "to have spent their time in an unprofitable inspection of Mr. Rothenstein's [later Rutherston's] costumes and Mr. Norman Wilkinson's decoration" (391). These sets and dresses were so stunning that the costumes for *The Winter's Tale*, which betrayed an exotic, Byzantine influence, were placed after the production in public exhibition at a London art gallery. "People who would have blushed to speak of going to His Majesty's to see the scenery," Bridges-Adams writes, "spoke without shame of going to the Savoy to see the décor" (*Lost Leader* 10).

Barker's intention was to merge the intimacy of thrust with the scenic possibilities of the picture-frame stage. He sought to create Elizabethan immediacy downstage, while simultaneously maintaining elaborate visual imagery on his set's upper level. For Norman Marshall, this meant that the audience was continually "jolted to and fro between two separate theatrical conventions" (*Producer* 150). Mazer similarly calls Barker's "Savoy double stage" a "dismal failure, perhaps the result of a confusion of goals" (*Refashioned* 136). Actors on the apron were literally upstaged by the complex sets and decorations. Kennedy concludes that many "spectators found that the new scenography did exactly what Barker had condemned about the old: it interposed itself between the play and the reception" (*Looking* 79). Barker vented frustration at the furor provoked by the Savoy designs in his response, from the *Play Pictorial* letter, to a journalist who had expressed reservations about the "confoundedly-puzzling scenery" in *Twelfth Night*. "I ask you," Barker queried his critic, "when you yourself are trying to set down something important, to have your handwriting admired, or to be tripped over a mistake in syntax – what are your feelings?" (rpt. in *Granville Barker and his Correspondents* 529). Barker apparently viewed the visual elements of his productions as peripheral. To focus attention on such matters was as foolish as to analyze a writer's penmanship rather than the words he wrote. Barker did not grasp that a public trained to appreciate the spectacular splendor of Beerbohm Tree would naturally consider ocular content to be of paramount importance.

The director eventually came to regret the stylistic excess of his Savoy productions. "Barker's distrust of décor, as expressed in the 1920s," Mazer writes, "is profound" (*Refashioned* 132). Yet many later scholars have idolized these early efforts. This is in part because most critics writing after 1950 had not been at the Savoy, and instead sought to reconstruct these stagings through the lens of Barker's *Prefaces to Shakespeare*. Muriel St Clare Byrne, for instance, frequently associates the Savoy productions with principles that Barker expounded only later in his critical writing. A minute but telling example comes when she claims that Barker "allowed only one break in the action" (Foreword xi). In reality, the Savoy *Midsummer* contained two intervals, which were scheduled not for audience comfort but to facilitate scene changes (Kennedy, *Granville Barker* 163). Barker thus committed the cardinal sin of "butchering Shakespeare to make a stage-carpenter's holiday" for which Shaw and Poel had condemned Beerbohm Tree (Shaw quoted in Styan, *Shakespeare Revolution* 26). While Byrne may be correct that "but for the productions the *Prefaces* might never have been written" (Foreword x), the relationship between the two is not what she assumes. Byrne believes that Barker learned how to stage Shakespeare at the Savoy. I suggest instead that what he learned was how *not* to stage Shakespeare, at least according to the standards Barker subsequently advocated in his critical writing. In the remainder of this section, I will look in detail at each of the Savoy productions as well as Barker's 1940 *King Lear* at the Old Vic.

The Winter's Tale

The Winter's Tale, which premiered in September of 1912, was Barker's first Shakespeare at the Savoy. Rather than Elizabethan methods, it featured what George C. D. Odell described as "modern staging with a vengeance" (466). *The Winter's Tale* was a financial failure and ran for only six weeks. Critical response was mixed, but tended toward the negative. The *Times* on 23 September gave the production a qualified endorsement, calling it "distinctly amusing" and pronouncing, "On the whole we like it." The review approved of Barker's eclectic mix of styles, which it defined as "Post-Impressionist Shakespeare":

> The busbies and caftans and deep-skirted tunics of the courtiers come from the Russian Ballet, and the *bizarre* smocks and fal-lals of the merrymakers at the sheep-shearing come from the Chelsea Arts Club Ball. Warriors are stuck all over with plumes, and look like fantastic and expensive toys. At Hermione's trial the officers of the court wear comically exaggerated birettas ... the whole scene suggests Beaumarchais ... Leontes reclines upon a seat which is frankly Art Nouveau. The Bohemian peasants are genuine Thomas Hardy ... Yes, there is no other word for it save the word that in popular usage denotes a special kind of artistic assault on conventionalism; it is Post-Impressionist Shakespeare. (review of *Winter's Tale* 7)

The critic took exception, however, to some of the more extreme visual elements. He described the wigs worn by Hermione and Leontes as an incongruous mixture of "Shakespeare and the fuzzy-wuzzy Tahitians." The reviewer dismissed the shepherd's cottage as "a model bungalow from the Ideal Home Exhibition with Voysey windows," which "strikes us as a joke, and not a good one," and derided the costumes in the Bohemia scenes as "superfluously, wantonly, ugly." The *Times* acknowledged one Elizabethan aspect of Barker's staging, the "set speeches" addressed "directly to the audience," and defined this as "the proper method, of course, of the old 'platform.'" But the review also correctly dated the production's practice of "the act-drop occasionally descending upon the actors when they are speaking" to "the theatre of the restoration" and not to Shakespeare's age (review of *Winter's Tale* 7).

Other notices were less tolerant of Barker's catholic vision. The *Athenaeum* wrote, "Mr. Granville Barker, in a distressful striving after the artistic, has achieved that mingling of discordant, ill-related elements, that impossible jangling of different keys, which can never be far removed from vulgarity." The anonymous critic acknowledged the intent, and the failure, of Barker's attempt to merge thrust and proscenium. He lauded "the device of extending the boundaries of the stage so as to provide a fore-space with side exits," which "rendered distinct and original service to the interpretation of the play." But while "that part of the action which takes place in front of the drop scene" was "generally recognizable as Shakespearian," the same could not be said for much of the remainder. The reviewer specifically rejected the "country revels" of the Bohemia section, which he felt had "no claim to consideration." "Mr. Barker," the *Athenaeum* concludes, is "strangely capable of being wearisome" (review of *Winter's Tale* 351). Not impressed by the originality of Barker's methods, J. T. Grein in the *Sunday Times* dismissed the Savoy *Winter's Tale* as "an orgy of new ideas grafted on classic soil" and as an exercise in "snobbist slavery" (7). As John Palmer noted, most of the journal critics focused largely on the production's scenic and costume effects. Descriptions of spectacle similarly dominate other first-hand accounts. "The first appearance of Miss Lillah McCarthy under a tremendous gold umbrella was so stunning," Bridges-Adams wrote years later, "that I cannot remember as much of her Hermione as I would like to" (*Lost Leader* 10–11).

Barker's confusing pronouncements regarding visual style make the task of analyzing his design choices more difficult. "As to scenery," he wrote of the Savoy *Winter's Tale*, "I would have none of it." The apparent contradiction between Barker's stated position and the elaborate scenic effects described in reviews is partly explained by a distinction between "scenery," which he rejected, and "decoration," of which he approved. Unfortunately he was maddeningly vague about these two categories. "The difference," he wrote, "is better seen that talked of" (*More Prefaces* 24). Dennis Bartholomeusz explicates thus: "Decoration for Barker was not illustration, or the mere play of fancy, but the revelation of an inner world behind the visible surface of reality" (145). Despite this supposedly non-illusionist intent, Barker's settings were frequently more illustrative than his advocates have acknowledged. The Bohemian shepherd's dwelling, a full-scale building which Dennis Kennedy nevertheless refers to as "metonymic" (*Looking* 73), has been particularly minimized in later accounts. Karen Greif describes it as "simply a cut-out shepherd's cottage with a wicker fence, set against an unadorned back-cloth" (126). It provided, according to Bartholomeusz, "only a hint of the representational" (143). But a house on stage is more than a hint, and this structure was as realistic as anything used at His Majesty's (Figure 4). A photograph of Hermione's first entrance (Figure 5) shows her descending beneath that giant gold umbrella onto a stage filled with what looks like a three-piece sectional of richly upholstered furniture and a coffee table topped with a giant fruit basket. This suggests that the Sicily scenes were also more elaborate and realistic than has been generally recognized.

Many later scholars have blamed contemporary observers for their inability to appreciate Barker's work. "Most reviewers of the time," Kennedy writes,

4　The Shepherd's Cottage in Barker's Savoy *Winter's Tale*

5　Hermione's First Entrance in Barker's Savoy *Winter's Tale*

"were conservative in their dramatic tastes, and should not be completely trusted about challenging innovation" (*Granville Barker* 133). Styan suggests that "the critics groped for points of reference" but did not realize that the "extravagance and eccentricity, of course, was planned for the release of the imagination into the world of artifice" (*Shakespeare Revolution* 87). Mazer, however, attributes the failure of *The Winter's Tale* to the indeterminacy of Barker's method. During the first half of the play, the nominal notion of a universal set was compromised by periodic rearrangements of curtains and furniture to signify various locations within Leontes's palace. Barker "could not decide whether he was creating a space or a room, and so created contradictory results" (Mazer, *Refashioned* 144). The published letter to *Play Pictorial* suggests that Barker had not completely broken with the traditional stagecraft of the Victorian era. With regard to the infamous pastoral abode, he admits that the "cottage of the shepherd was much blamed" by critics, but asserts that "the play demanded a cottage; to be put in conventional surroundings, and therefore a conventional cottage" was required (rpt. in *Granville Barker and his Correspondents* 530). Barker's use of "conventional" here refers not to the practices of the non-localized Elizabethan stage but rather to the representational paradigm of Tree and Irving. This position seems at odds with Barker's stated rejection of "scenery" and confirms the confusion sensed by Mazer, who writes that the Savoy productions "were often miscalculated and self-contradictory, more so than adulatory theatre historians ... have been willing to admit" (*Refashioned* 123).

One non-scenic element that provoked extensive comment at the time of the Savoy *Winter's Tale* was the rapidity with which the actors spoke Shakespeare's lines. Response to this "gabbling" was uniformly negative. J. T. Grein wrote that, because of the extreme speed of delivery, "Not a soul, unfamiliar with the play, could follow its drift and pace" (7); and Arnold Bennett complained that "half the words" were "incomprehensible" (248). Barker deliberately intended this galloping pace of speech. He said in a 1914 interview with *The New York Times*, "In the matter of speed I am adamant" ("A Talk About the Stage" 9). Cathleen Nesbitt, who played Perdita, confirms Barker's "mania for speed" (quoted in Elliot 52). Byrne ties this vocal velocity to Barker's desire to avoid cutting the play. "Granville-Barker presented unabridged texts," she wrote in 1949. "For this to be possible, in what was, after all, an evening's entertainment and not a test of scholarly endurance, the whole tempo of production had to be speeded-up" ("Fifty Years" 8). In order to present a full text Barker willingly compromised the public's ability to receive the play's language. Kenneth Branagh did the same thing with his uncut cinematic *Hamlet*, in which the filmmaker retained obscure passages (such as the reference to the "little eyases") but had them delivered at such blinding speed that there was little opportunity for interpretation from the actors or comprehension by the audience. Like Branagh, Barker employed an "eat your vegetables and you'll get dessert" approach to textual fidelity. He asked the audience to listen to an uncut text played at incomprehensible speed, in compensation for which he offered the elaborate spectacle of the production's sets and costumes. *The Winter's Tale* thus created a textual monument for literary cognoscenti and simultaneously attempted to appease the masses with stunning scenic effects.

Another aspect of the inaugural Savoy production reveals an anxiety that informs much of Barker's career. All his biographers note Barker's lack of formal education and subsequent efforts to ingratiate himself into the world of high culture in order to become "more respectable" (Dymkowski 140). In the Introduction to the acting edition of *The Winter's Tale*, Barker describes how he and his costume designer, Albert Rothenstein, arrived at one element of their visual concept:

> I suddenly thought and said to Rothenstein, "Giulio Romano! There's our pattern designer recommended in the play itself." It's little I know of Giulio Romano. Ought I to confess that Rothenstein could remember little more? But Giulio Romano was looked up, and there the costumes were much as we had forethought them. (rpt. in *More Prefaces* 24)

This passage describes the aspirations of two upwardly mobile theater practitioners eager to ascend into the bourgeois world. Barker's shame at the "little" he and Rothenstein knew is erased by the facility with which the cultural icon can be "looked up." In 1923 these two would collaborate on a literary project, the *Players' Shakespeare* series, for which Barker wrote prefaces and Rothenstein served as art director. By this time, both the director and the designer had changed their names in quest of middle-class respectability. Rothenstein Anglicized his patronymic to the gentlemanly "Rutherston," and Harley adopted the scholarly hyphenate "Granville-Barker" (for simplicity's sake I have consistently used the unhyphenated version of his name, even when referring to later events). As Ralph Berry writes, Barker "adopted the hyphen in 1918, around the time when he married Huntington money and effectively withdrew from active stage work ... The hyphen bears all the symbolism of this change" ("Two Great" 376). The onset of Barker's professional identity crisis is, I believe, suggested by the aggressive excitement he expresses in his discovery of Giulio Romano.

Twelfth Night

According to G. Wilson Knight, "*Twelfth Night* was the best" of Baker's Savoy stagings (*Shakespearian* 221). It was a popular and financial success, running for 137 performances. *Twelfth Night* was also, unlike *The Winter's Tale*, generally well received by critics, who perceived it as more mainstream than Barker's previous effort. The *Times* wrote on 16 November 1912 that in this production "Mr. Granville Barker sets out chiefly to please rather than, as in the *Winter's Tale*, chiefly to make us 'sit up.' There is no deliberate challenge now to the scoffer, no flaunting eccentricity, no obvious search for quaintness for its own sake." The review also praised "Mr. Norman Wilkinson's 'decoration,'" which it described as "simple, flat, [and] conventional" unlike the more experimental set for *The Winter's Tale* (review of *Twelfth Night* 10). The *Illustrated London News* on 23 November likewise found *Twelfth Night* "more conciliatory" than its predecessor (review of *Twelfth Night* 780).

Many later scholars have rejected the notion that Barker modified his methods to make *Twelfth Night* more palatable. The conventional wisdom by 1980 was that *The Winter's Tale* served "to break the critical ice," preparing critics and audiences for what was essentially more of the same in the second Savoy offering. "What had appeared disconcertingly radical and modern in September," Karen Greif writes, "in November was hailed as 'a breath of fresh air'" (131). Christine Dymkowski similarly asserts that this "revival was actually no different from the first" (46); and Edward M. Moore writes that the "critical about-face when *Twelfth Night* opened two weeks after *The Winter's Tale* closed substantiates the integrity of what Barker was doing" ("Introduction" 14). The second Savoy production, however, represented a greater compromise with popular expectations than these remarks acknowledge.

One reason that theater historians have not viewed *Twelfth Night* as acceding to the demands of contemporary taste is that it opened so soon after *The Winter's Tale* was withdrawn from the evening bill (matinee performances continued through the end of November). Two weeks does not at first seem time enough for Barker to have significantly altered his methods, even if he had so desired. Preparations for *Twelfth Night* began, however, during the six-week run of *The Winter's Tale*, and Barker notoriously worked his cast and production staff very long hours. As Nesbitt wrote of her work at the Savoy, "We rehearsed until three or four o'clock [in the morning]–there was no Equity in those days" (quoted in Elliot 52). Barker had sufficient opportunity during this period to change the play following *The Winter's Tale* from *Macbeth* to *Twelfth Night*. The company had rehearsed the Scottish Tragedy throughout the summer, but when *The Winter's Tale* failed at the box office *Macbeth* was dropped in favor of the more popular comedy. Felix Aylmer (today best remembered as Polonius in Laurence Olivier's 1948 film adaptation of *Hamlet*) was a bit player at the Savoy and later found himself performing on a set from the aborted *Macbeth* in Birmingham, where it "had become the Ogre's castle in *Puss in Boots*" (Aylmer 33). The shift in program suggests that Barker also had time to alter his visual style to make it more acceptable. He later asserted that he had chosen *The Winter's Tale* as a sacrificial lamb, which he knew would be devoured by the critics as they grew accustomed to his methods. "We shall have to throw one play to the wolves," Barker claims to have said when planning his Savoy season (quoted in "A Talk About the Stage" 9). But his decision to change the second play from the challenging *Macbeth* to the more accessible *Twelfth Night* demonstrates that Barker was more deeply affected by the negative response to *The Winter's Tale* than this cavalier quotation implies. This concern also resulted in a move toward greater localization and realism in the subsequent production's set design.

Many scholars have stressed the minimalism and non-representational quality of the Illyrian garden which formed the central set of Barker's *Twelfth Night*. Hugh Hunt writes, "Instead of the traditional garden setting with its grass and shrubs, there were one or two cut-out trees with some formal steps" ("Granville-Barker" 47). J. L. Styan describes a setting of "pale green yew trees with box hedges in a topiarian arrangement [which] reminded spectators of a child's Noah's Ark toy-box" (*Shakespeare Revolution* 91). He then, without irony, describes *Twelfth Night* a few pages later as a "production unimpeded by detail" (95). Dennis Kennedy states that only "one full-stage set was built, showing Olivia's formal garden, and it was even more non-illusionist than the sets for the previous play" (*Granville Barker* 145). In contrast to these descriptions, Olivia's garden was actually quite representational. This setting was dominated by trees that Kennedy describes as "futuristic space needles" (*Granville Barker* 145) which, while abstract, were still identifiably trees and therefore served the traditional Victorian function of localizing theatrical action. As in the case of pop-art in the 1960s, Barker's set reassured his spectators by providing them with recognizable, though distorted, objects.

Tying the design of Barker's *Twelfth Night* to traditional Edwardian stagecraft, Mazer claims that the production's main set had much in common with Beerbohm Tree's realistic staging of this comedy. Barker's garden was permanent like Tree's "unstrikable" terrace, and "the other built scenes were placed before it or inserted into it." These other settings, for Mazer, were highly representational. "The 'kitchen' scene was a small tapestried room," he writes, "the prison was a simple grate with curtains on either side" and "the final scene was placed before a gate to Olivia's property." Mazer suggests that "Barker thoroughly intended, in his production of *Twelfth Night,* to ape the success of Edwardian fashionable drawing-room comedy, such as was playing elsewhere in the West End" (*Refashioned* 145). The photographic record supports Mazer's analysis. While Greif claims that the configuration for the midnight carousal used the "simplest essentials" to "suggest the outlines of a

6 Malvolio interrupts the revelers in Barker's Savoy *Twelfth Night*

room" (133), the photograph she reproduces (Figure 6) show that this setting used realistic furniture to recreate the kind of "fourth-wall" ambiance familiar to contemporary audiences.

The shepherd's cottage may have been more realistic, but Olivia's garden formed the backdrop for a larger portion of its respective play, and the extensive use of furniture placed *Twelfth Night* even further than *The Winter's Tale* from the Elizabethan ideal of a bare stage. Instead of advancing the cause of non-localized staging which he would later champion in his *Prefaces*, Barker's *Twelfth Night* represented a retreat toward the traditional stagecraft of the theatrical status quo. This compromise with popular expectations was efficacious, as the production proved the only unqualified success among Barker's Savoy offerings.

Twelfth Night gave Barker an opportunity to explore some of his ideas regarding women players in Shakespeare. The "breeches part" of Viola/Cesario was a perfect test case for his notion that women in Shakespeare should act like boys. Lillah McCarthy (married to Barker at the time of the production) recalled that "the producer" insisted on having Viola "played as a leading man," which she initially found to be a "big strain." "During rehearsal," she observed, "I must have stressed too much the poetry of the part, and by so doing let Viola betray the woman in her. The producer would not have it so. I must play the man." Eventually, she struck a balance, managing "at last to make Viola steer clear of the shallows of sentimentality and safely past the hard rocks of extreme mannishness" (161). While McCarthy's performance was successful, there is something disturbing about Barker's attempt to contain his wife's femininity on stage. This effort to manipulate her behavior did not end with their marriage. When McCarthy wrote her autobiography after the couple's divorce, Barker threatened legal action and "made it clear that there should be no reference whatever to himself anywhere in the book" (Purdom 191). This accounts for McCarthy's odd references to her ex-husband as simply "the producer."

A Midsummer Night's Dream

Like his production of *Twelfth Night*, Barker's *A Midsummer Night's Dream*, which opened at the Savoy in February 1914, was a popular success. It ran for ninety-nine performances, but many critics did not like it. While Lillah McCarthy later claimed that the "press was unanimous in its praise" (175), actual contemporary reviews were largely unfavorable. As in the case of *The Winter's Tale*, observers objected to the production's elaborate and abstract design. The *Era* wrote that *Midsummer* was "too bizarre, too grotesquely imaginative even for a dream; in fact, at times it becomes dangerously akin to a nightmare" (review of *Midsummer* 13). John Palmer, who approved of both *The Winter's Tale* and *Twelfth Night*, felt that this time Barker had ruined the play. Palmer wrote for the *Saturday Review*, "I would have been quite happy in Mr. Wilkinson's forest had it not been for the unfortunate coincidence that Mr. Barker's company of players were therein trying to present a play purporting to be by William Shakespeare." He had read Barker's early Preface to

Midsummer (published in the 1914 Acting Edition), and concluded from this essay that the director "really loved and understood Shakespeare as a practical dramatist writing for a stage and an audience." After seeing the production, however, Palmer felt that "the play now running at the Savoy, though it be almost everything by turns, and nothing long, is never Shakespeare's 'Dream.'" Barker's *Midsummer* represented "Shakespeare being slaughtered to make an intellectual and post-impressionist holiday." The playwright, Palmer wrote, "never had a chance" (review of *Midsummer* 202). These comments are instructive when compared to the writings of later scholars like Byrne and Styan, who have portrayed the Savoy stagings as a triumph of literature in performance. The *Illustrated London News* sensed a disconnect between Barker's stated reverence for the text and the production's emphasis on outlandish décor. "This mistake of audacity in Messrs. Barker and Norman Wilkinson's scheme is the more vexing," the *ILN* reviewer wrote, because "we are given the whole text of the play" (review of *Midsummer* 449).

Desmond MacCarthy, who reviewed *Midsummer* for the *New Statesman*, eventually endorsed the production, but had to see it twice to get over the scenic elements. He suggests that, as in the case of *The Winter's Tale*, *Midsummer*'s design caused more comment than Barker would have wished: "I am sure (the newspaper criticism confirms this) that the majority of the audience thought as much about scenery at the Savoy Theatre as ever did an audience at His Majesty's. It was a different kind of scenery, but just as distracting to most people" (rpt. in MacCarthy, *Drama* 11). MacCarthy wrote that on his first visit he "did not think Mr. Norman Wilkinson's scenery beautiful," and instead felt "that it was distracting and not in harmony with the spirit of the play." He enjoyed *Midsummer* "a great deal more the second time," and wrote that the "merits of this production came out clearer when surprise at the scenic effects ... has subsided" (10). The fact that MacCarthy required repeated viewings to arrive at a critical judgment suggests that the visual effects were more of a hindrance than an aid to comprehension.

This mixed reaction in London was replaced with outright scorn when Barker restaged *A Midsummer Night's Dream* in New York in 1915. George G. C. Odell attended the 16 February performance at Wallack's Theatre and described the setting of Titania's bower thus:

> The fairy scene was built up to a round mound in the middle of the stage, and covered with bright green velvet carpet. Just above the mound was suspended a large terra-cotta wreath of flowers that would have been the envy of a German pastry cook, and from it depended a veil of white gauze, lighted within by vari-colored electric bulbs, hanging at irregular lengths. At the back and sides of the stage fluttered curtains of chintz or silk, designed to suggest forest branches. Like forest branches they waved vigorously in the breeze, so that one felt disposed to ask some one to shut the windows in heaven in order that the trees might not blow out so violently into Titania's bower. (467)

Odell was sympathetic to Elizabethan staging. "Anyone who has imagination," he wrote, "can get the poetic illusion by seeing these things acted on a bare stage or on a stage hung with curtains or with just a conventional unchanged setting." But he saw no connection between this minimalist aesthetic and Barker's production. "No human being," he continued, "can be expected to be anything but worried and annoyed by pink silk curtains that are supposed to be the roofs of houses, or green silk curtains that are supposed to be forest trees" (468). While he is perhaps unnecessarily cantankerous, Odell correctly notes the difference between Barker's elaborate methods and the simplified approach of practitioners like Poel and Monck.

More harsh in his criticism than even Odell, William Winter described Barker's New York *Midsummer* as a "nauseous admixture of mental decadence and crotchety humbug," which "reveal[ed] a deplorable proclivity for frivolous and fantastic innovation" (281–2). Winter was near the end of his life in 1915, and would die two years later at age eighty-one. His comment that *Midsummer* "should be made to move with ease and celerity through a sequence of handsome scenes" (295) and his complaint that because of the apron stage "illusion was destroyed" (284) betray Winter's allegiance to the traditional stagecraft of an earlier generation. Nevertheless Barker's lack of a coherent philosophy of staging gives credence to Winter's assertion that the "pretence that Granville Barker's productions show *any advance* in the producer's art is preposterous. At their best ... they indicate nothing higher than a commercial purpose to profit, if possible by ministering to a craze for 'something different,' merely because it is different" (294).

The outrageous portrayal of Oberon, Titania, and their followers suggests that novelty for novelty's sake may have indeed been one of Barker's goals. The costuming of these fairies was the feature which attracted the most attention from both proponents and detractors. The *Times*, which liked *Midsummer*, thought the fairies its most brilliant element and began a review on 7 February 1914, subtitled "Golden Fairies at the Savoy Theatre," with their description:

> Is it Titania's "Indian boy" that has given Mr. Barker his notion of Orientalizing Shakespeare's fairies? Or is it Bakst? Anyhow, they look like Cambodian idols and posture like Nijinsky in *Le Dieu Bleu* ... they are all gold ... One with a scimitar stalks like the black marionette, with *his* scimitar in *Petrouchka*. Evidently the Russian ballet, which has transformed so much in London, has transmogrified Shakespeare ... One might perhaps have had misgivings about the thing in advance ... But the thing turns out to have been an inspiration.

The *Times* critic quickly dismisses the production's other elements. Of the four lovers, he writes that if "they escape being bores, they may be said to have succeeded. We are not sure that the men did altogether escape." The reviewer then returns to his favorite topic. "But it is not of these one thinks in the end," he writes. "The mind goes back to the golden fairies, and one's memories of this production must always be golden memories" (review of *Midsummer* 8).

Not all observers were smitten with Barker's sprites. The *Illustrated London News* wrote that they looked "neither pretty nor poetical," and seemed "the invention of calculated eccentricity and of the resolve to do something new at all costs" (review of *Midsummer* 449). Edward M. Moore, who generally argues for the success of the Savoy productions, concedes that Barker "always insisted that any kind of scenery, scenic decorations, or settings were wrong if they called attention to themselves at the expense of the text, and his gilded fairies certainly seem to have done so" ("Introduction" 16). Odell grumbled that by "the aid of their bronze you could tell at a glance whether any person in the play was a fairy or a mortal, and as Mr. Barker evidently had no faith in Shakespeare or the imagination of the audience, this was an advantage" (468).

Many contrasting descriptions of these fairies have been offered at the time and since. Norman Marshall, without specifying his sources, cites contemporary press reports which referred to them variously as " 'nickel-plated sprites,' 'lacquered leprechauns,' 'peroxidised pixies,' [and] 'tawny Hindus" (quoted in *Producer* 157). Several observers noted their mechanical movements including MacCarthy, who describes them as "ormolu fairies, looking as though they had been detached from some fantastic, bristling old clock" (*Drama* 11). Some later scholars also emphasize this quality. Samuel L. Leiter's identification of the sprites as "robot-like beings" (37) suggests that Barker may have sought to create the same kind of futuristic fantasy he had explored in 1913's *The Harlequinade*. Perhaps perceiving a similar connection to Craig's "*ubermarionetten*" as that advanced by Gary Taylor (274), Dymkowski describes the fairies' movements as "jerky" and "puppet-like" (60). Hugh Hunt, while acknowledging the similarity to puppets, identifies these spirits as principally "connected with some vaguely Eastern folklore" ("Granville-Barker" 48). Photographs (Figure 7) reveal a mixture of Middle Eastern, Himalayan,

7   Eight fairies from Barker's Savoy *Midsummer Night's Dream*

and Indian elements in their costumes. Robert Shaughnessy, writing in 2005, reads Barker's fairies as an expression of imperial anxieties in early twentieth-century Britain ("Dreams" 114).

All accounts agree that the fairies were "golden," a description literally achieved by Barker and his production team. "The makeup was gold leaf," Kennedy writes, and "applied from small sheets with the fingers" (*Granville Barker* 160). Lillah McCarthy recalled that "it cost a shilling each time the gilding was done and, for economy's sake, the elves had to keep their faces golden between the matinees and evening performances" (175). No better example illustrates the chasm which separated Barker's approach from that of Nugent Monck. Monck, like Poel before him, rejected extravagant expense in his stagings of Shakespeare. Barker, on the other hand, covered his performers with money.

Barker's attempts to merge traditional and abstract scenography were as confusing in *A Midsummer Night's Dream* as they had been in *The Winter's Tale*. While Theseus's palace was fairly representational, the forest scenes "made no attempt at realism" (Marshall, *Producer* 156). Trevor Griffiths describes the pains Barker took to establish the play's locations visually:

> The action thus moved from the white silk curtains with conventional gold design, which represented the palace, to the salmon pink curtains of the carpenter's shop, with steel blue masses supposed to represent the roofs of the city, and thence to the non-naturalistic wood … From the wood the scene returned to the carpenter's shop and ultimately to the palace, where the fairies reappeared to mingle with the solid columns and blend the fairy and mortal worlds against a star-spangled backdrop. (79–80)

Far from employing an unlocalized stage, Barker's *Midsummer* was therefore highly specific in its semiotics of place. Kennedy for his part acknowledges "some concessions to atmosphere," but seeks to minimize any connection to the representational tradition. He writes that the mound built for Titania's bower was "green (but not grass)" (*Looking* 77). While this distinction rightly separates Barker's *Midsummer* from the verdant staging of Beerbohm Tree, Kennedy glosses over the fact that any set built to signify a specific location is an embrace of realism.

A Midsummer Night's Dream was Barker's last Shakespeare production at the Savoy. Even with long runs for *Twelfth Night* and *Midsummer* Barker was losing money, and his budget depended on philanthropic support. With the outbreak of war in 1914 this source of funding evaporated. Barker went to New York and attempted a failed season at Wallack's Theatre, which included a remounting of *Midsummer*. The two Greek tragedies he staged outdoors in American college football stadiums also lost money. Barker despaired deeply and wrote to Gilbert Murray, "One feels about once a day that the trenches would be a welcome relief to the crass anxiety of it all" (quoted in Purdom 171). He had pronounced in 1912, "We shall not save our souls by being Elizabethan" (*Granville Barker and his Correspondents* 530). Yet Barker may have come to feel that he had lost his soul through his Savoy attempts at theatrical compromise. In 1917 Barker published a short story set in New York titled "Souls on Fifth." The narrator wanders the streets of Manhattan in a state of despondency similar to Barker's own during this period. This storyteller is possessed, Barker writes, of "forty years growing contempt for the human race" ("Souls" 60) and calls his life "a black and hollow thing, a wasted thing" (73). The narrator magically becomes able to converse with the dead souls of New Yorkers, who float up and down Fifth Avenue. One of these, the spirit of a minister, tells a story of self-betrayal which parallels Barker's experience at the Savoy. The clergyman had come to Fifth Avenue with the intent of turning his materialistic congregation toward a more spiritual path. "But looking back," the minister says, "I see quite clearly now what happened. I had set out to convert Fifth Avenue," but instead, "it was Fifth Avenue converted me" (63).

King Lear (1940)

Following his Savoy productions, Barker did not stage Shakespeare for twenty-five years. He nevertheless greatly influenced Shakespearean production during this period through his scholarly writing, particularly his *Prefaces*. Chastened by his unsuccessful Savoy compromise with representational staging, Barker advocated a stricter adherence to Elizabethan conventions in his critical essays than he had ever followed as a director. Before withdrawing from the stage in 1915, Barker frequently dismissed the importance of early modern practices. "There is no Shakespearean tradition," he wrote in a 1912 letter to the *Daily Mail*. "At most we can deduce from a few scraps of knowledge what Elizabethan methods were" (rpt. in *Granville Barker and his Correspondents* 528). Nor did he hold great reverence for the architecture of Shakespeare's theater. "I do not care to go in for an exact reproduction of the Elizabethan stage," he told *The New York Times* in 1914. "It is archeological and unattractive" (quoted in "A Talk About the Stage" 9). By 1923 he attached greater importance to early modern staging, writing in the Introduction to *The Players' Shakespeare*, "If I am asked whether, with all the scene devising and designing in the world, we shall do better for Shakespeare than he did for himself upon his own plain stage, backed by a curtain and an inner room, surmounted by a balcony, I will answer that I doubt it, and do rather more than doubt" (rpt. in *More Prefaces* 54). He wrote of this same "plain stage" in his 1927 Preface to *King Lear* that a producer "cuts from [its] anchorage at his peril." Attempts to devise an alternative, "atmospheric sort of background, which does not positively conflict with the play's stagecraft," such as Barker had essayed at the Savoy, would likely not "be worth the risk and the trouble" (Preface to *Lear* lxxviii).

Barker's writings helped convince Tyrone Guthrie (along with Guthrie's visits to Nugent Monck's Maddermarket Theatre) to adopt Elizabethan methods at the Old Vic in the 1930s. Guthrie wrote that he "had read Granville-Barker's Prefaces to Shakespeare" (*Life* 120) and therefore decided to "have no scenery except a 'structure,' which would offer the facilities usually supposed to have been available in the Elizabethan theatres" (121). Barker's admirers made many efforts to draw him out of retirement to direct an Eliza-bethan production. For years he refused. Barker replied to one such request from John Gielgud in 1937, "As to me – oh, no I have put it all into books now … I doubt if I'd *be* any good as a producer any longer – other reasons apart. I doubt if I've energy and patience left" (*Granville Barker and his Correspondents* 416). In 1940, however, Barker finally agreed to stage an Old Vic production of *King Lear* featuring Gielgud in the title role.

Barker's Preface to *King Lear* was particularly influential. In it he refuted the argument, advanced since the time of Charles Lamb, that *Lear* was impossible to stage. Barker has since been given much credit for restoring the play to the theatrical canon. T. C. Worsley, for instance, wrote in 1953 that *Lear*'s return to theatrical prominence in the mid-twentieth century was due "as much to Granville Barker as to anyone" (100). The 1940 production was an attempt to bring Barker's critical ideas to life on stage. The program announced that the performance was "based upon Harley Granville Barker's Preface to *King Lear* and his personal advice besides" (rpt. in *Granville Barker and his Correspondents* 424–5). The *Manchester Guardian* in its review of 17 April acknowledged this connection. "In the very first sentence of his famous preface to 'King Lear,'" the *Guardian* wrote, "Mr. Granville-Barker declared it to be his business to justify the tragedy's place in the theatre." The reviewer added, "In this production this claim is vindicated at almost every point" (review of *King Lear* 6).

While Barker was lured out of retirement partly by the urge to incarnate his theories about *Lear*, there were other exigencies. London was at war, and the blitzkrieg raged. The Old Vic had been scarred by fire and bombs, and *King Lear* was staged "in aid of the rebuilding fund" (Nesbitt 177). Soon afterward, the theater was seriously damaged by other air raids and rendered unusable for the duration. William French suggests that Barker's "sense of the Nazi threat to civilized values surely affected his decision" to work on the pro-duction (47) and asserts that the opportunity to bring *Lear* back to the Eng-lish stage under these perilous conditions proved "an irresistible temptation" (52). Barker nevertheless restricted the extent of his involvement. While the *Manchester Guardian* claimed that it "was Mr. Granville-Barker himself who supervised this production [and] ordered each movement and intonation of it" (review of *King Lear* 6), John Gielgud recalls that "Barker refused to have his name officially announced as director, and only agreed to supervise some rehearsals, using his own preface to the play as a foundation" (*Stage Directions* 51). Barker devoted limited time to the production. Lewis Casson and Tyrone Guthrie held several rehearsals before Barker arrived from France. Gielgud writes that Barker then "worked with actors for ten days, but he left after the first dress-rehearsal and never saw a performance with an audi-ence" (51). In spite of these constraints, Barker was still effective. As demon-strated during the two-week interval at the Savoy between *The Winter's Tale* and *Twelfth Night*, he was capable of achieving meaningful results in a short period of time. Gielgud notes that the actors were "constantly dismayed" by Barker's high standards "and by the intense hard work to which he subjected them without showing any appearance of fatigue himself" (53).

For many years scholars did not grant much significance to the 1940 *King Lear* at the Old Vic. G. Wilson Knight called it "a half-hearted collaboration with Lewis Casson and John Gielgud" to which Barker "was unwilling to give his name" ("Producer" 794); and C. B. Purdom wrote that it "had a mixed reception" and possessed "little of the real Barker quality, for the production was uncertain and confused" (263). In recent decades this *Lear* has received more recognition. Dennis Kennedy, for instance, writes that Barker's "hand helped make the performance one of the most successful revivals of the play in the twentieth century" (*Granville Barker* 156). Positive reviews in the *Manchester Guardian* and in the *Times*, which called the production the "first genuine theatrical occasion of the war" (review of *King Lear. Times* 4), support Kennedy's view. I disagree, however, with one aspect of this favorable interpretation. Kennedy sees the 1940 production as a continuation of the Savoy approach, which demonstrated that Barker "had lost nothing of his genius for the stage despite the years of disuse" (*Granville Barker* 156). I suggest instead that the Old Vic *King Lear* signaled a radical departure from Barker's earlier efforts, and that this change in methods was the major reason for this production's success.

In this *Lear*, Barker for the first time employed an approach consistent with the principles of the Elizabethan movement. Christine Dymkowski writes that the "stage made use of a permanent set." While there was also "a variable backdrop at the back of the stage" (145), photographs illustrate that, with the exception of scenes staged in a fairly representational tent during Act V, the settings were unlocalized and unadorned (Figures 8 and 9). Unlike

8 The "Happy King of Nature" in Barker's 1940 *King Lear*

9 Cordelia's tent in Barker's 1940 *King Lear*

its reviews for the Savoy productions, the *Times* notice made no mention of *King Lear*'s settings, costumes, or other visual effects, suggesting that these elements did not attract undue attention to themselves or upstage the actors (review of *King Lear* 4). The application of early modern methods may have been partly because Lewis Casson, Barker's principal collaborator and the production's titular director, had previously worked with William Poel. Casson's prior experience combines with Barker's limited involvement to raise the question of how much this minimalist style can be attributed to Barker's influence. But his 1927 Preface, which argued that the test of the tragedy's performability must be made "in the strict terms of [Shakespeare's] stagecraft" and "in no other" (Preface to *Lear* xi), was unquestionably a major source of this *King Lear*'s Elizabethan design.

Barker returned home to Paris before opening night. Gielgud wrote that "it seemed something of a disaster that he did not feel free to stay and guide us to the end, either to final victory or defeat" and attributes Barker's early departure to the director's temperament. "I suppose he was no longer prepared to face the tedious anxieties of the last days before production," Gielgud observed. "I think he had ceased to care about the reactions of audiences or the opinions of dramatic critics. The actual working life of the theatre with its petty involvements no longer concerned him" (*Stage Directions* 54). Kennedy cautions that, while it is "tempting" to interpret Barker's return to Paris "as a sign of his utter detachment from the affairs of the theatre," other considerations were involved (*Granville Barker* 157). Letters from Barker to Gielgud after *King Lear*'s premiere contain very specific questions and recommendations, indicating that Barker remained highly interested in the production (*Granville Barker and his Correspondents* 425–7). Anxieties about the war, rather than artistic ennui, may have motivated Barker's premature exit from London. Kennedy cites correspondence from across the Channel, in which Helen urges Barker to come home. "Less than a month later France was occupied," Kennedy writes, "and the Barkers escaped barely in time" (*Granville Barker* 157). Barker had hidden from the world for a quarter century. It seems that, just when he tried to reconnect with the practical life of the theater, the world caught up to him with a vengeance.

Barker and Literature

IN 1934 Harley Granville Barker warned against the "dangerous heresy that there is a kind of absolute art of the theatre, the task of which is not simply to interpret the author's play, but to re-create it in its own terms" (*Study of Drama* 20). He admonished that to "exalt the theatre, as this heresy does, at the expense of the drama is a retrograde step" (22). These pronouncements justify Barker's inclusion in what W. B. Worthen calls "the 'directorial' mode of dramatic criticism" (*Authority* 223 n), which perceives performance "as supplemental to the designs of the text" ("Deeper" 444). Barker is the only major figure associated with Elizabethanism to embrace this derivative view of theater's relationship to literature. His motivation, however, did not stem from any advocacy of early modern staging conventions, but rather from Barker's increasing personal connection to the academic establishment.

Barker's critical essays reveal a complex and at times contradictory attitude toward performance. While his scholarship initially advocated the stage as the primary site for understanding Shakespeare, over time Barker came to view theater as a mere adjunct to literary criticism. In his early Preface to *Macbeth*, written in 1923, Barker mocked a critical method that he later imitated. Commenting on M. F. Libby's theory that Ross was "the motive force and the real villain" of *Macbeth*, Barker writes that to "bring this home in performance" the actor playing this role "would, one fears, have to be accompanied throughout by an explanatory chorus" (rpt. in *More Prefaces* 83). Yet in his later *Prefaces to Shakespeare* Barker frequently indulges in similarly non-theatrical analysis. An example is his 1937 speculation as to the degree of physical intimacy in Gertrude and Claudius's relationship. Of the king's speech to Laertes in Act IV, scene 7 of *Hamlet* which begins

> Not that I think you did not love your father;
> But that I know love is begun by time,
> And that I see, in passages of proof,
> Time qualifies the spark and fire of it. (110–14),

Barker asserts, "Of what does that covertly speak – those 'passages of proof'– but of Gertrude's mute obedience to Hamlet's behest to deny herself to his bed?" (*Prefaces* 1: 224). He then admits a few lines later that such a reading cannot "be very clearly brought home to the audience" (225). This would render such an interpretation useless in terms of Barker's original stated intention for his *Prefaces*, which in 1923 had been to present the plays in the context "of their performance upon the stage" (rpt. in *More Prefaces* 43).

Barker's gradual embrace of a theatrically impractical approach took place during the decades following his retirement from the stage. His early writings sometimes defy the traditions of academic criticism. In 1923 he bemoans "the scholar's indifference to the theatre" and suggests that much dramatic scholarship has been "written by people who, you might suppose, could never have been inside a theatre in their lives" ("Some Tasks" 17). The stage was "where a play belongs" (18), and he claims that any Shakespearean drama will come to life if "shout[ed]" by "a company of schoolboys" but remain "inert under the touch of the most learned professor" (19). By 1934, his tone was more conciliatory. In his *Companion to Shakespeare Studies* (co-edited with G. B. Harrison) Barker describes the actor as a "foolish Greek" ("Shakespeare's Dramatic Art" 85), a necessary evil in the theatrical process. Barker implores his readers to "learn to listen through as well as to the actor" (86) in order to overcome the "intrusion" (85) of this thespian. He came to identify himself more closely with his scholarly readers than with his former theatrical colleagues. His changing attitude toward the work of E. K. Chambers illustrates this transition in sympathy. In 1925 Barker wrote dismissively of Chambers and his fellow "theorists" that if they "could be set to acting a play or so upon a stage ... they would learn more in a week than they will persuade each other of in a generation" ("A Note" 70). In 1932, by contrast, Barker justified the activities of the Shakespeare Association by announcing that this organization had planned "an elaborate analytical index to the six volumes of Sir Edmund Chambers's *Elizabethan Stage* and *Life of Shakespeare*" (*Associating* 4). In less than a decade, Barker went from attacking Chambers to indexing him.

In the 1925 essay "From *Henry V* to *Hamlet*," first delivered as the British Academy Annual Shakespeare Lecture, Barker displayed his own growing dislike for the stage by attributing to Shakespeare an anti-theatrical bias. There were, he suggested, two Shakespeares. One was a "complaisant" theatrical professional and the other a "daemonic … genius bent on having his own way" who resented the limitations of his work as a "popular play-provider" (rpt. in *More Prefaces* 139). Of this eccentric literary genius Barker wrote, "*This* is the Shakespeare who was finally to people, not his little theatre only, but the whole intellectual world for the next three hundred years with figures of his imagining" (140). This pejorative reference to Shakespeare's "little theatre" is difficult to reconcile with the position of Barker's later champions that he "believed in the power of the stage" and that his "unswerving principle was that Shakespeare is understood best and appreciated fully only in the theatre" (Kennedy, *Granville Barker* 154). "From *Henry V* to *Hamlet*" goes on to dismiss *As You Like It, Much Ado about Nothing,* and *Twelfth Night* as "bones thrown to the dogs of the audience, that wanted their plot and their ear-tickling jokes" (rpt. in *More Prefaces* 147), which is particularly odd considering that *Twelfth Night* was Barker's only unqualified success as a director of Shakespeare. Barker does not, however, reject the stage completely. Instead he argues for establishing professorial rigor within the theater, and proposes a new guild of actors and directors, "grave and sober men" (166), who would be "scholars in their kind" and achieve respectability by working "side by side" with "scholars of the printed page" (167). There is logic in an approach to Shakespeare that coordinates the efforts of academics and theater practitioners, but Barker displays throughout this essay contempt for the stage and for himself as a former showman who must now seek redemption as a man of letters.

"In associating with professors," C. B. Purdom wrote, "Barker became (almost) one of them" (220). This is not necessarily a bad thing, but it led Barker to a supercilious attitude toward the theater. By 1934, he felt that he had to plead with his fellow scholars to frequent the playhouse. Employing the first person plural with his academic readers, Barker wrote, "The art of drama makes a primary demand upon us: to leave our armchair throne of judgment and descend into the mellay [*sic*]" of live performance. He warned of play-going that "far less of literature or art there will seem to be in the experience than of the vulgar emotions of life." Barker acknowledged that "a case can be made against the theatre; artistically, and sometimes morally too" when a play is dominated by actors with their "imperfect human embodiment" and "immediate emotion." But he assured his literary readership that "when great dramatists were about" the vulgarities of human performers were inevitably held in check ("Shakespeare's Dramatic Art" 87). In *The Study of Drama*, published that same year, Barker damned thespians with faint praise when he noted that a performer "will not have, perhaps, the brains of a first-rate philosopher or scientist, a lawyer or financier – but then he has not chosen those paths in life!" (35). Actors were smart enough, apparently, for the theater.

Barker's transition from practitioner to scholar was possible in part because the literary establishment needed Barker as much as he needed it. Douglas Lanier suggests that "the rise of performance criticism is a recuperative response of literary institutions" to "the decline of the book in an increasingly post-literate society" (191). While Lanier connects this phenomenon principally to cinema and not the theater, anxiety about the shrinking importance of the written word also led critics to welcome the participation of a former stage director like Barker in the hope that his expertise would give their endeavors new relevance and credibility. This was particularly the case for scholars writing after Barker's death during the post-World War II technological boom, when new media took an increasing toll on readership. Critics like Muriel St Clare Byrne were so eager to have a representative of the theater as an ally that they exaggerated Barker's stage accomplishments and, perhaps, the value of his writings.

Ironically, the quality for which Byrne most admired Barker, his advocacy of "unabridged texts" ("Fifty Years" 8), diminished over time. The Savoy productions were virtually uncut. Barker acknowledged in his 1914 *New York Times* interview that he "did cut just a little." But all accounts generally agree with Barker's estimate that these excisions "amounted, perhaps to less than two dozen lines in all three plays" (quoted in "A Talk About the Stage" 9). The very notion of a "complete text," however, presumes that there is a definitive master copy which should not be violated. James C. Bulman notes instead that "Shakespeare left no originary text – no perfect, authorially sanctioned script – for performance" (2). While this notion is a commonplace today, it was still something of a novelty in Barker's time. Gary Taylor writes that the First Folio was generally considered a uniquely authoritative version until A. W. Pollard's advancement of the "good" quartos in 1909 (279). In his second career as an academic critic, Barker embraced this new scholarship and moved away from his earlier simplistic endorsement of "full text" productions.

In the 1927 Introduction to his *Prefaces*, Barker expressed dissatisfaction with the Folio as a definitive text. He wrote that there "is much to be said for turning one's back on the editors, even, when possible, upon the First Folio with its demarcation of acts and scenes, in favor of the Quartos – Dr. Pollard's 'good' Quartos – in their yet greater simplicity" (*Prefaces* 1: 8). In his Preface to *King Lear* that same year, Barker employed what Christine Dymkowski calls "courageous discretion" (137) in arguing for a mixture of Folio and Quarto in assembling a performance text of that play. He recommended the excision of certain passages appearing in both editions, which he claimed were not written by Shakespeare. Barker also urged the cutting of Edgar's soliloquy at the end of Act III, scene 6 even though he did not doubt its authorship, because "Shakespeare may afterwards have repented of it as sounding too sententious" (Preface to *Lear* lxxii).

Barker was influenced by the contemporary challenges to textual authority defined by E. K. Chambers in 1924 as "The Disintegration of Shakespeare"
(Chambers 7). Chambers refers to "the speculations started by Professor
Pollard and pursued by Mr. Dover Wilson" (14) regarding collaboration and
revision in Shakespeare's plays. He rejects these ideas, but identifies them in
terms that would become, against Chambers's wishes, conventional wisdom
by the end of the century:

> We arrive at the notion of the long-lived manuscript in the tiring-house
> wardrobe, periodically taken out for a revival and as often worked upon
> by fresh hands, abridged and expanded, recast to fit the capabilities of
> new performers, brightened with current topical allusions, written up
> to date to suit the new tastes in poetic diction. Additional scenes may
> be inserted. If the old pages will no longer hold the new matter, they
> may be mutilated and replaced by partial transcripts. In the end hardly
> a single line may remain as it was in the beginning. Yet, in a sense, it is
> the same play, even as our human bodies, the cellular matter of which is
> continuously renewed, remain our bodies from the cradle to the grave
> … Who is the author of such a play? We cannot tell. (16)

This "disintegrationist" argument had a great effect on Barker. In 1934 he
wrote that there was "now sufficient agreement as to which of the plays in the
First Folio may be called early work, but discussion still as to whether the
earliest of these are wholly or only partly or merely nominally Shakespeare's"
("Shakespeare's Dramatic Art" 44). "And surely it is time," Barker wrote in his
Preface to *King Lear*, "that all editions of Shakespeare put certain passages,
whose fraud can be agreed upon, in expurgatorial brackets. We are ready for
another – and another sort of – Bowdler" (lxiii n).

One drawback to this vision of indeterminate textual transmission is that
it can allow biased scholars to reject a scene or passage they do not like on
the grounds that it is spurious. In his Preface to *Macbeth*, Barker acknowledges this "weakness in criticism to be always maintaining that what is well
done is by Shakespeare and what is ill done is by somebody else" (rpt. in
More Prefaces 86), yet he was guilty of this very vice in rejecting Shakespeare's
authorship of the witches' scenes. Barker is, of course, not the only critic to
doubt the authenticity of some of this material. Even as ardent an advocate
for the authority of the First Folio as Neil Freeman concedes that there "is
consensus that Shakespeare did not write any of the Hecat sequences" (Freeman xli). G. Wilson Knight suggests that Barker merely "succumbs to the
disintegrating scholarship rampant in his day" by dismissing the play's opening scene as non-Shakespearean ("Producer" 794). But Barker went beyond
these schools of critical thought in rejecting the second witches' appearance
as "spurious" (*More Prefaces* 63) and in asserting that "we do not meet Shakespeare's true text till Macbeth's own entrance" (61). While the witches' scenes
may not be objectively "ill done," they inspired personal antipathy in Barker.
He may have been moved to banish the weird sisters by the same urge to contain femininity that made him exhort Shakespearean actresses to deny their
womanhood on stage.

Barker's attitude toward the First Quarto of *Hamlet* shows how much he was guided by literary rather than theatrical concerns at the time of his 1937 Preface to this tragedy, an essay which according to J. L. Styan illustrates Barker's "academic atrophy and his divorce from stage experience" (*Shakespeare Revolution* 118). Barker rejects the First Quarto's order of events, even though he acknowledges that there "is much to be said, from a narrowly dramatic point of view, of Q1's scene-sequence" (*Prefaces* 1: 63). Barker's 1923 goal of presenting the plays in the context "of their performance upon the stage" (rpt. in *More Prefaces* 43) would suggest that a "narrowly dramatic point of view" should be the only one considered. Instead, Barker prefers the Second Quarto because "Q2's scene-sequence is the more favorable to the exhibiting of Hamlet's character" and therefore represented Shakespeare's "subduing and adapting of the story and the storytelling to this maturer end" (*Prefaces* 1: 66). This preference for literary character over dramatic action indicates how far Barker had drifted from his theatrical moorings.

Barker first advanced this inversion of Aristotelian hierarchy in the 1925 essay "From *Henry V* to *Hamlet*," in which he argues that "*Hamlet* is the triumph of dramatic idea over dramatic action and of character over plot" (rpt. in *More Prefaces* 150). Not confined to *Hamlet*, this notion increasingly dominated Barker's critical writing as time went on. Even Eric Salmon, who consistently argues for the *Prefaces'* theatrical relevance, acknowledges that Barker was "perhaps unduly influenced by the 'character-drawing' school of scholarly criticism" (222). Purdom is less kind, suggesting that Barker becomes "concerned with the characters in the plays as they may have been as living men or women, which takes him far outside the sphere of drama, and makes most of his commentary beside the mark and seriously misleading" (219). Character is an important element in the plays and arguably the factor that distinguished Shakespeare from his contemporaries and that has allowed his work to endure for centuries. But Barker's excessive advocacy of character at the expense of plot ultimately renders much of his critical writing anti-theatrical.

The Usefulness of the Prefaces for Actors and Directors

Critics have long disputed the value of Barker's *Prefaces to Shakespeare* for theater practitioners. For Knight, Barker's *Prefaces* "lack the glamour, the tang and smell as it were, perhaps even one might say the vulgarity, of theatre art; despite their stage references, they are products of the academic rather than the histrionic intelligence" (*Shakespearian* 225). Robert Speaight similarly sees the *Prefaces* as being of little practical value, and writes that against them "any director will break his teeth in vain" (*Shakespeare* 144). Barker wrote that his "prefaces themselves may best be thought of as the sort of address a producer might make to a company upon their first meeting to study the play" (rpt. in *More Prefaces* 43). Styan considers these essays "strangely academic" in light of this stated purpose (*Shakespeare Revolution* 108) and follows Purdom in asserting that Barker "devoted too much of his energy to scholarly issues of little account, like the discussion of the time-scheme in *Othello*, or act-division in *Hamlet,* or the separation of Shakespeare's hand from a collaborator's" (112). Others contend that Barker's *Prefaces* are consistently stage-centered. In direct response to Styan's assertion, Salmon writes that "even looked at from the strictest of practical stage viewpoints, only the middle of these three instances seems to me to be an issue 'of little account'; the other two, surely, have immediate and important implications for the interpretation and the playing of the play" (227). Yet Barker himself dismisses one of these two concerns, the "discussion of the time scheme in *Othello*" which Salmon calls "immediate and important," as irrelevant to stage production. "When it is acted," Barker writes in his Preface to this play, "we notice nothing unusual, and neither story nor characters appear false in retrospect" (*Prefaces* 4: 141). Salmon nevertheless asserts that "there is no point" at which Barker "lost touch with the stage" (204); and Edward M. Moore incongruously contends that "Barker never forgets that he is dealing with a play meant for the theatre, and he approaches it as a director" ("Introduction" 17).

Some of Barker's critical comments could be of use to an actor preparing a Shakespearean role. His observation of the "commanding hardness and firmness in the rolling r's and final d's" in the Prince's first speech in *Romeo and Juliet,* which by "its sound alone ... does half its business" (*Dramatic Method* 72), and his analysis of how the naturalistic pattern of the Nurse's first speeches in this play give the verse a prose-like verisimilitude, share this potential for practical application (73–4). His description of Antony's rage at Thidias in *Antony and Cleopatra* microscopically defines the optimal timing for this moment on stage. "The caesura-pause of two beats that the short line allows is followed by the repeated crack of two more short phrases," Barker writes, "the first with its upward lift, the second with its nasal snarl and the sharp click of its ending; the last line lengthens out, and the business finished with the bitter *staccato* of 'Take hence this jack and whip him'" (*Prefaces* 3: 49). Few actors, however, could make use of Barker's commentary on the Lysander and Hermia exchange in Act I of *A Midsummer Night's Dream* which begins, "The course of true love never did run smooth." Barker writes:

> The whole passage is conventional in form. Conceit answers conceit. The pretty antiphony is convention itself. Lysander's apologue is conventionally rounded and complete. But how nicely it is charged with emotion, with enough to illumine the form, but not with so much, nor of such a complexity as would warp it. (rpt. in *More Prefaces* 113)

This passage is coherent but, even taking into account differences in diction between Barker's age and our own, his language seems esoteric for "the sort of address a producer might make to a company upon their first meeting."

Directors pursuing an Elizabethan style can find some inspiration in the *Prefaces.* In the 1923 Preface to *Macbeth,* Barker offers a strong illustration of the power of early modern staging in his analysis of that tragedy's climactic combat:

> We may be fairly certain that the play is meant to end on the lower stage. If Macduff and Macbeth are to have a good fight, this – or at least

the best part of it – should take place on the lower stage too. Now the double stage direction [*Exeunt fighting. Alarums.* Followed immediately by *Enter Fighting and Macbeth Slain*] will be made clear if they can leave the lower stage fighting, and re-appear in the gallery. If Macbeth is killed on the inner upper stage the drawing of its curtain would conceal his body. And if young Siward had been killed there too, there would be no pressing necessity for the removal of his. (rpt. in *More Prefaces* 66)

For a rapid succession of scenes such as this, Barker writes, "No swifter movement is well possible than that for which the Elizabethan stage provides" (67). While Barker's assumption of a curtain hung in front of the on-stage balcony does not jibe with a twenty-first-century understanding of early modern conventions, his description of *Macbeth's* finale is nevertheless stimulating and specific enough to inspire imitation by sympathetic directors.

In his 1927 Preface to *Julius Caesar*, Barker demonstrates an intuitive understanding of the Elizabethan stage that anticipates more recent scholarship. Of the Folio stage direction "*Enter Brutus in his Orchard*" Barker writes, "This looks like a discovery upon the inner stage" (*Prefaces* 1: 213), and then entertains a digression on this architectural feature:

I think that scenes were more often played "in relation to" the inner stage than consistently within its boundaries; that is to say, the actors, having gained the effect of a discovery, would be apt to advance upon the main stage, where their movements would be less cramped, where they would be in closer touch with the audience ... One need not suppose that the Elizabethan actor ever saw the division between inner stage and main stage as a fixed boundary. (*Prefaces* 2: 215)

As Byrne notes, Barker here uses his "instinctive playwright-producer's grasp" to see beyond the contemporary understanding of the "inner stage" as a false proscenium behind which complexly staged scenes could be played in their entirety toward the more limited notion of a "discovery space" endorsed by later theater historians (Byrne, "Foreword" xx).

By the time of his 1930 Preface to *Antony and Cleopatra*, however, Barker seems to have wearied of discussing the practical ramifications of Elizabethan staging. Early in this essay, he shows the same zeal for exploring original methods that he had applied to *Macbeth* and *Julius Caesar*. But he abandons his description of the play's action at the moment which constitutes the greatest challenge for an early modern approach. His discussion of Cleopatra's apprehension by Gallus and Proculeus (Act V, scene 2) is inconclusive. He assumes that Cleopatra must appear at the time of her capture "on the inner stage behind a barred gate" (*Prefaces* 3: 39). Barker then rejects the solution (which he cites from the Arden edition) of Gallus climbing to the balcony while Proculeus distracts Cleopatra, thereafter appearing behind her on the inner stage. For Barker this "climbing up and climbing down again" would take too much time. He instead suggests that Gallus and the other guards might somehow "be upon the inner stage by the back way" and surprise Cleopatra from behind while she speaks to Proculeus (*Prefaces* 3: 40). Barker's idea violates the logic of theater. If the audience sees Cleopatra behind a barred gate, they will assume that one cannot simply walk backstage to get around this barrier. Barker's long absence from the stage leads him to overlook the possibility of leaving Cleopatra on the balcony for this scene, and having Gallus quickly scale the *frons scenae* to ascend to her. The skilled tumblers of Shakespeare's company could have found a creative way to achieve this effect, perhaps similar to that employed in the 1972 cinematic adaptation directed by Charlton Heston. In this film, Roman soldiers turn their shields to construct a temporary ramp to the balcony, up which Proculeus sprints. Barker in the end dismisses this issue, perhaps because he sensed the inadequacy of his proposed solution. "The discussion is fairly barren from a modern producer's point of view," he writes (*Prefaces* 3:40). This reluctance to engage with the mechanics of theatrical practice is typical of Barker's later Prefaces, in which he consistently eschewed considerations of *mise-en-scene*. His 1937 Preface to *Hamlet*, for example, is longer than the play itself but contains no section devoted to staging.

Barker, Shakespeare, and Retirement from the Stage

In "From *Henry V* to *Hamlet*" Barker, embittered by his experience at the Savoy, attributes an anti-theatrical bias to Shakespeare. Elsewhere in his critical writing, Barker often moves up the date of the playwright's retirement to Stratford, perhaps seeking to justify his own abandonment of the stage at a comparatively young age. In his Preface to *Cymbeline*, Barker writes of "the shifting from outdoors in" (2: 85) which occurred in 1608 when The King's Men took over the Blackfriars Playhouse. "Shakespeare is an old hand when the change comes," Barker comments, "and will live out the rest of his life retired, more or less, from the stage." (2: 87). 1608 is an early date for Shakespeare's withdrawal from London. The playwright's 1613 purchase of a gatehouse near the Blackfriars Theatre is evidence that he maintained some connection to London until the final years of his life. Barker nevertheless frequently seems eager to pack Shakespeare off to the country. In his Preface to *Coriolanus*, Barker writes that this play's extensive stage directions "stand among the items of evidence of a retirement to Stratford" (3: 238). Scholars generally concur that *Coriolanus* had been written and performed by 1609, yet Barker claims that Shakespeare composed this tragedy as "a manuscript to be sent to London" for "a staging which the author did not expect to supervise himself" (3: 238). Barker attempts to end Shakespeare's career even earlier when he suggests that soon after *Macbeth* the playwright "was retiring to Stratford" (*Dramatic Method* 113). 1606 is the likely date of composition for this play. In that year Shakespeare was forty-two, only slightly older than Barker when he married Helen Huntington and bid farewell to the stage. Barker seems to have wanted Shakespeare to retire early, as Barker had done, to a life of gentlemanly leisure.

3 Nugent Monck

DURING his lifetime, Nugent Monck's fame was international. Hugh Hunt, a noted West End director who also worked at the Old Vic, wrote in 1934, "I have been asked by numerous friends in France and Germany if I ever visited the Maddermarket Theatre at Norwich, while most American tourists, interested in the theatre, make this one of their pilgrimages" ("Maddermarket" 48). This global renown spread in the years following World War II, when a replica of Monck's playhouse was built in Graz, Austria. Critics and practitioners saw the Maddermarket as "the only genuine Elizabethan theatre" in Britain (Miller 326), and as a laboratory for testing ideas about early modern staging. Hunt, for instance, directed half of the 1933–4 season at the Maddermarket and applied this experience to the scholarly controversy surrounding the nature of the "inner stage" (*Live Theatre* 76). Barry Jackson was so taken with Monck's efforts that, when Jackson became director of the Shakespeare Memorial Theatre in 1946, he immediately hired Monck to stage *Pericles*. In 1953 a distinguished group of theater artists and critics including Ivor Brown, Lewis Casson, Barry Jackson, Paul Scofield, Edith Evans, T. S. Eliot, and John Gielgud wrote a letter to the *Times* soliciting support for Monck's theater. "The work of the Norwich Players at the Maddermarket Theatre," they wrote, "is of international repute, it has done much to spread the ideals of William Poel, and it has had a notable influence on modern methods of Shakespeare production in the professional theatre" (Brown *et al.* Letter. *Times* 15 Oct. 1953: 9).

While contemporary observers considered Monck "a link in a chain" connecting William Poel's early experiments "to the Old Vic and Stratford-upon-Avon" (Hills 24), in recent decades he has been largely overlooked. Dennis Kennedy dismisses Monck's significance, noting merely that he "built a small Elizabethan Theatre in Norwich, the Maddermarket, where he staged reconstructed performances of small interest and smaller effect" (*Looking* 153). More has been written about Granville Barker's three productions at the Savoy than about the hundreds of plays staged by Monck over the course of his career. One cause of this near oblivion was Monck's unwillingness to write extensively about himself or his work. Charles Rigby, perhaps referring to Monck's tenuous status as a homosexual in a conservative environment, wrote in 1933 that "Nugent Monck out-oysters the oyster" (6) and "knows the value of reticence and minding his own business" (7). Monck was in fact too reticent for the good of his reputation with posterity. He started but never finished an autobiography, announcing on his eightieth birthday, "I have lived the life, and I find it dull" (quoted in Hildy, *Shakespeare* 5). Monck's reluctance to leave a written record hindered the dissemination of his ideas. His brief 1959 article for *Shakespeare Survey* (published posthumously) provides a fascinating glimpse into his methods, and leaves the reader wanting more. Monck's legacy has also been impaired by the fact that he worked in provincial Norwich, where his productions did not attract the press coverage they might have garnered in London. Fortunately, Franklin J. Hildy's exhaustive archival research, culminating in the 1986 volume *Shakespeare at the Maddermarket: Nugent Monck and the Norwich Players*, documents Monck's career and makes possible its examination.

Monck's given name was Walter, but he preferred to go by Nugent. Unlike Harley Granville Barker, who was forced on the stage by his mother at an early age, Monck chose a theatrical career of his own volition. His family wanted him to be a musician, and Monck was a Music student at the Royal Academy before changing his principal course of study to Drama in 1899. At that point, he later recalled, "My parents decided they would have nothing more to do with me, and I must go my own wicked way" (quoted in Hildy, "Reviving" 18). Barker was by all accounts quite talented, but Monck had no real gift as an actor. "I called myself a professional," he said of his early life as a performer, "but my acting ability was small and I seldom had any work to do" (quoted in Marshall, *Other* 92).

Monck was the son of an Anglican minister, but he rejected the faith of his father and eventually found an alternative to organized religion in the theater. "As a spiritual force," he told a government committee studying the arts, "nothing can touch drama," because "it can 'get' people who – for some reason or other – are religiously dead" (quoted in *The Drama in Adult Education* 8–9). Monck's sense of the spiritual mission of the stage began when he was cast in William Poel's 1902 production of *Everyman*. Monck later wrote that this production was so powerful that audience members often knelt in prayer after performances. Mariette Soman describes an early production of the Norwich Players as an expression of Monck's transcendent vision. "The few feet that separated audience from players was bridged by spiritual imagination," Soman writes, "and the whole room was thinking and feeling in unison" (10). Yet the intent was not to spread the Christian faith. Nugent Monck appears as a character in David Holbrook's 1978 coming-of-age novel *A Play of Passion* set in and around the Maddermarket during World War II. This fictionalized Monck declares, "I'm really an atheist – or, rather, I suppose an agnostic" (Holbrook 123). The founder of the Maddermarket was normally too circumspect to issue such bold proclamations, but Holbrook's reconstructed quotation nevertheless accurately expresses Monck's views on religion. He offered the theater as a substitute faith for those who, like himself, no longer felt connected to the established churches.

In their youths, Harley Granville Barker and Nugent Monck shared a leftist outlook and socialist leanings. Barker's political turn to the right paralleled his move away from work in the theater toward a life of literary study. Nugent Monck, in contrast, remained an active stage practitioner his entire life and never surrendered his populist vision. According to Hildy, Monck developed "social consciousness" during "his years in the Liverpool slums" ("Reviving" 19). Monck's father had been banished from an affluent congregation to an inner-city parish for preaching social activism. The son of this radical cleric followed in his father's political footsteps. Haden L. Guest wrote of Monck's 1907 play *The Hour*, "Every Socialist … should go and see it" (49). Monck never wavered from his belief that the working class could benefit from theater and deserved the opportunity to do so. He pursued this potential audience with the zeal of a missionary. Monck refused to accept the cynical advice offered him by George Bernard Shaw in a 1923 letter, who wrote, "First rate art cannot be pushed beyond a certain percentage of the population" (quoted in Hildy, *Shakespeare* 90). Monck always insisted that his work at the Maddermarket was not "high-brow," and that it could be appreciated by anyone with a basic education.

Monck's experience in World War I best illustrates his indefatigable urge to bring theater to as broad a public as possible. When the conflict broke out, he was in Norfolk producing plays with the Norwich Players. His company all joined the war effort, but Monck at thirty-six was too old to enlist. He therefore lied about his age in order to be accepted into the medical corps and was sent to Egypt where he worked as an orderly in an operating room. He attributed his success in this position to thespian discipline. "I was not a good orderly," he admitted, "but I could hold limbs steadily, being able to stand quite still from my long theatrical training'" (quoted in Hildy, "Reviving" 126). Soon after learning his new job, Monck set about staging all-male amateur theatricals in his spare time. He went to great lengths to assure the quality of these productions and on one occasion even commandeered two naval searchlights to illuminate a performance. One of Monck's efforts, an adaptation of *A Midsummer Night's Dream*, garnered sufficient attention for John Booth to mention it in "Shakespeare in the English Theatre," a 1919 summary of the "principal stage productions of Shakespeare's plays in this country in the last hundred years" (Booth 212). According to Hildy, Monck's Poelesque revivals may have inspired Robert Atkins, who was stationed in Egypt and saw Monck's *Macbeth*, to institute Elizabethan methods at the Old Vic after the war (*Shakespeare* 37).

A letter from Monck in March 1917 gave the impression that these theatrical activities turned his war-time experience into something of a lark. "My only interest," he wrote, "is in *The Importance*, in which I'm playing Lady Bracknell and fighting with my clothes" (quoted in Hildy, "Reviving" 129). Another missive from August of that same year gives a more accurate picture of Monck's service during the conflict:

> Tremendous excitement because a hospital ship may soon be going to England. All the legless men are rushing about trying to get ready. The legless men are helping the armless and the armless usually have a legless hanging on to them. It is rather wonderful and beautiful to see them each other, all so joyously happy. It is quite pathetic for the others with enough body left to be sent back to the firing line. (quoted in Hildy, "Reviving" 130)

Shakespeare had a special resonance for the military audience in Egypt because, as Monck later noted, "all this silly old fighting and dying business seemed much less silly when you yourself were nearly killed last week in a scrap" ("Shakespeare and the Amateur" 321). That Monck was able to continue producing plays under such circumstances is a testament both to his personal resilience and to the healing power of theater.

Monck wrote of producing Shakespeare during the first war that the task was easier because "he wrote mostly for men (though there was plenty of competition among the soldiers to play the few women's parts)" ("Shakespeare and the Amateur" 321). An observant reader might correctly suspect from this comment, and from Monck's excitement at playing Lady Bracknell, that he was homosexual. He lived as openly as he could in a comparatively intolerant age. While Hildy suggests that "Monck's sexual proclivity" had "little influence on his life's work" ("Reviving" 12), some in Norwich saw Monck and the Maddermarket as a rallying point for what would later be called Gay Pride. The Nugent Monck of *A Play of Passion* is openly gay; and Reyner Banham in a 1964 reminiscence of life in Norwich called Monck one of his "favorite queers" and celebrated the director's "equivocal presence" and "refusal to go native" (372). Monck's status as a member of a persecuted minority gives added significance to his inclusive vision of a theater accessible to all.

Monck shared with William Poel the longing to return to the simplicity of a pre-industrial world. He sought to "work as the Pre-Raphaelites did in painting and evolve a new outlet for dramatic sense which would not be hampered by stock traditions, scenery, curtains, footlights, paint, and the other things that make for technique" (Monck quoted in Hildy, *Shakespeare* 10). Like Poel, Monck feared that film, through its relentless emphasis on the visual, was robbing audiences of their ability to listen. Monck anticipated Tyrone Guthrie in his assertion that, to survive in the cinematic era, theater would have to abandon naturalism and move in another direction. "The one great thing," Monck wrote, "that the kinema [*sic*] has done for the theatre is that it has stopped it attempting to compete with realism" (quoted in Hildy, *Shakespeare* 162). Throughout his long career, Monck's appreciation of the growing challenge from cinema combined with the inclusiveness of his populist vision and belief in the spiritual mission of theater to shape his artistic endeavors.

Early Work

NUGENT Monck began his theatrical career in London at the start of the twentieth century. He performed in several productions of the Elizabethan Stage Society and also worked for William Poel as a stage manager. Following the collapse of Poel's organization in 1905, Monck formed his own group, the English Drama Society. This company articulated its aesthetic in a 1907 brochure, which states the desire to "revive something of the early simplicity of the Drama, banishing as much as possible unnecessary and cumbersome scenery and properties" (quoted in Hildy, "Reviving" 37). Desmond MacCarthy's description of Monck's 1906 *Love's Labour's Lost* suggests the low-budget nature of the production and the influence of William Poel:

> The Bloomsbury Hall, Hart-street, is a long, oblong room, with a level floor. At one end of it is a kind of dais of two different levels, winged with tapestry curtains, and led up to on each side by to or three steps.

Two little, formal trees, in tubs, showing that the scene was out of doors, stood on this stage, which was crowded, when I entered, by five gentle-men in Elizabethan costume … I sat so near that I felt almost like an Elizabethan gentleman perched on the stage itself. (review of *Love's Labour's Lost* 91)

Monck's amateur theatrical organization was no more financially success-ful than Poel's had been, and in 1909 the English Drama Society was forced to disband. Strapped for cash, Monck entered into the lucrative sideline of staging civic pageants, which brought him to Norwich for the first time as the director of some "Historical Tableaux" (Hildy, "Reviving" 50).

In 1910 Monck made his greatest impact on the London theater scene as stage manager for William Poel's production of *The Two Gentlemen of Verona* at His Majesty's Theatre. This staging employed two innovations, an apron stage and direct lighting, which were adopted in subsequent productions by that theater's operator, Herbert Beerbohm Tree. While no electronic illumi-nation can ever be "Elizabethan" in a historical sense, direct lighting, in which instruments are aimed at the stage from the back of a performance space, facilitated the extension of the proscenium stage into an apron or thrust con-figuration. Before direct lighting, performance spaces were lit either from the wings or by footlights at the stage's front edge. This meant that performers moving downstage of the proscenium arch would inevitably be left in the dark. Direct lighting, by contrast, allowed illumination to be focused on actors no matter where in the theater they went. Monck had previously used this effect in his Norwich pageants and, as Hildy argues convincingly, was responsible for its application at His Majesty's in 1910 (*Shakespeare* 12). This innovation greatly influenced the staging of Shakespeare in the decades to come, and Monck played a key role in its dissemination.

Poel had extended his platform beyond the proscenium before, but these efforts had frequently been dismissed as irrelevant antiquarianism. The intro-duction of direct lighting made possible the acceptance of the apron stage by traditional practitioners like Tree, who was impressed by the configuration for *Two Gentlemen*. W. Bridges-Adams writes:

Tree, at the height of his supremacy, was sensitive to the winds of change. I watched him once while William Poel … was building a fore-stage out over the stalls of His Majesty's and placing his arc-lamps in the upper circle … when, not long after, Tree staged *Henry VIII* it was apparent that he had imbibed Poel's sense while rejecting his aberra-tions. There was an unmistakable forestage. ("Proscenium" 28)

By Poel's "aberrations," Bridges-Adams means the absence of scenery. In his own variation on an Elizabethan approach, Tree maintained elaborate sets upstage while expanding the playing area forward on an apron lit by instru-ments from the back of the house. Harley Granville Barker used basically these same methods at the Savoy. While he deserves some credit for replac-ing realistic "scenery" with abstract "decoration," the basic configuration of Barker's productions had already, by the time of the Savoy *Winter's Tale* in

1912, been adopted by as conventional a theatrical figure as Herbert Beer-bohm Tree.

Even with these innovations, the days of large-scale Shakespeare on the professional London stage were numbered. By the end of World War I, such lavish endeavors were no longer economically viable. Hildy notes, "In 1917 Henry Irving [*fils*] was forced to withdraw a successful production of *Hamlet* after only two weeks in spite of very good houses because the cost of pro-ducing it was double that of a modern play and his theatre simply could not afford it." This financial pressure helped to make the inexpensive Elizabethan style "the new direction of the theatre" (Hildy, *Shakespeare* 40). Poel had pre-dicted this eventuality in 1912, when he wrote that "increasing railway rates, together with the additional cost of labor and cartage involved in moving scenery from town to town, are becoming a serious tax on the managerial purse." Poel concluded that, because of these economic pressures, "any dis-position shown by the public to dispense with scenery will, without doubt, find, sooner or later, ready acceptance in the theatre" (*Monthly Letters* 82). Old habits die hard, however, and the West End was by no means ready for the minimalist aesthetic of Elizabethanism. It would be two decades before such an approach became a regular feature on the professional London stage, and even then it would be largely confined to theaters like the Old Vic, which today would be considered part of the "not-for-profit" sector. Monck, for his part, despaired of ever being able to do the kind of work he wanted in the professional theater. He decided instead to devote his life to working with amateur actors, accepting a small remuneration and supplementing his income with work as a freelance director. His base of operations would not be London, but rather the provincial city of Norwich.

"Why Norwich?" Ralph Hale Mottram asks in examining the career of Nugent Monck. "For no logical reason" (Mottram 7). This is not completely true, as Monck had a very practical motivation for moving to East Anglia. While he was there producing "Historical Tableaux" in 1909, "a wealthy and rather eccentric old lady" named Mrs M. E. Pym, acting on a caprice, pur-chased a house for Monck to live in at the very low rent of six shillings per week (Hildy, "Reviving" 53). This dwelling was a Tudor structure ominously called "The Crypt." For a while Monck split his time between this abode and London accommodations. Then, in the spring of 1910, he moved to Norwich for good. After the death of Mrs Pym title passed to Monck, and he lived in this ancient home the rest of his life.

The Crypt was the first meeting place of the Norwich Players, and their early productions were staged in Monck's living room. This group came together in 1910 and originally consisted of nine male members, all under the age of thirty. It had for Mottram "at different times the characteristics of a male salon, a stage school, and a secret society" (10). Monck's own description is less sinister. "We began in such a small, humble way," he recalled years later, "five of us around a fire discussing plays we should never see, because they were plays which no one in the early 20th century would expect a public to pay to see" (quoted in Fowler 349). This group of amateur enthusiasts began to investigate alternative methods of staging. They arrived at an approach that emulated Poel's Elizabethan revival: "Footlights, proscenium, drop curtain and scenery were discarded and an astonished audience found itself thinking less of upholstery than of the play-wright" (Stephenson, *Theatre Arts Magazine* 203). The Norwich players, however, began not with Shakespeare but with plays in the medieval tradition. Their first performance in November 1910 was of *The World and the Child*, a Tudor morality play. This was followed by Monck's adaptation of *St George and the Dragon* early in 1911.

Monck soon received an offer to work at the Abbey Theatre in Dublin. William Butler Yeats attended the English premiere of *The Countess Cathleen*, which Monck staged in 1911 for the Norwich High School Old Girls' Association. Yeats was impressed by Monck's treatment of the play and soon returned to Norwich for a second visit. When the playwright walked into the final rehearsal for a theatrical adaptation of the *Book of Job*, Monck allegedly pressed him into service tying ticket numbers onto the seats. "Yeats decided," Andrew Stephenson writes, "that a man who could casually persuade an Irish poet to undertake such a task was obviously the right man to run the Abbey Theatre" (*Maddermarket Theatre Norwich* 5). The anecdote regarding Yeats's adventures in House Management may be apocryphal, but in October 1911 Monck was nevertheless offered the job of running the Abbey Theatre School while the company toured America in *Playboy of the Western World*. This educational project eventually led to the formation of the Abbey Second Company. For the next two years Monck spent most of his time in Ireland and on tour in America. While he was away, the Norwich Players performed under the direction of W. Bridges-Adams, who had originally come to town in 1910 to design a "water-frolic" staged by Monck (Stephenson, *Maddermarket Theatre Norwich* 4), and who later became director of the Shakespeare Memorial Theatre at Stratford-on-Avon.

Monck had some success at the Abbey. He introduced that company to the innovations of direct lighting and an apron stage, which he had employed in Poel's *Two Gentlemen* at His Majesty's. At Yeats's request, Monck incorporated a set of canvas and wood screens Gordon Craig had donated to the Abbey into a production of Lady Gregory's *The Canavans*. These flexible screens represented "the culmination of [Craig's] innovative theories on stage design," and Monck's production was one of the few times they were ever employed to practical benefit (Hildy, *Shakespeare* 27). This demonstrates that while Monck generally strove for a minimalist approach in theatrical production, he was also capable of mastering the most innovative features of the New Stagecraft. In direct contrast to the visual effects of Barker's Savoy productions, which distracted the audience from the spoken text, Monck's designs at the Abbey served to increase comprehension. Hildy notes that "most critics would say that the actors spoke so well that not a word was missed," but that "it took the poet Yeats to notice that it was not only the training Monck gave the company which accounted for this; of equal importance was the way Monck's visual artistry made the audience listen" (24).

Monck did not, however, stay at the Abbey long. He later claimed that he left because he "wanted to produce Shakespeare and not Irish peasant plays" (quoted in Fowler 349). More diplomatically, Monck said of the Abbey in a

1952 interview with the BBC, "Although I learned much from that institution – how to run a small theatre cheaply – I felt the limits of the Celtic twilight and my heart was really in the Shakespearean experiments that Mr. William Poel was making" (quoted in Hildy, *Shakespeare* 32). This emphasis on Shakespeare is somewhat puzzling, considering that, up to this point, Monck had staged exclusively medieval (and medieval-themed) drama with the Norwich Players. Monck's newly fortified passion for Shakespeare and Elizabethan staging may be explained by his 1912 visit to the reconstructed Globe playhouse at the Earl's Court exhibition. While Poel had attempted to reconstruct the Fortune stage within the boundaries of a proscenium structure, the Earl's Court Globe represented the first attempt, however flawed, to build an entire theater in an Elizabethan manner. In his next two performance spaces, Monck would attempt a similar feat.

When Monck returned to Norwich from the Abbey, his ambitions had outgrown his living room. In December 1913 he rented the "upper floor of what had once been a medieval banqueting hall" in a building known as the Old Music House to serve as a theater for the Norwich Players (Marshall, *Other* 93). In this space Monck built a stage approximately 15½ feet wide and 16½ feet deep. This is an intimate playing area, to say the least. Mariette Soman observed that the Music House stage would "barely take an average-sized dining room carpet" (25). There was no proscenium arch or wing space, and the audience sat exclusively in front of the platform. About a third of the way back from the downstage edge of the stage, Monck placed two pillars from which he hung a "hessian" (burlap) curtain. Monck would set up one scene behind this curtain while another was played in front. He would then open the hessian drapery to segue instantly from one scene to another.

Monck's use of a curtain in this manner is similar to the traditional Broadway musical technique of playing "in one" scenes or musical numbers downstage of a traveler or scrim, which then lifts to reveal a more complex set upstage. This device is at odds with a twenty-first-century understanding of early modern staging. But in Monck's era, even the most ardent Elizabethanists were conditioned by centuries of proscenium tradition to accept the notion of a "traverse curtain." They looked at the onstage pillars portrayed in the "de Witt" drawing of the Swan playhouse and assumed that a curtain must have been strung between them to allow for the "alternation theory," a plan of staging similar to that employed by Monck at the Music House. The historical invalidity of the traverse curtain and the alternation theory are immediately apparent in a thrust configuration. Spectators on the sides observe the scenes being set behind the traverse and, depending on their position, are blocked by this curtain from seeing action downstage of it. This was demonstrated at the new Globe in 1998, when director Lucy Bailey's use of "a curtain strung between the stage pillars" at the beginning of *As You Like It* "meant that spectators behind the line of the pillars, especially those in the first gallery, missed several minutes of the show" (Proudfoot 216). Monck's Maddermarket Theater had seating on the sides, and this forced him to discard the simple traverse curtain he had employed at the Music House in favor of a more complex system of draperies which sought to maintain proper sightlines. He never completely abandoned the alternation theory, however, and this remains the most serious flaw in Monck's attempts at historical accuracy.

The miniscule playing area of the Music House combined with the lack of a fly system and an absence of wing space to keep Monck's productions very simple. Rather than chafing at this lack of scenic resources, Monck used it to his advantage. As the *Times* noted, "It is not merely that he understands the limitations of both stage and actors. He does more. He realizes their possibilities" ("Norwich Players: Amateurs" 8). On the comparatively bare stage of the Music House, the Norwich Players departed from their early repertoire of medieval drama and made their first attempt at Shakespeare with a production of *Twelfth Night* in February 1914. They were off to a good start in their new home, but World War I soon intervened and put their endeavors on hold. After the war, Monck had to build a company from scratch, since none of his original players returned to Norwich. Most had moved on to new lives elsewhere and "Victor Earles, who had played most of the major parts, was killed" in the conflict (Stephenson, *Maddermarket Theatre Norwich* 15). Undeterred, Monck assembled a new group and allowed women to participate for the first time.

In keeping with the emphasis on Shakespeare established after their move to the Music House, the Norwich Players began their first postwar season with *Much Ado About Nothing* in September 1919. Mariette Soman describes the simple effectiveness of Monck's staging for this production:

> Charm is the producer's chief characteristic – quaintness and charm. Take the church scene in "Much Ado" as an example. The priest accompanied by his acolytes in red came on and stood with his back to the audience, while the curtains opened discovering the whole of the cast who moved slowly forward to the priest, the two principals a little in advance of the rest on a small white stage-cloth. The effect of this cloth was, when Claudio waves the priest on one side, to isolate Claudio and hero for the tragic scene as no other method on so tiny a stage could possibly do. (29)

If staged by Tree at His Majesty's or Barker at the Savoy, this scene would likely have been dominated by a realistic or expressionistic representation of a church. Instead, there is no mention of any kind of scenic backdrop in Soman's description.

Architecture, Design, & Staging Practices at the Maddermarket

BY 1921 the Norwich Players had once again outgrown their performance space, and Nugent Monck went in search of a new venue. He found an eighteenth-century edifice originally built as a Roman Catholic chapel and used most recently by the Salvation Army. Most commentators, including Monck himself, also mention the building's history as a baking powder factory, but Hildy disproves this assertion ("Reviving" 155). The new theater was named "The Maddermarket" because of its location adjacent to Norwich's medieval market, where madder roots were once sold for dyeing the city's famous wool. Monck said of his first visit, "The place was not prepossessing and ludicrously decorated. When I looked at it first I exclaimed 'what awful blue paint' and as I said it I discovered the acoustics were perfect" (quoted in Hildy, "Reviving" 149). Sufficiently impressed, Monck bought the building and began renovation. While Eric Fowler writes that the Norwich Players collectively "pawned their boots" (349) to make this purchase, it was Monck who assumed the bulk of the risk, investing everything he had and borrowing to the limit of his credit. The renovation, achieved in just five weeks, was a mammoth undertaking. "The architect and contractor donated many late night hours to the attempt," Hildy writes, "the workmen defied a union ban on overtime in order to keep on schedule, and the Norwich Players helped build up the stage around themselves as they rehearsed for opening night" ("Reviving" 157–8). Monck observed that by the time the work was finished, "I was already broke, without a penny in the world, and fed by my Players" (*Shakespeare Survey* 72).

Monck built the Maddermarket on an Elizabethan model. He did not intend, however, to create a lifeless museum that would be frozen in the past. For Monck, Elizabethanism was "not mere antiquarianism; it was the wave of the future" (Hildy, "Playing Spaces" 83). He believed that a minimalist, early modern model would serve not only for Shakespeare, but also for Greek tragedy, medieval drama, restoration comedy, and modern works. Hugh Hunt summarized the scope of Monck's repertory as of 1934:

> Greek drama is represented by Euripides, Sophocles, Theocritus and Herodias; Indian, Japanese, Norwegian, Spanish, French, Italian, German and Russian are here to show, while British drama is represented from the Wakefield Cycle down through the Elizabethan, Restoration, Georgian and Victorian ages; nearly two hundred plays, many of them plays which have never been presented before in our lifetime, have run their week on the Maddermarket stage. ("Maddermarket" 48)

Monck wrote in 1949, "Practically any play (in which the setting is not more important than the text), can be given on our stage" (Monck, *Drama* 20). This privileging of dramatic language ("the text") over visual elements ("the setting") may alarm those who fear that Elizabethan staging advances an agenda of literary hegemony. But Monck's desire to emphasize interpersonal communication over visual spectacle is common to most avant-garde attempts to redefine live performance in the cinematic age.

Despite the broad range of plays from diverse periods presented on its stage, Monck strove for historical accuracy in the early modern design of the Maddermarket. He particularly adhered to the conjectures of W. J. Lawrence regarding Shakespeare's original indoor performance space (Figure 10). For this reason, Monck's theater resembles the recently reconstructed Blackfriars Playhouse in Staunton, Virginia. One main difference between the Maddermarket stage and that of the new Blackfriars is a large decorative canopy 18 feet above the playing area supported at the back by posts in the *frons scenae* and at the front by two pillars 9 feet downstage. "Such canopies were known to exist in the open-air stages of Shakespeare's day," Hildy writes, but "would have been unnecessary in an indoor playhouse" (*Shakespeare* 46). Poel's Fortune fit-up included a similar structure, and Monck may have initially intended its posts to anchor the kind of traverse curtain used by Poel and by Monck himself at the Music House. In practice, however, Monck generally employed a more subtle and complex system of tapestries at the Maddermarket, which were hung upstage of the canopy supports.

During Monck's career, the nature and/or existence of the "traverse curtain" came to be disputed, and the critical consensus shifted toward the notion of an extensive "inner stage" which would accomplish the same revelatory function as the traverse, only further upstage. Barker in his Preface to *Julius Caesar* conflates these two notions, using "traverse" to describe the curtain which closes this area under the balcony (*Prefaces* 2: 215). The Maddermarket differs from the Staunton Blackfriars in the presence of such an inner stage. The Blackfriars has a small discovery space in this position, approximately 7 feet wide and of an adjustable depth normally set at 6 feet. Monck's inner stage was almost twice as wide at 13½ feet, but was fixed in depth at less than 5 feet. Hildy writes that there "is no historic evidence for the existence of an inner stage in the playhouses of Shakespeare's day" (*Shakespeare* 62). But he also points out that the "idea of an inner stage has its origins in the fact that there

10 A model of the Maddermarket Theatre Stage

are some scenes in Elizabethan plays which need to be 'discovered', such as that of Hermione's statue in *The Winter's Tale*, and that "the need for even the smallest curtained space necessitates a decision on how this might have been managed in the theatres of Shakespeare's day" (65). The distinction between a historically accurate "discovery space" and a spurious "inner stage" may therefore be subtle. Hildy notes that many "producers brought up on the conventions of the picture frame stage" overused the inner stage as a kind of false proscenium, assembling elaborate stage pictures behind its curtain (62), as Barker did with the upper level of his Savoy configuration. Monck resisted this tendency, although he may have been forced to do so because the architecture of his building limited the depth of his alcove to only 5 feet, making it "too small to accommodate more than the shortest tableau" (63).

Monck employed a removable staircase for some productions that allowed actors to move from the upper level to the main stage in sight of the audience. He explained that

> Certain plays seem to need steps direct from the stage to the balcony, so that you can see the performers going up or down. Many writers have suggested this, but have never settled the exact position. Originally the steps may have been temporary, pushed into position according to the need of the play. Such a staircase – in three parts – is in use at the Maddermarket. It can be placed under the balcony if not required throughout a play, or otherwise stored in the scene dock. (Monck, *Shakespeare Survey* 72–3)

The notion of such a staircase, for Hildy, "may represent Monck's first major contribution to modern notions of Shakespeare's stagecraft." He points out that Lawrence first proposed such a feature as historically accurate in 1927, three years after Monck's initial use of a portable stairway at the Maddermarket (Hildy, *Shakespeare* 232 n). Tyrone Guthrie, who first observed this practice at Monck's playhouse, later incorporated on-stage staircases into all of his Elizabethan designs. More recently, Eric Binnie has pointed to the presence of a removable staircase unit among Philip Henslowe's inventory of properties for the Lord Admiral's Men as evidence that such a device may have also been employed by Shakespeare's company (91).

Monck's canopy was historically accurate for the early modern period, although inappropriate for indoor use. His inner stage was too large according to twenty-first-century understanding, but not so big as to serve as a false proscenium. His removable staircases, while innovative, have been later acknowledged as a historically viable alternative. The architecture of Monck's stage was therefore functionally consistent with later, more authentic, reconstructions. The great pitfall of the Maddermarket with regard to Elizabethan practices, however, was the positioning of the audience. The theater was originally constructed with 206 seats in front, divided between the floor level and an upper tier, and approximately thirty on each side in elevated galleries. This configuration is disproportionately skewed to favor the audience in front. The number of side spectators decreased even further when sight lines for the second row of gallery seats proved poor, leading to the removal of these places soon after the theater opened. Seats overlooking the stage were soon eliminated as well, after unfortunate incidents of patrons dropping objects on the actors. This left the Maddermarket with only twelve chairs in each side gallery. Hildy notes that this lack of a significant side audience was "not without scholarly support," because "the authority Monck had turned to, W. J. Lawrence, had argued that there was no side audience at all at the Blackfriars except for a few nobles who possibly sat on stage" (Hildy, *Shakespeare* 48). The current reconstruction in Staunton, however, accommodates a much higher percentage of its public on the sides, with seventy-eight out of a total of 300 seats located right or left of center.

Monck took seriously his obligations to the small audience on the sides of the Maddermarket. Bridges-Adams writes, "It was from [Monck] that I learned all I know about what is now called acting in the round" ("Proscenium" 26). Yet over time the lack of an appreciable side audience tempted Monck toward over-production. Without a significant number of spectators right and left to keep him honest, Monck eventually gravitated "toward significant scenic adjuncts" in quest of "visual variety" (Hildy, "Reviving" 254). Many of these elements, such as a set of revolving flats, would have been impractical with an audience overlooking the stage. As it was, Monck's "policy of hanging his traverse curtains halfway back between the posts and the rear façade" (Hildy, *Shakespeare* 66) acknowledged the sight lines of his public in the side galleries. A greater number of spectators seated further upstage right and left, as at the twenty-first-century Globe and Blackfriars, would have prohibited the use of these tapestries altogether and led the Maddermarket closer to the Elizabethan ideal of a bare stage.

Monck's draperies were a metatheatrical device. "All curtains were opened or closed by the actors in character in full view of the audience," Hildy writes. "It was a frankly theatrical convention" (*Shakespeare* 67). Monck's practice shared this Brechtian quality with a moment in Barker's Savoy *Midsummer* described by Styan:

> When Oberon gave Puck his final orders to put right the mistakes of the night, Puck ended the scene by seeming to stage-manage the production himself ... Puck came down center and motioned for the lights to be dimmed, and then bent down as if raising the drop cloth as it ascended to bring in Demetrius and Lysander. For Puck to be physically aware of the mechanics of the Savoy stage was an extra-dramatic device by which Barker's audience could be compelled to accept the mode of the play as one of conscious non-illusion. (*Shakespeare Revolution* 102–3)

A distinction exists, however, between Barker's Puck signaling the operation of mechanical stage equipment and Monck's actors manually positioning their curtains. One involves the technological resources of the modern era, the other employs a method utilized on Shakespeare's own stage. Monck's Pre-Raphaelite rejection of the industrial age found expression in his staging, while Barker's anxiety regarding technology, expressed in *The Harlequinade*, did not impact his work at the Savoy.

Critical response to the Maddermarket was mixed. The *Times* announced on 27 September 1921 that "the opening to-night of the first Elizabethan theatre to be constructed in this country since Cromwell ordered the closing of the playhouses, is one of the brightest spots in the dramatic history of this country." Monck's playhouse would "afford a great deal of comfort to those who are genuinely concerned for the future of the English stage" ("Norwich Players' New Theatre" 8). William Butler Yeats, who attended the inaugural performance, said that he hoped Monck's theatre would inspire him to write "a bustling play in the manner of Shakespeare's historical plays with 'trumpets' and 'alarums and excursions,' and resounding defiance and everybody murdered at the end and no damned psychology" (quoted in Hildy, *Shakespeare* 47). Andrew Stephenson noted Monck's anachronisms but forgave them. Of the downstage pillars supporting the incongruous indoor canopy he wrote, "These may not have been used in an Elizabethan private theatre, but they have proved so useful for bits of 'business,' so important in the adaptability of the stage, and present so pleasing a line to the eye, that their existence is fully justified" (*Theatre Arts Magazine* 204). Of Monck's historical accuracy in general Stephenson elsewhere summarized, "The Maddermarket Theatre, while it cannot pretend to be an exact reconstruction of what we presume the Elizabethan playhouse to have been like, combines aspects of both the private and public theatres of the time" (*Maddermarket Theatre Norwich* 8).

Others critics were less positive. William Poel, probably the most severe arbiter of Elizabethan methods among theater practitioners, had reservations about the Maddermarket. Monck said of Poel's initial reaction, "He hated it" (quoted in Hildy, *Shakespeare* 48). But Poel nevertheless wrote in the *Manchester Guardian* on 1 October 1921, "No one has got closer to the essentials that give scope for the successful presentation of Elizabethan drama than have Mr. Nugent Monck and his able assistants" ("Elizabethan Playhouse" 7). Muriel St Clare Byrne was more harsh in her critique. She claimed that the Maddermarket "had neither proscenium arch nor curtain, but it was no more an Elizabethan open stage than any platform that stretches across the end of a hall from one side to the other" (Introduction xxxiv). Nevill Truman describes Monck's take on this scholarly reaction:

> It was designed as an Elizabethan Theatre, and all the authorities had been consulted. But, as Mr. Monck says, no one really knows what an Elizabethan Theatre looked like, and he had to take all the practical parts of the experts' books and leave the rest. The experts attended. They said it was all wrong. Monck retorted that at least its principles could be found in their books. And the critics turned and rent each other. Monck pursued his way calmly, and left the critics to dispute amongst themselves. (144)

Whatever the limitations of its historical accuracy, the Maddermarket proved a versatile stage for presenting Shakespeare and also for applying Elizabethan methods to the work of other dramatists. Monck wrote in 1931 that the Maddermarket "was designed in order that Shakespeare's plays could be presented with the staging and production for which they were originally intended," but that he "soon discovered that practically any piece that did not depend upon Realism could be played upon this open stage" (*Theatre Arts* 581).

Shakespeare, however, remained the Maddermarket's primary focus, and Monck's productions of his plays were marked by speed and clarity. Norman Marshall wrote, "It is remarkable how fast an actor can speak without becoming inaudible in a theatre like the Maddermarket where he is playing almost among the audience." In contrast to accounts of Barker's Savoy productions, Marshall claimed that at the Maddermarket, "There is no gabbling." The speed of speech was matched by swiftness in scene transitions. While in "the normal Shakespearian production it is amazing how much time is wasted between the innumerable scenes," Monck instead used "his Shakespearean stage exactly as Shakespeare intended it to be used, each scene following on the other without even an instant's pause." Marshall concluded that until "one has seen a production by Monck it is difficult to realize how essential it is for the full effect of any Shakespearian play that it should flow along without the slightest interruption" (*Other* 96).

The immediacy and intimacy of the Maddermarket experience inspired Herbert Farjeon to exclaim, "The Maddermarket Theatre in Norwich is a revelation." "You do not look on at the feast through a crack in the wall," Farjeon claimed, "You are actually present at it. You come upon it as you might come upon a fight in the street" (61). Eric Fowler believed that Monck sought "to rescue Shakespeare" from "the schoolmen who treated his works as books to be studied rather than as plays to be enjoyed" (349). While Monck never expressed an anti-literary attitude in his limited writings, his work as a director convinced at least one critic of the primacy of performance. "If you prefer to read *Macbeth*, the preference becomes inadequate," wrote Charles Rigby for the *Eastern Daily Press*. "There is too much atmosphere imparted by the spoken lines, the hues of the costumes, and settings that achieve their effect by understatement, to leave any longer the meal at the printed page satisfying" (rpt. in Rigby, *Maddermarket Mondays* 58).

Not everyone was enamored of Monck's methods. Terence Gray, director of the Cambridge Festival Theatre, wrote of the Maddermarket in terms that recall Max Beerbohm's earlier criticism of William Poel. "Cannot Max Reinhardt, Jessner or Hilar," Gray asked, "make more of Shakespeare, producing him with all the forces of modern continental stagecraft at their command, than can some archaeologist reviving the conditions of the Elizabethan stage?" (quoted in Hildy, *Shakespeare* 114). More commonly, observers complained that Monck cut too much of Shakespeare's plays in performance. The *Observer* critic wrote of Monck's 1925 *Romeo and Juliet* that he had been surprised to find the text "rather ruthlessly slashed," particularly as he considered the Maddermarket "the Mecca of true Shakespearians" (quoted in Hildy, "Reviving" 284). Both Soman and Fowler also claimed that Monck cut Shakespeare "ruthlessly" (Fowler 350); and the director admitted that the great advantage to staging Shakespeare came from having "no author to bother about – you could cut and perform just as much as you liked" (Monck, "Shakespeare and the Amateur" 321). Farjeon suggested a highly practical objective behind Monck's editorial practice. "Norwich," he wrote, "likes to be in bed by ten o'clock" (61). Some of Monck's cuts, however, suggest an aggressive agenda of adaptation beyond the bounds of pragmatism, as when he cut the entire first act of *Pericles* and created a chorus for *Titus Andronicus* in order to consolidate the action of that tragedy. Whatever his exact motivations, Monck never subscribed to the kind of fetishistic reverence for a "complete text" advocated by Byrne and employed by Barker in his Savoy productions.

With his 1933 *Henry VI* Monck had staged the entire Shakespearean canon. Up to this point, he later maintained, Monck's productions had all been "strictly Elizabethan" (Monck, *Drama* 20). Now however he began to experiment more broadly because, as he told the *Times* in 1953, "after six productions of *Twelfth Night* the audience got nearly as bored with it as I did" (quoted in "Shakespeare at the Maddermarket" 9). Monck once went so far as to stage a production of "*What You Will* (in very large letters) or *Twelfth Night* (in very small), in which Viola breathed her lines to a typewriter and Orsino called 'What ho, Cesario!' into the telephone" ("Shakespeare at the Maddermarket" 9). Besides Monck's temptation to stray from his core artistic vision, the Maddermarket also had to cope with the challenges posed by the Great Depression and World War II. This latter catastrophe nearly destroyed the Norwich playhouse.

The British government closed all theaters at the start of the conflict in 1939. Monck was able to reopen soon afterwards, partly through the assistance of Tyrone Guthrie, who was working for the government's Council for the Encouragement of Music and the Arts. While it remained open thereafter, the Maddermarket's situation in the early years of the war was precarious. Hildy writes that "by 1943 Monck found himself running the box office, making the costumes, designing and building the sets, cleaning the theatre, and even spending night after night sleeping in the Maddermarket as part of the fire watch" (*Shakespeare* 143). But this saga had a happy ending, as American troops stationed in the area after 1942 provided the Maddermarket with a badly needed public.

Monck wrote for the journal *War-Time Drama* in 1944, "We are getting a new type of audience these days, strangers to our city, and their enthusiasm gives the performers great encouragement. Some have never seen good plays before, and, like many of the American troops, have never seen Shakespeare acted" (3). While some of these Yanks were no doubt as unsophisticated as Monck suggests, others according to Reyner Banham were "college-educated top-sergeants who knew all about the man and his theatre from reading *Theatre Arts*." Some were accomplished actors themselves. "The first and only time I ever met James Stewart," Banham recalls, "he was with some other uniformed thespians, swapping tall memoirs with Nugent Monck on the stage of the Maddermarket Theatre." These international playgoers inspired the locals to a greater appreciation of Monck's institution. "Norwich," Banham writes, "discovered that it had a famous theatre and a producer of genius in its midst. Discovered just in time, for he was pushing 70 by then" (372). This new popularity continued after the war when, for the first time, Maddermarket audiences were made up primarily of locals and not of theater enthusiasts driving in from other parts of England. Monck retired as head of the Maddermarket in 1952, but continued to direct regularly until his death in 1958. In 1953, he staged *A Midsummer Night's Dream* outdoors in Norfolk. It was his last Shakespearean production.

Populism and Ideology

ALTHOUGH almost everyone at the Maddermarket worked on a volunteer basis, Nugent Monck always paid his cleaning crew. "Heaven defend us," he said, "from an amateur charwoman" (quoted in Truman 144). Although this comment is pragmatic, it also reflects a lifelong respect on Monck's part for the working class, an attitude developed during his boyhood in Liverpool. He extended similar consideration to his actors, although he could not compensate them monetarily. Once, while staging a pageant at Winchester College, Monck was offered an opportunity to dine with the event's sponsors. "What about the Players?" he asked. When told the performers would be eating in the servants' quarters, Monck announced, "So will I" (quoted in Hildy, "Reviving" 116). While Harley Granville Barker in his later writings adopted a superior attitude toward performers, Monck never thought of actors as "the help."

Monck's approach to financing was equally egalitarian. He believed that "all theatre should depend on the box office in order to keep it from becoming too elitist" (Hildy, "Reviving" 237). In securing funding, he sought the support of citizens who would advance small sums of money in the expectation of recompense once a production succeeded. "It is better to have a hundred poor patrons at a guinea each than one rich man who is willing to throw away a hundred guineas," he explained, because while "the rich man does not mind if he loses his money" the "guinea guarantor has not the slightest intention of losing his" and therefore becomes "an active and excellent publicity agent" (quoted in Marshall, *Other* 93). Monck's financial method was the opposite of Barker's reliance on patronage. The Savoy productions were made possible by a gentleman farmer named Lord Lucas who sold his pig-farm and gave the £5,000 in proceeds to produce Shakespeare because, he said, "I like his pearls better than my pigs" (quoted in Purdom 139).

While stationed in Greece following the 1918 armistice, Monck requested permission to visit the ancient theater at Delphi. He later recalled, " 'Certainly Not!' I was told. 'No N.C.O. could possibly want to see it.' It was a sight reserved for officers and nursing sisters" (quoted in Hildy, "Reviving" 137). Mottram wrote in 1936 of Monck's reaction to this snub, "I think he has never forgiven the British Army" (9). Monck sought in his efforts at the Maddermarket to combat this kind of cultural snobbism and to make his art available to the broadest possible segment of society. The stated goals of the Norwich Players were "to produce plays of literary and artistic merit in the best and most vital manner possible" and "to bring such within the level of the democracy" (quoted in Cook 212). After long years of effort, Monck succeeded in building a local following that spanned demographic divisions. He described in *Shakespeare Survey* the difference between his Maddermarket public and a more typical Shakespeare audience. "At Stratford-Upon-Avon," Monck observed, spectators

> know what they are going to see, and treat what they are shown with reverence. This situation is different if you are giving Shakespeare to a working-class audience between the ages of sixteen and twenty. There is no knowing what will raise a loud burst of ironic laughter, for these audiences are intelligent and quick to take up points; they are also readily moved by sincerity. (75)

In 1933, Charles Rigby suggested that Monck was "ahead of his time" in seeking to serve a population that was becoming "better and better educated" and would consequently "demand from the drama more and more intellectual diversion and sustenance" (8–9). While the intervening decades in theatrical history have not consistently borne out this hope, Monck's work anticipated the achievements of the new Globe in bringing Shakespeare to a wide audience.

Ideologically, Monck's populist approach to Shakespeare has a potentially repressive component. If its function were to indoctrinate the lower orders into an elitist hegemonic discourse, then Monck's agenda would be essentially reactionary. At least one element of his production style, however, suggests that he did not seek to contain the expression of Norwich locals within the limits of "high-brow" Elizabethan language but instead offered Shakespeare to his Players and public as a medium for communicating their own culture. I refer to Monck's consistent use of Norfolk dialect in the staging of comic roles.

In his essay "Shakespeare, Voice, and Ideology: Interrogating the Natural Voice," Richard Paul Knowles argues that the twentieth-century paradigm of vocal training for actors, which advocates "open" speech that is free of regionalisms, is politically regressive. This "movement away from the accidentals of cultural conditioning that constrain the voice," Knowles asserts, "allows for the *effacement* of cultural and other kinds of difference" (100). The supposedly culturally neutral vocal style modeled by teachers like Kristin Linklater, Patsy Rodenburg, and Cicely Berry is for Knowles "filled by the unquestioned because naturalized assumptions of (dominant) ideology" (94). These voice teachers force aspiring actors from various class backgrounds and disparate geographic locations to speak in a vaguely anglophilic "Mid-Atlantic" dialect, thereby subtly leading these performers and their audiences to emulate and respect the values of the Anglo-American elite. Knowles connects this repressive agenda in voice training to "the fundamental precepts of the 'Elizabethan revival.' " He believes that both schools erroneously endorse the notion that " 'free' and 'open' principles of staging," whether in vocal work or scenography, " 'allow' contemporary audiences direct access to Shakespeare's transcendental intentions"(102). Knowles's argument has great value for understanding the ideological ramifications of contemporary actor training. It falters, however, in its attempt to connect an agenda of cultural effacement to the practices of the Elizabethan movement. Nugent Monck was the most prolific and consistent practitioner of early modern methods in the first half of the twentieth century, yet his approach to vocal work was radically different from that described by Knowles.

"The producer," Monck wrote in 1937, "should never be afraid of provincialism, for nothing is more awful to listen to than an unnaturally refined voice; standardized English is as dull as a baker's loaf. The home-made variety is more interesting" ("Shakespeare and the Amateur" 323). In his Shakespeare productions, Monck consistently used one variety of non-standard English, the Norfolk dialect, for portrayals of comic characters. Reyner Banham offers a phonetic rendering of this speech pattern, which shows its deviation from the BBC norm. "Come yew haer, gal Gloria, do else I'll lump ya one!" Banham transliterates, "Yew only want me outa the house so yew can goo off with that bleedin' Yank." (372). The use of this accent exclusively for low comic parts could have been construed as insensitive and demeaning, particularly since Monck was not a native of Norfolk. Local observers, however, consistently approved. Mariette Soman wrote of Monck's early *Much Ado About Nothing* at the Music House that a "pleasant innovation was the use of the Norfolk dialect for all the low comedy parts," adding, "One felt indeed that Dogberry was a Norfolk man" (27). Charles Rigby similarly wrote of the comic lead in Monck's 1933 *A Midsummer Night's Dream*, "His broad Norfolk adds another cubit to his stature, whereby he out-Bottoms Bottom" (16). Rather than using non-standard speech to belittle a social group, as was the unfortunate case in American minstrel shows, Monck intended his application of Norfolk dialect to celebrate linguistic diversity in the same way that the Italian actor-playwright Dario Fo employs the patois of his native Lombardy.

Nugent Monck was not overtly political in his work, although some productions betrayed an ideological slant. Hildy notes that (like William Poel before him) Monck turned *Troilus and Cressida* into "an anti-war play" and advanced a similar pacifist message in *Romeo and Juliet* ("Reviving" 422). Monck also "created quite a stir" in 1950 colonial Jamaica when he "staged a production of *The Merchant of Venice* with an all-black cast" (389). Yet Monck's individual stagings didn't normally proclaim specific political statements. Monck's general philosophy toward the theater and its relationship to society, however, strongly resembles the approach of a later and more avowedly radical practitioner, the Polish director and theorist Jerzy Grotwoski. This seems at first an unlikely connection. Monck's work, as Hildy writes, was generally "too tame" for those seeking an "emotionally demonstrative experience" (*Shakespeare* 89). Grotowski, on the other hand, exhorted his actors to unveil their primal emotions and was openly confrontational with his audience. But the strategic similarities in the approaches of these two theatrical visionaries outweigh their tactical differences. Both men believed in breaking the proscenium wall and establishing intimate contact between actors and spectators. They also shared a sense of the spiritual mission of theater, and both embraced minimalist, low-tech staging in an attempt to define their medium in contrast to cinema.

In spite of having abandoned the Anglicanism of his minister father, "Nugent Monck," as Eric Fowler wrote, "was a deeply religious man" (348).

Monck recognized a metaphysical longing in his audiences, and saw theater as an alternative to the established churches. He said his public came to the Maddermarket because "the theatre was giving them things" of a spiritual nature which "they could find nowhere else" (quoted in Hildy, "Reviving" 338). Some in Norwich seem to have attended performances in lieu of traditional religious services. The pseudonymous "Hotspur" who reviewed Monck's 1930 *Pericles* for *Shakespeare Pictorial* went before that well-attended Maddermarket production to Evensong at the Cathedral where, he writes, "Two ladies and myself formed the total congregation" (15). Nevill Truman noted of Monck's work that the "Church is preparing us for another world, and to do so, it damns this; the Stage is trying to make the best of the world we live in." Truman concluded that in "the hurry and bustle of today, the Norwich movement has a spiritual value" (144). Grotowski, writing in 1968, describes his own vision in similar terms:

> I do not think that the crisis in the theatre can be separated from certain other crisis processes [*sic*] in contemporary culture. One of its essential elements – namely, the disappearance of the sacred and of its ritual function in the theatre – is a result of the obvious and probably inevitable decline of religion. What we are talking about is the possibility of creating a secular *sacrum* in the theatre. (49)

This notion of a quasi-religious quest, which Grotowski called "an intentional return to 'ritual roots' " (18), was common to the Polish director and the Elizabethan movement, as evidenced by the fact that Poel, Monck, and Grotowski all chose to stage Kalidasa's sacred Hindu drama *Sankuntala*. Tyrone Guthrie similarly emphasized the ritual nature of theater in his writings and in his design of the Stratford Festival stage.

Monck would have been in sympathy with the spirituality and asceticism expressed in Grotowski's notion of "a 'holy' actor in a poor theatre" (41). Of the Maddermarket's poverty Truman wrote, "Those who think nothing can be achieved without money should note that the Norwich Players began with ten pounds" (144). Hildy writes that Monck saw his low-budget efforts as a "crusade" (*Shakespeare* 87), and Grotowski likewise suggests that renewal in the theater can only come "from amateurs working on the boundaries of the professional theatre" (50). His description of these optimal theater artists as "a few madmen who have nothing to lose and are not afraid of hard work" (Grotowski 50) accurately describes the Norwich Players, especially in their early years. Like Monck, Grotowski believed that the magic of theater was available to anyone. Access was "not determined by the social background or financial situation of the spectator, nor even education. The worker who has never had any secondary education can undergo this creative process of self-search" (Grotowski 40). Monck similarly insisted that his work at the Maddermarket could be appreciated by any open-minded person, regardless of education level.

Monck and Grotowski both understood the need for theater to redefine itself in response to the challenge from cinema. Each rejected what Grotowski terms "the wrong solution" to this problem, which consists of making theater "more technical" in order to compete with motion pictures. Instead, Grotowski writes, "the theatre must recognize its own limitations. If it cannot be richer than the cinema, then let it be poor" (41). Monck similarly advocated in response to film a simpler theater in which "there will be less noisy action on the stage" (quoted in Hildy, "Reviving" 213). Grotowski's assertion that "no matter how much theatre expands and exploits its mechanical resources, it will remain technologically inferior to film" (19) echoes Monck's earlier pronouncement that theater must stop "attempting to compete with [the] realism" of cinema (quoted in Hildy, *Shakespeare* 162). Monck shared with his fellow Elizabethanists this willingness to concede realistic and technological superiority to film. "Authenticity spared the theatre from a competition it could not win," Gary Taylor writes of the movement's relationship to cinema. "The Elizabethan stage," he continues, "had no sets, no artificial lighting, [and] no period costumes" (274). This paucity of resources allies the recovery of early modern practices to Grotowski's "poverty," in which "Theatre can exist without make-up, without autonomic costume and scenography, without a separate performance area (stage), without lighting and sound effects, etc." (19).

Monck and Grotowski both rejected standard forms of praise and accolades for theater artists. The Norwich Players performed anonymously, a practice which according to Hildy "did a great deal to encourage ensemble acting" (*Shakespeare* 77). No "calls" were ever taken at the Maddermarket. Legend has it that, in spite of "cries for the author," Monck even denied a curtain call to George Bernard Shaw at the premiere of that playwright's *Getting Married* (Hildy, "Reviving" 261). Grotowski wrote that in the "Poor Theatre" artistic satisfaction "does not mean flowers and interminable applause, but a special silence in which there is much fascination" (44). Monck's audiences typically offered this kind of undemonstrative recognition. As an anonymous Maddermarket patron claimed in a letter to the local newspaper, "Our silence is a far higher tribute of appreciation than applause can be" (quoted in Rigby 12). Lillah McCarthy offers a more typical metric for theatrical success when she writes of her performance in the Savoy *Midsummer*, "As Helena in a golden wig, I was again beloved. Presents showered upon me. Nice chocolates, bad verses, flowers, [and] bracelets" (174). Ms. McCarthy was no more mercenary than the vast majority of her fellow performers at the time or since, but she would not have enjoyed working for either Monck or Grotowski.

The Legacies of Monck and Barker

IN 1928 Charles F. Smith, the founding producer of the Leeds Civic Playhouse, wrote, "Some time ago I asked a very distinguished producer a characteristically indiscreet question: 'Who in your opinion are the three greatest producers of this generation?' 'Gordon Craig, Granville Barker, and Nugent Monck,' was the prompt reply" (quoted in Hildy, "Reviving" 274). Smith's anecdote suggests that at the time Barker and Monck were considered equally significant. In recent decades, however, scholars have seen Barker's influence as predominant. In his 1977 *The Shakespeare Revolution*, for instance, J. L. Styan devotes two entire chapters to Barker (one examining the Savoy productions and another Barker's early criticism) but less than two pages to Monck's work at the Maddermarket (*Shakespeare Revolution* 124–5). Monck's reputation has suffered in part because it is difficult to separate his influence from that of Barker. A group of productions and Prefaces between 1926 and 1940 illustrates the complex web of association between these two Shakespeareans.

In his Preface to *Antony and Cleopatra*, Barker advocated the use of Renaissance costumes for those plays of Shakespeare set in earlier eras, to be augmented by small sartorial touches from these more distant periods. He wrote:

> In the National Gallery hangs Paolo Veronese's "Alexander and the Wife and Daughter of Darius." This will be very much how Shakespeare saw his Roman figures habited. Antony would wear Alexander's mixture of doublet, breastplate, sandals and hose. Here too is something very like Octavia's costume; and though Cleopatra might be given Egyptian stigmata, there would still be laces to cut. (*Prefaces* 3: 42–3)

Monck used this style of dress for his 1926 *Julius Caesar*. Hildy writes that this production "was probably the first time anyone had put on stage the idea of costuming that Granville-Barker advocated in his preface to *Antony and Cleopatra*, which had appeared in 1925" ("Reviving" 199). Complications arise when one considers that Barker does not appear to have actually published his Preface to *Antony and Cleopatra* until 1930 (Purdom 303). This is a small point arising from a Byzantine sequence of revision and reprinting with regard to Barker's *Prefaces*. It would be cruelly ironic if Hildy, who has undoubtedly done more than any other scholar to resurrect the reputation of Nugent Monck, were led by the unclear record of Barker's publication dates to, in this one instance, give Monck less credit than he deserves. Nevertheless, this later date of publication for Barker's Preface to *Antony and Cleopatra* raises the question of who influenced whom in the use of Renaissance costuming for Shakespeare's ancient plays.

Barker did not use early modern dress in the two plays set before 1500, *The Winter's Tale* and *A Midsummer Night's Dream*, which he staged at the Savoy. Rather than influencing Monck in this design choice, Barker may have actually been led to advocacy of Elizabethan costumes by the work he saw at the Maddermarket. Monck, Hildy writes, "like Poel before him, conceived of all the characters from Troilus to Hamlet, as essentially Elizabethan people and he dressed them accordingly" ("Reviving" 198). He therefore used Renaissance costuming for his 1926 *King Lear*, which Barker saw at the Maddermarket in September of that year. Barker was sufficiently impressed with Monck's production to mention it in his 1927 Preface to this tragedy. Complaining in a footnote of "modern scenic productions" which "lengthen the plays considerably," Barker observed:

> Mr. Nugent Monck recently produced *King Lear* at the Maddermarket Theatre Norwich, upon an unlocalized stage. He cut approximately 750 of the 3340 lines of text (the Folio will give authority for the cutting of

some 200), allowed a ten minutes interval, did not play over-rapidly, and the whole performance only lasted two hours and twenty-five minutes. (Barker, Preface to *Lear* xviii n)

The *Times Literary Supplement* in its June 1927 review of the Preface to *King Lear* found Barker's admiration for Monck's production significant. The reviewer attributed to Barker the notion that "the Maddermarket Theatre at Norwich appears to be the only place at which Shakespeare's *King Lear* has been acted, since the seventeenth century, as Shakespeare meant it to be acted" ("*King Lear* for the Stage" 437). This is a strong conclusion to reach from the brief expository footnote cited above. Perhaps other passages in the Preface also suggested homage to Monck. Barker's thoughts on costuming in *King Lear* comprise one such possibility.

Barker wrote of this play that while "the prevailing atmosphere and accent is barbaric and remote," Shakespeare's "own seventeenth century" asserts itself in many aspects, including Edmund's "Italianate flavor." Oswald was similarly "a topical picture" that would be "all but obliterated" by an ancient British costume. The presence of a Renaissance Fool "in a barbarous king's retinue" was for Barker a typically Shakespearean anachronism similar to that of "Henry V in doublet and hose" (Preface to *Lear* lxxix). Overall, Barker advocates the same mixture of Elizabethan and earlier elements that he would later endorse in his Preface to *Antony and Cleopatra* and employ in his 1940 *King Lear* at the Old Vic. The *Manchester Guardian* described this production's "rich Renaissance costumes," which "exactly communicate the tragedy's barbaric temper and yet at the same time contrive to make each player look as though he or she had been painted thus by Moroni or Moretto" (review of *King Lear* 6). This was the same style that Barker had seen in Monck's 1926 *King Lear* at the Maddermarket. While Barker's 1940 staging of *King Lear* derived from his own Preface to this tragedy, this Preface had in turn been influenced by Monck's earlier production.

The impact of Barker and Monck on later stage directors is similarly intertwined. They both influenced Tyrone Guthrie in his adoption of Elizabethan methods. Guthrie got his job running the Old Vic largely on the strength of his staging of *Love's Labour's Lost* at the Westminster Theatre in 1933. He freely acknowledges that this production was based on Monck's 1930 revival of this comedy. Guthrie wrote in *A Life in the Theatre*:

> I had seen the play not long before in a delightful production by Nugent Monck directing a semi-amateur cast in the little Maddermarket Theatre in Norwich. In Monck's production a permanent set suggested no clearly identifiable locality; [and] there were no breaks between scenes; ... Most of the good ideas in my production were culled from Monck's at Norwich ... From Monck I absorbed various points of style, and a point of view about this particular play. (84)

"I confess my debt to Nugent Monck," Guthrie concluded, "not with a blush but with pride that I had the sense to pick so good a model" (*Life* 84). Elsewhere, Guthrie wrote of Monck's 1930 *Doctor Faustus*, in which "scenery there was none" and "the costumes were exact copies of Elizabethan dress," that it was "more than archeologically interesting. It was stimulating because it suggested the possibilities of a technique that, being old, was not lost but new" (*Theatre Prospect* 49). Guthrie's comments recall George Bernard Shaw's review of William Poel's 1896 production of this same Marlovian tragedy, in which Shaw claimed that early modern methods created a "picture of the past" which "was really a picture of the future" (Shaw, review of *Doctor Faustus* 37).

Monck, however, is conspicuously absent from the roll of influences Guthrie cites in *A Life in the Theatre* to justify his application of Elizabethan principles at the Old Vic. "We would follow Poel and Barker and Shaw," Guthrie claims (121) and specifically cites Barker's *Prefaces to Shakespeare* as an inspiration (120). Nevertheless, Guthrie obliquely acknowledges Monck slightly later in this section. In a list of "the facilities usually supposed to have been available in the Elizabethan theatres" Guthrie includes as the first item "stairs, leading to a balcony" (121). These are not a universally accepted feature of early modern stagecraft. Neither the new Globe nor the reconstructed Blackfriars have such stairs, and Barker does not consider them in his *Prefaces*. Monck, on the other hand, often used a removable staircase in his Maddermarket productions, and it was in Norwich that Guthrie came to see this device as a useful component of Elizabethan staging.

No one can completely separate the respective influences of Harley Granville Barker and Nugent Monck on the Elizabethan movement. Barker's reputation has grown over the years, largely because his writings continued to speak for him after his death. Monck's frustratingly brief article in *Shakespeare Survey* demonstrates that he could, if he wished, have composed highly specific descriptions of the mechanics of early modern staging. In this piece, Monck describes the function of the Maddermarket's architectural features:

> In *Romeo and Juliet*, the balcony has several uses. It is, of course, kept for the first balcony scene, and for the second when Romeo secures his escape by the rope ladder, which Juliet unties, and throws after him … For the last scene of all, you return to the balcony. Juliet is upon the tomb below; there is a grating before the balcony so that the impression is given that you are looking down into a crypt … Juliet's head should be towards the audience, so that when Romeo addresses her he is facing the audience. Juliet can easily turn when the Friar awakens her. The Duke and the crowd speak from the balcony; only the parents are below, save for their torch-bearers, who close the curtains after everyone has filed out. (73)

The pragmatic style of this essay is a welcome contrast to the opaque verbosity of many of Barker's *Prefaces*. A book-length exploration by Monck of the issues touched on in his *Shakespeare Survey* article would have been invaluable for theater practitioners wishing to emulate an Elizabethan style. The manner in which Monck's contributions have been overlooked by subsequent generations provides a cautionary tale for stage directors, whose work is inherently ephemeral. As twenty-first-century scholarship increasingly embraces performance as a legitimate alternative to written criticism, Monck may eventually gain the recognition he deserves.

Like Jerzy Grotowski, Nugent Monck rejected the trappings of technology and overproduction and believed that simpler methods could yield spiritual results. Grotowski claimed that the practices of the "Poor Theatre" revealed "not only the backbone of the medium, but also the deep riches which lie in the very nature of the art form" (21). Monck similarly saw his minimalist efforts at the Maddermarket as an antidote to the over-stimulation of the cinematic age and as a means of maintaining spiritual community in a modern society increasingly afflicted with alienation. He inherited this quest from William Poel but surpassed his teacher by constructing an architectural solution that enabled greater audience engagement. Nugent Monck therefore represented an important (but often overlooked) transitional phase between the idealism of Poel and the eventual achievements of Tyrone Guthrie and the new Globe.

4 Tyrone Guthrie

TYRONE Guthrie's theatrical designs frequently incorporated early modern features. Historical accuracy was not, however, his primary concern. There was "no need" in his view for "an exact replica of the Globe Theatre." Instead his chief goal in imitating the Elizabethans was "to make the contact between players and audience as intimate as possible" ("The Theatres" 9). He believed that theater was descended from ancient religious ceremonies, and the placement of the public in close proximity to the playing area created a sense of unity that enhanced what he perceived as the sacramental quality of drama. This concern led him to become a major proponent, in both theory and practice, of the "open stage." For Guthrie this term referred to "an auditorium arranged not *in front* of the stage, but, to a greater or less extent, wrapped *around* the stage." He distinguished between an "Arena" format, where the audience completely surrounds the playing area, and a "Thrust" or "Open" model, in which the public only partially encircles the platform. Guthrie believed that the presence of spectators on three sides of the stage created a "social, shared aspect of performance," through which the public is constantly "reminded that one and all are sharing the same occasion, taking part in the same rites" (Guthrie, "Do We Go" X3).

While Guthrie frequently employed an Elizabethan-style permanent set and sometimes experimented with the early modern convention of "universal lighting," his major influence in the recovery of Shakespearean staging was as a founder of the open-stage movement. The thrust configuration is generally considered to have been a key feature of early modern theaters. The new Globe in London and the reconstructed Blackfriars in Staunton, Virginia both place audience on three sides in an arc of approximately 180° from the front of each theater's *frons scenae*. In his most famous performance space, the original tent at Stratford, Guthrie pursued a more circular form by arranging the public in a 240° crescent (Somerset xiv). This allowed him to better imitate those ancient celebrations which had been enacted in the round.

There was a political dimension to Guthrie's advocacy of this alternative theatrical form. He believed that the proscenium arose as a manifestation of society's increasing division along class lines. It "marked the social chasm, which separated the predominantly courtly and aristocratic audience in the stalls and boxes from the socially inferior persons who were paid to entertain them" (Guthrie, *Life* 197). During the Cold War, Guthrie wrote that the danger of fire in proscenium theaters had led to the introduction of "yet another barrier, the iron curtain, now a world-famous symbol of political separation" ("Do We Go" X3). This conflation of political and theatrical boundaries is typical of what Robert Shaughnessy calls the "generally anti-authoritarian character of Guthrie's repudiation of the picture frame" (*Shakespeare* 93) and the director's "relentless drive to abolish the line between audience and performer and auditorium and stage" (94). Guthrie contrasted the hierarchical arrangement of the picture-frame stage with "the intimate, daylit relation of the Elizabethan actor to his audience and, at any rate in the public theatres, the far more democratic character of that audience" (197). He sought to emulate this early modern ambiance through his use of the thrust configuration.

Guthrie also had a more practical reason for championing the open stage. He believed that live theater could only survive the competition from cinema and television by adopting this alternative design. These new media, Guthrie felt, had raised audience expectations beyond the capabilities of the proscenium format. "When there was no better alternative," he wrote for *The New York Times* in 1962, "the public was prepared to buy seats where the best that could be expected was a dim and distant relation with the stage." People began to demand more "as soon as it was found that in the movies everyone could see and hear fully." Guthrie warned that "the theatre will not survive unless the fact is faced – and that right soon – that live acting is not indefinitely expansible. It is my belief that anything subtle or intimate cannot be projected much beyond fifteen rows" ("The Case for 'Live' Theatre" 210). Guthrie's design for the Stratford Festival, which holds 2,262 people with no spectator more than 65 feet from the stage (Somerset xiv), provides the visual and aural closeness required by a public accustomed to cinema while simultaneously allowing enough revenue from ticket sales to enable economic viability.

Guthrie's arguments for the open stage, coupled with his practical example, convinced many that this model represented the way of the future. The decision to build the Chichester Festival Theater in a thrust configuration typically reflects Guthrie's influence at mid-century. The *Times* reported in 1960 that the Chichester trustees had "been convinced by the example of the Festival Theatre at Stratford, Ontario," to adopt a three-quarter plan because such a stage was "most likely to keep 'live,' three-dimensional theatre in existence in the age of films and of television with their two-dimensional screens" ("Chichester Festival" 3). For a while it seemed that proscenium's days were numbered. Some commentators sounded like Marxist revolutionaries heralding the inevitable downfall of capitalism. "While these Roman mobs are at it," Walter Kerr wrote of the Stratford Festival's 1955 *Julius Caesar*, "they can tear down the proscenium arch theatres from coast-to-coast" (quoted in Pettigrew and Portman 108). Two years earlier, Brooks Atkinson invoked similar imagery of upheaval when he wrote that the "whole theory of the proscenium stage" had "begun to crumble" ("Shakespeare" X1).

In 1966 Guthrie could justly boast, "Most of the new theaters in North America with any serious policy have been built with an open stage" ("Do We Go" X3). As in the case of Communism, however, this forward progress stalled. Proscenium today remains the dominant theatrical format in North America. Commercial theater, as represented by Broadway productions and the auditoriums throughout the continent to which they tour, has remained largely untouched by the open-stage movement. New theater construction in the not-for-profit sector has also failed to consistently reflect Guthrie's vision. While some theaters built since the director's 1966 proclamation, such as Chicago Shakespeare's home at Navy Pier, have employed a thrust configuration, many others have stuck to the picture-frame model. One example of this retrenchment was the 1992 decision by Washington, DC's Shakespeare Theater to leave a thrust configuration at the Folger Library (albeit one with serious deficiencies) to move into a custom-built proscenium space at the Lansburgh building. Educational theater has also been slow to embrace open staging. Most college theater departments (even those with new facilities) still mount their most important productions on picture-frame stages, with any thrust work relegated to smaller "black box" spaces capable of various configurations.

Many factors have contributed to the failure, or at least the delay, of the open-stage revolution. Commercial theater in general and the Broadway musical in particular have continued to pursue what Grotowski called "the wrong solution" (41) to the challenge from film, employing ever more complex technological resources in an effort to create cinematic spectacle. Such illusionistic effects can only be achieved within the copious wing and fly space of a proscenium venue. Not-for-profit theaters often imitate the elaborate stagecraft of Broadway in an attempt to attract a broader public, and this has contributed to their continued reliance on the picture-frame. The vested interests of set designers in both professional and educational theater have also led this important theatrical constituency to resist three-quarter experimentation. While these practical and economic concerns have had the greatest impact in delaying the advance of open staging, performance scholars have also been ideologically critical of this format. These critics see the thrust stage as a conservative adjunct of the commercial status quo rather than as an alternative to this paradigm, and their negative interpretations have impeded acceptance of Guthrie's vision, at least within the academy. This critique focuses primarily on the Stratford Festival, which functions in this view as an Althusserian "Ideological State Apparatus" (Knowles, "Shakespeare, 1993" 225) that serves a reactionary agenda. These critics accuse Guthrie of adopting a "lavish and luxurious production style" (Groome, "Affirmative" 144) that "accented visual richness ... and spectacle at the cost of all else" (Cohen, Nathan, "Theatre" 235) in a celebration of bourgeois consumerism. This notion of Guthrie as a purveyor of visual excess seems at odds with the supposedly Spartan aesthetic of Elizabethanism and points to a key contradiction in the director's work.

Throughout his career, Guthrie frequently aligned himself with the minimalist stagecraft practiced by William Poel and Nugent Monck. He rejected the commercial paradigm with its "elaboration of spectacle," in which to "give the public something for its money, a Pageant is mounted to the accompaniment of a Shakespearean text" (*Life* 214). In Ontario, Guthrie achieved his vision of "a stage without sets" (Pettigrew and Portman 76). All of his Stratford productions were staged on an undecorated, purely functional platform. Guthrie was also sparing in his use of stage lighting. He eschewed colored gelatins and the use of lighting for interpretive purposes, and advocated instead a merely utilitarian approach to stage illumination. Yet while Guthrie followed a "path of artistic austerity" (Whittaker x) when it came to sets and lighting, this philosophy did not hold in matters of costume.

In theory Guthrie sometimes advocated minimalism in stage dress, as when he wrote of *The Tempest*, "Let Ariel and Caliban appear as what they are – two actors; and let them persuade the audience that they are spirits by the art not of the dressmaker but of the actor" ("Introduction to the *Tempest*" 448). In practice, however, his productions featured elaborate and expensive costumes, which Nathan Cohen describes as "more lavish than the most lavish settings" ("Theatre" 235). Alec Guinness's gigantic crimson coronation robe, which literally filled the Stratford stage during 1953's inaugural production, typifies this tendency toward sartorial extravagance. Props were also ornate, picturesque and sometimes macabre. During rehearsals for *Richard III* the director "kept sending Henry's corpse back to the properties department for more gore, telling it to 'ladle on the pus'" (Pettigrew and Portman 5); and Guthrie's *Tamburlaine* was dominated by "machines of death and cages of torture" (Williamson, *Old Vic Drama 2* 78). This excess clashed with Guthrie's professed rejection of scenic splendor. For unsympathetic scholars, his visual achievements went beyond good showmanship to perniciously invert theatrical values. Richard Paul Knowles suggests that Guthrie's early efforts created a "tradition of splendour" at Stratford in which "visual elements have competed with, or overwhelmed, the text" and "quality of design" has often taken "priority over clarity of directorial vision" ("Legacy" 41).

Guthrie saw himself as an anti-establishment figure who challenged the passive mindset of postmodern consumerism. Yet Margaret Groome believes that Guthrie's embrace of opulent spectacle negated any agenda of radical reform the director may have espoused. She challenges the notion "that Guthrie was a tradition-breaker" along with "the idea that the technical innovation of the open stage would be a progressive, even experimental, enterprise by which to advance Shakespearean production" ("Stratford" 124). Instead Groome argues that the "Guthrie variant of 'spectacle' frequently meant that the transgressive potential of the Shakespearean text (that is, the potential of both performance texts and dramatic texts to play a role in political and social transformation) was subverted by the physical and technical elements of the performance text." Because of its reliance on a "predominance of facile effects," the Stratford Festival under Guthrie "failed to give any indication that theatre might function as a commentator on the social situation, that theatre and culture possess the capability to resist society" (125).

If I understand Groome's argument, it is similar to my own position regarding Herbert Beerbohm Tree and Edward Gordon Craig, and to the ideological interpretation of the Stuart masque offered by Stephen Orgel and Barbara Lewalski. Only those in positions of power can mount elaborate and expensive theatrical productions. Such stagecraft therefore inherently supports the status quo. A radical challenge can only come from what Grotowski calls a "Poor Theatre." I have argued that the work of William Poel and Nugent Monck represented such an alternative. Tyrone Guthrie imagined a similarly provocative mission for his own theatrical endeavors, but his work has been interpreted by critics like Groome to mean the opposite of what Guthrie intended. My goal is not to blame Groome or Guthrie for this, but rather to understand how this miscommunication occurred.

I believe that Elizabethan theatrical practices in general, and the open stage in particular, can offer the kind of "transgressive" ideological experience which Groome finds lacking at the Stratford Festival. To advance a progressive vision, however, practitioners employing early modern conventions must avoid the pitfalls which led Guthrie's work to be received, against his wishes, as politically and artistically conservative. Several factors contributed to this confusion, including Guthrie's conflicted relationship with commercial theater, and aspects of his personal character that led him to contradictory behavior in matters of austerity and opulence.

For much of his life, Tyrone Guthrie defined his endeavors in stark contrast to the practices of commercial theater. Describing his attitude in the 1920s, Guthrie wrote in his autobiography, "I heartily despised a good deal of the professional theatre for its blatant commerciality, its playing down to what I considered ignorance and bad taste" (*Life* 68). Guthrie desired a theater of his own, "which would make no concessions to popular vulgarity, which would be a temple" (69). His disdain for Broadway in the 1960s recalls William Poel's earlier critiques of the West End. Guthrie claimed that commercial theater was "no longer a business in which wisdom, thrift and honesty eventually pay dividends" but rather "a fantastic, speculative game" (*New Theatre* 19). He called instead for a new paradigm "that is less concerned with making money than with the expression of ideas" ("Why I Refuse" X5). Guthrie's actual relationship with the theatrical mainstream is, however, more complex than these comments suggest.

Throughout his career, Guthrie went back and forth between the commercial theater and what would become the not-for-profit sector. After his first stint at the Old Vic in 1933–4, Guthrie worked for two years on Broadway and in the West End. He wrote that he returned to the Vic in 1936, "to attach myself to something more significant than my own career; to feel part of something more permanent, and rooted in more serious intentions than ... commercial theatre" (*Life* 179). Guthrie does not accentuate that his forays into mainstream entertainment had to that point been largely unsuccessful. He was not inundated with other offers when Lilian Baylis called with an opportunity to return to the South Bank. Following his triumphant establishment of the Stratford Festival in 1953, Guthrie used the notoriety gained in this non-commercial venture to once again pursue work on Broadway, this time with more success. Leonard McVicar referred to Guthrie in 1955 as "the foremost director in the J. Arthur Rank organization" (110); and Eric Bentley announced that "the 1955–6 season will go down in stage history as the one in which Mr. Guthrie took Broadway by what can accurately be called storm" (20). In that year he staged productions on the Great White Way of *The Matchmaker, Six Characters in Search of an Author*, and *Tamburlaine*. Everything went well until Guthrie's financially disastrous production of Marlowe's tragedy, which survived only twenty-one performances of its scheduled eight-week run. Only after his Broadway star began to fade following the *Tamburlaine* debacle did Guthrie begin to adopt the position that quality work could not be done within the constraints of commercial theater. In 1964 he wrote a piece for *The New York Times* called "Why I Refuse Invitations to Direct on Broadway." The title is unintentionally ironic, since

Guthrie had accepted more than a dozen such invitations in the ten years preceding this article. Herman Shumlin, responding in the same New York daily, asked, "Where does he come off?" and wondered why Guthrie should bite the Broadway hand that had fed him so well (Shumlin X3).

Ultimately, Guthrie sought to create a hybrid form which would address his dissatisfaction with both commercial and non-commercial practices. He summarized the weaknesses of each format in the following passage written shortly after the founding of the Stratford Festival:

> Theatre is divided into two directly opposed categories: first, Show Business, which is fun, sexy and frivolous, educational only in the same sense as drunkenness or rape; second, the Serious Theatre, which is educational in the same sense as quadratic equations, and is a thundering, pompous, unmitigated but anemic bore. ("Long View" 152)

Although his reference to the educative potential of intoxication and sexual assault is puzzling, Guthrie apparently envisaged a theater which could be as "fun" and "sexy" as Broadway while at the same time aspiring to a serious artistic mission. While purists might disdain this policy of artistic appeasement, it was in many ways successful. Guthrie brought two key components of early modern staging – the thrust configuration and the permanent, non-decorative set – to widespread international attention in a way that William Poel, hampered by his lack of a theater, and Nugent Monck, geographically isolated in Norwich, could not. This achievement would not have been possible without some compromise with popular expectations, and Guthrie better understood the needs of the public because of his experience in commercial theater.

Guthrie's contradictory attitude toward spectacle, in which he championed the austerity of Elizabethan staging while delighting in luxurious props and costumes, reflects a similar paradox in his personal character. Guthrie's maternal great-grandfather was Tyrone Power, an illegitimate and impoverished Irishman who became, before his death in 1841, a wealthy and successful actor with an international reputation. The film star Tyrone Power, also a descendant of this nineteenth-century thespian, was Guthrie's cousin. On his father's side, Guthrie's great-grandfather was "Dr. Thomas Guthrie, a nationally famous minister of the Scottish Kirk" (Guthrie, *Life* 5). Throughout his lifetime, the director imitated these two very different ancestors. Like the Irish actor, he was a risk-taker and a non-conformist. Like the Scottish Minister, he was a figure of authority who styled himself "Doctor" (although the younger Guthrie possessed only an honorary degree).

Scottish thrift and Irish profligacy are the stuff of cultural stereotypes, but Guthrie's background contained both nationalities and his behavior displayed both attributes. His personal life was marked by extreme austerity. "I think his *entire* luggage consisted of something like a very small string bag," recalled Coral Browne, who played Zabina in the New York *Tamburlaine* (quoted in Rossi, *Astonish* 107). On his first trip to Stratford, Ontario Guthrie brought only two shirts, one of which he washed by hand and hung to dry while wearing the other. When he directed *Henry VIII* at Stratford-on-Avon in 1949, Guthrie lived on the river in a covered punt with his wife, Judith. Following the death of his mother in 1956, the Guthries moved their permanent residence to the family home at Annagh-ma-Kerrig on the northern border of the Irish Republic. At this time the house had no electricity and only intermittent telephone service. To demonstrate the beautiful rigors of country life, Guthrie frequently made visitors pick blackberries and flowers in order to barter this produce at local shops. Yet what actor Stanley Baxter calls the "cult of simplicity" in Guthrie's private life did not carry over to his work on stage (quoted in Rossi, *Astonish* 122). Instead he often swung to the opposite extreme. Robert Morley recalls that "this insistence on asceticism, on economy, on cut out the frills, in his private life, was equated in his production by putting in as many frills as possible. He was never happy unless he could find someone to ride a donkey on the stage" (quoted in Rossi, *Astonish* 86).

According to his obituary in the *West Australian* on 17 May 1971, "Tony Guthrie was a true Irishman in that he was agin [*sic*] the government on principle and loved thumbing his nose at the powers that be" (quoted in Shaughnessy, *Shakespeare* 92). In keeping with this rebellious and anti-authoritarian side of his personality, Guthrie often felt the need to shock. "Guthrie's offenses are chiefly against bourgeois convention," wrote Robertson Davies. "He loves to make people jump" ("Director" 39). Guthrie told *The New York Times* in 1956 that "one cannot be afraid to be thought a little odd, a little bit of a freak. I greatly admire people who aren't always asking, 'What will the neighbors say?'"(quoted in Peck 105). Harry Andrews, who played Wolsey for Guthrie at the British Stratford in 1949, recalled that when living in their punt on the Avon the Guthries would "always be naked. It didn't matter who was coming up the river" (quoted in Rossi, *Astonish* 117). Guthrie never appeared publicly nude in Ontario, but he frequently rehearsed in nothing but "underwear shorts and a see-through plastic raincoat" (Pettigrew and Portman 61). Robert Cushman reports that when angered Guthrie would take this raincoat off to berate the cast (27). No physical exhibitionism has been reported in connection to Guthrie's work on Broadway, but he could not refrain from announcing to a group of VIPs assembled for the first rehearsal of *The Matchmaker* in 1956, "Distinguished guests, we are now going to get to work, so will you kindly fuck off?" (quoted in Rossi, *Astonish* 188).

Many scholars have analyzed the ideological implications of Guthrie's work at the Stratford Festival but, while excellent descriptive accounts exist of his early career, there have been comparatively few attempts to scrutinize Guthrie's efforts prior to 1953 from any kind of theoretical perspective. In an attempt to redress this imbalance, I will chronologically examine Guthrie's career and trace the sporadic and irregular development of his commitment to Elizabethan staging.

Before Elsinore

IN reviewing Tyrone Guthrie's life it is helpful to remember that he was born in 1900. As old as the century, Guthrie's age is therefore easy to calculate at any point in his career. His first regular theatrical employment came in 1926 as producer/director of the touring Scottish Players. The goal of this nationalist group was "to encourage the initiation and development of a purely Scottish drama" through "the production of plays, national in character, written by Scottish men and women of letters" (Forsyth 69). Guthrie spent two years trekking through Scotland with this "group of tartan amateurs" (66). While these efforts were undistinguished, the experience eventually enabled Guthrie's landmark involvement with the Edinburgh Festival. After leaving Glasgow at the end of 1928, Guthrie split his time for a few years between radio and live theater. He succeeded Terence Gray as director of the Cambridge Festival Theatre for a season before spending six months in Montreal, where he worked for the Canadian National Railways on a radio series titled "The Romance of Canada." According to James Forsyth, Guthrie was at this time already developing "his own idea of how Shakespeare should be staged" and frequently doodled designs for a new kind of theater on café napkins (106).

After leaving Montreal, Guthrie returned to England to work at the new Westminster Theatre, founded by Anmer Hall. He staged his first major theatrical success, *Love's Labour's Lost*, at the Westminster in 1932. Guthrie had seen Nugent Monck's revival of this comedy, which had "no breaks between scenes" and featured "a permanent set" that suggested "no clearly identifiable locality" (Guthrie, *Life* 84). This was Guthrie's first direct contact with any variant of Elizabethan staging, and he was very impressed. "All the good ideas in my production," Guthrie wrote, "came from Monck's at Norwich" (*Life* 84). Harcourt Williams, then the Old Vic's artistic director (or "resident producer" in the parlance of the time) was currently searching for a successor. The Vic staged primarily Shakespeare, so Williams needed someone proficient in early modern drama. He saw *Love's Labour's* and recommended the director to Lilian Baylis, who hired Guthrie for the 1933–4 season.

Guthrie writes in *A Life in the Theatre* that he was determined to implement early modern practices at the Old Vic. His tone suggests that Guthrie was the first to introduce such staging to Waterloo Road, but the Vic already had an Elizabethan tradition. Lilian Baylis had inherited control of the theater from its founder, her aunt Emma Cons. Miss Baylis's frugality was legendary, and this predisposed her to Elizabethan methods. As Dennis Kennedy writes, "Extremely limited finances and a prejudice against elaboration justified one another; the result was a Shakespearean stage with a distrust of the visual" (*Looking* 122). Robert Atkins served as resident producer following World War I and, perhaps inspired by Nugent Monck's war-time productions in Egypt, moved the Vic toward William Poel's minimalist vision. Atkins built out a platform in front of the proscenium in an attempt to recreate some of the intimacy of a thrust configuration. He also used curtains and a "selective use of painted scenery" to create "non-representational settings" for Shakespeare's plays (Rowell 104). Harcourt Williams, who assumed artistic leadership of the Vic in 1929, produced what John Gielgud called "Elizabethan productions which preserved the continuity of the plays" through "light and imaginative settings allowing quick changes of scene" (*Early Stages* 126). Guthrie's plans for the Old Vic were therefore hardly revolutionary, but rather an extension of the "Elizabethan theatrical values" (Howard 139) already in place at the theater. In some ways, Guthrie moved away from the path of Poelesque austerity toward more commercial practices. The Old Vic had traditionally developed its own talent. Harcourt Williams instead began a policy of hiring better known actors when he engaged the up-and-coming Gielgud, and Guthrie accelerated this trend by bringing in established performers from the West End and the world of cinema. Specifically, he engaged Flora Robson, Elsa Lanchester, and Charles Laughton.

Guthrie wrote of his plan for simple, early modern staging that the "money saved was to go into costumes" (*Life* 121). Wardrobe, of course, was an important component of Shakespeare's own theater and there is nothing "un-Elizabethan" about beautifully dressed productions. But Guthrie's push for a bigger budget in this area meshed with his plan to recruit cinematic talent. "It would be a condition of Laughton's joining," Forsyth writes, "that the company would improve its costumes" (129). Guthrie's high-profile company and more luxurious production values provoked suspicion in the Old Vic's matriarch, and the director's inaugural season "was blighted by uncertainties of trust between himself and Lilian Baylis" (Bate and Jackson 148).

In *A Life in the Theater*, Guthrie wrote that he planned to "have no scenery except a 'structure,' which would offer the facilities usually supposed to have been available in the Elizabethan theatre." This set would "serve as a permanent background" throughout each play in the Old Vic's season (121). Guthrie commissioned a design from the architect Wells Coates (whose name is sometimes hyphenated to Wells-Coates in published accounts). It consisted of two pillars with a balcony between them, a central entrance under the balcony, and two curved staircases connecting the two levels. J. C. Trewin said in 1974 of this "built-up central structure" that "these days it happens everywhere, but it was a sensation then and everybody talked about it" (quoted in Rossi, *Astonish* 31). The experiment, however, was not successful. In its review of Guthrie's first Old Vic production in September 1933, the *Times* described "a scene of the utmost austerity, massive, stony, [and] bare," which was "satisfactory as an arrangement of architectural forms, but not in all things pleasing as a design for *Twelfth Night*" (review of *Twelfth Night* 10). Guthrie acknowledged in retrospect that the set was "obtrusive" and "proclaimed itself, almost impertinently, to be modern" (*Life* 122), a conclusion supported by the *Times'* observation that "Olivia's bath-taps [we]re of chromium plate" (review of *Twelfth Night* 10). "Whatever color it was painted, however it was lit," Guthrie complained, this structure became "a powerful, stridently irrelevant competitor for the audiences' attention" instead of "a merely functional background to the play." Painted in unfortunate hues of gray and rose, the set for *Twelfth Night* "suggested not Illyria but a fancy dress ball on a pink battleship" (*Life* 122).

Guthrie abandoned the Wells Coates set for his second Shakespeare production at the Vic. In *Henry VIII*, which followed *Twelfth Night*, Guthrie used traditional settings from the Lewis Casson-Sybil Thorndike production of this play at the Empire. "Suddenly, with a bang," Trewin notes, "we were back in spectacular Shakespeare" (quoted in Rossi, *Astonish* 31). The permanent set had been tactically flawed, but Guthrie's willingness to abandon it and return so quickly to traditional stagecraft suggests that he was not at this point in his career strongly committed to Elizabethan staging. He instead pragmatically tested different approaches in pursuit of a viable method. The pictorial splendor of *Henry VIII* was followed by a bare setting for *The Tempest* which "denuded Prospero's island of practically everything" (Trewin 159) and merely "consisted of a log and a few strands of seaweed" (160). Charles Morgan complained in *The New York Times* that Elsa Lanchester's brilliant performance as Ariel had been "undone by the shocking inappropriateness of the scenery and many of the dresses" (X3). Morgan's comments indicate how resistant mainstream observers still were to non-traditional approaches in 1934 and suggest that, while Guthrie was inconsistent, he did not lack courage.

The 1933–4 season at the Old Vic drew large houses, primarily due to Laughton's celebrity. This public, however, was no longer made up of the theater's South Bank neighbors but consisted primarily of "serious and predominantly young working people from all over London" (Guthrie, *Life* 111). This alienated the Vic's traditional customer base. "One tough old regular – Miss Pilgrim," Forsyth reports, "started collecting signatures for a petition: to send young Mr. Guthrie back over the river where he belonged" (134–5). Elizabeth Schafer cites John Gielgud's assertion that Ms. Pilgrim tricked the actors in the company into signing this petition by pretending to ask for their autographs (149). In any event, Lilian Baylis had never been comfortable with Guthrie's methods and had positively feuded with Laughton. At the end of the season she eagerly accepted Guthrie's resignation.

After leaving the Vic, Guthrie spent two years working in the commercial theaters of London and New York without any great success. Henry Cass followed Guthrie as resident producer of the Old Vic and led the theater for two undistinguished seasons. "Perhaps his lasting legacy," George Rowell writes of Cass, "was convincing Lilian Baylis that Guthrie had a great deal more to him than she had previously allowed" (125). In 1936 Baylis offered Guthrie the opportunity to return, and he quickly agreed. This time they got along much better. Schafer writes that Baylis's health was deteriorating and that she was "anxious about planning her succession" (149). Despite their artistic differences, Baylis came to see Guthrie as "the best option available" to take over the Old Vic once she was gone (150). He therefore assumed leadership of the organization following her death in 1937.

During his second period of service, Guthrie continued to recruit celebrity talent. In place of Laughton, he now convinced Laurence Olivier to come work at the Old Vic. Olivier played Toby Belch in a production of *Twelfth Night* that demonstrated the director's growing penchant for creative staging. Guthrie cast Jessica Tandy as both Viola and Sebastian and, according to the *Times*, employed theatrical sleight-of-hand during the play's recognition scene:

> Mr. Tyrone Guthrie has used Miss Jessica Tandy, who is normally Viola, to represent Sebastian also, wherever the young man appears separately from her; and, where at the end the two are on the stage together, Miss

Tandy, as Sebastian, is embracing Olivia at one moment, and, as Viola, is chattering to the Duke at another, while an interchangeable double flits about the stage under cover of masking gentlemen in cloaks. It is ingeniously done. (review of *Twelfth Night* 12)

An outrageous gimmick, this device also advanced the play's theme of confusion regarding gender identity.

In 1933, Guthrie proclaimed that he would stage all Shakespeare plays on a permanent architectural structure but quickly retreated from this position when the Wells Coates set proved unworkable. In his second tenure at the Vic, Guthrie offered no such sweeping statements of intent. Instead, he made cautious and sporadic attempts to replicate early modern conditions. In April 1937, Guthrie staged a *Henry V* starring Laurence Olivier which, according to Tony Howard, inspired the director's later "experiments in open-stage Shakespeare" (149). Because this *Henry V* coincided with the coronation of George VI in May, there was a natural tendency for patriotic spectacle. The *Times* reported, "The stage of the Old Vic glows with colour from emblazoned shields and surcoats richly embroidered and from banners." This pageantry was not, however, supported by the kind of traditional stagecraft that Guthrie had employed in his 1933 *Henry VIII*. The "polychromatic splendour" was "set off not by realistically painted vistas but by a simple arrangement of curtains." The *Times* critic suggested that the appeal was therefore "to a more adult aestheticism" (review of *Henry V* 14). Audrey Williamson asserts that Guthrie showed admirable restraint and ties this prudence to the Elizabethan revival. "It was William Poel," she writes, "who first revolted against the type of spectacular production which twisted the whole point of the play by bedecking the English side with all the glittering pageantry of overwhelming numbers and equipment" (*Old Vic Drama* 89). In contrast to this scenic excess, Guthrie in the scene before Harfleur used "only a handful of actors, a shifting light and no visible scenery" to suggest "a whole body of men on the move" (90).

The most successful offering of the 1936–7 season was *Hamlet*. This revival is today best known for Olivier's Freudian interpretation of the title role, but at the time this psychological dimension "went generally unremarked" (Trewin 164). It was not until the 1948 film version of the play that Olivier's Hamlet was widely recognized as Oedipal. The Old Vic set design, by contrast, attracted a good deal of immediate attention. J. C. Trewin describes its gymnastic nature. "Guthrie had provided an extraordinary kind of up-and-down set," Trewin recalls. "The actors were skipping about on Alpine peaks during most of the evening. At the end the Queen fell backwards from a high rostrum into somebody's arms." Not surprisingly, "she was scared stiff every time" (Trewin quoted in Rossi, *Astonish* 33). Indeed, this 15-foot fall was a maneuver that today would only be attempted in a theme park stunt show. As Trewin suggests, it "might have been excessive" (164). Dorothy Dix, the actress originally cast as Gertrude, apparently thought so. She "fell ill (perhaps from a fear of excessive heights?) and was replaced by Esme Church early in the run" (Williamson, *Old Vic Drama* 85).

The Old Vic was invited to stage *Hamlet* outdoors at Kronborg Castle,

Elsinore during the summer of 1937. Expectations were high for this Danish visit. A *Times* correspondent wrote from Elsinore before the first performance, "there is a feeling here that theatrical history, and something more than theatrical history, is to be made on this day, June 2." Theatrical history would be made, but not in a way anyone expected. The journalist observed that "the courtyard is, of course, open to the skies and there is no alternative indoor site" ("*Hamlet* at Elsinore" 14). Rain came, however, and a substitute venue was found, one that would shape the future of Shakespearean production on two continents.

The Elsinore Hamlet

THE Old Vic *Hamlet* at Kronborg Castle was planned as an early modern reconstruction that would freeze Shakespeare's play in a distant historical moment, the kind of "museum" production bitterly derided by postmodern critics. Local officials stopped the tower clock so that its noise would not interfere with the scheduled outdoor performances, an action which to Robert Shaughnessy "seems almost too perfect a metaphor for a general collusion in the suspension of history" (*Shakespeare* 111). Largely by chance the Elsinore *Hamlet* also came to demonstrate the practical value of open staging for twentieth-century theater. This Danish excursion therefore illustrated two conflicting conceptions of the Elizabethan movement: the "theme park" vision of ersatz historical "authenticity" and the quest to find advantages in early modern practice that could help keep theater alive in the cinematic age. Ultimately, the events in Denmark advanced the more progressive of these paradigms. Rather than celebrating archaism, the Elsinore *Hamlet* presaged a new avant-garde.

The *Daily Telegraph* billed this revival as "Hamlet in his own home" (quoted in Shaughnessy, *Shakespeare* 108). It was intended as "a site-specific event exploiting the convergence between the cultural authority of the play and the magic of this 'authentic' location" (Shaughnessy, *Shakespeare* 108). There were, of course, problems with the notion of Kronborg as a historical setting for Shakespeare's play. The castle was built centuries after Saxo-Grammaticus wrote the legend on which *Hamlet* is based. This tragedy is, however, notoriously fluid in its mixture of medieval and renaissance elements, and the Danish palace existed at the time of *Hamlet's* composition. Kronborg's construction in 1580 allowed boosters of the Old Vic tour to engage in the "wild speculation" that Shakespeare might have traveled to the site as a boy player with a group of English players who performed there at the court of Frederick II (Shaughnessy, *Shakespeare* 109).

The planned outdoor setting recalled one kind of early modern theatrical venue. "What this stage resembled," writes Niels B. Hansen, "was perhaps not so much the Globe Theatre with its tiring-house and its roof supported by pillars as the pre-Elizabethan acting space consisting of a platform set up in an enclosed courtyard" (113). This design took advantage of Kronborg's sixteenth-century façade, allowing the castle to serve as a natural backdrop for the action of the play. But many elements of theatrical modernity intruded into this putatively Renaissance endeavor. The production's set, "which was essentially the same as had been used for the indoor performance in London" (114), was more complex than the simple configuration of the Globe or Blackfriars. This "stage consisted of several platforms at different levels, the highest of which was a kind of rostrum, a cube of about $6' \times 6' \times 6'$, which towered above the rest of the set. The various levels were connected by a quite elaborate set of stairs" (113). The assembled personnel also far exceeded the capabilities of an early modern touring company. Besides the cast of seventeen acknowledged in the *Times* review, the company included a hundred Danish military cadets to serve as extras. The installation of flood lighting and sound amplification also limited the production's historical accuracy, as did the placement of the audience exclusively in front of the stage, rather than on three sides.

The first night was to be a gala event. A special train was scheduled out of Copenhagen to bring VIPs to Elsinore. Among these were the Danish royal family, who had been invited to see *Hamlet*, Shaughnessy notes, "without any obvious sense of irony" (*Shakespeare* 112). Their anticipated presence raised the stakes for all involved, and the weather did not cooperate. The performance was scheduled for eight o'clock but, Guthrie recalls in his autobiography, "at seven-thirty the rain was coming down in bellropes" (*Life* 190). This presented a significant dilemma, as it was too late to cancel the performance. What happened next has become the stuff of legend. Olivier, recalling the event in 1986, almost paraphrases the Saint Crispin's day speech. It was, Sir Laurence claims, "a night that they will always remember. 'Were you there that night at Elsinore? I was.'" The actor then adds mischievously, "It is amazing how many people now think they were there" (87). Frantically searching for an alternate performance space, Guthrie came upon the ballroom of the Marienlyst Hotel and decided, "We would play in the middle of the hall with the audience seated all around us as in a circus. The phrase hadn't been invented, but this would be theatre in the round." Division of labor necessitated that Guthrie have no involvement in the staging of this impromptu *Hamlet*. He writes that "Larry conducted a lightning rehearsal with the company, improvising exits and entrances, and rearranging business." Meanwhile Guthrie, "assisted by the critics" set about arranging seats for the audience (*Life* 190).

Guthrie did not initially have very high expectations for this improvised *Hamlet*. He said to Olivier at intermission, "Thought we'd just do one act and apologize," but this was no longer possible. Everybody was "taking it *far* too seriously," Guthrie explained, the company would have to "go through to the end" (quoted in Rossi, *Astonish* 96). The impact of this effort was extraordinary. J. C. Trewin, among those critics pressed into moving chairs, said in 1974, "It remains to this day the most exciting performance of *Hamlet* I've ever seen" (quoted in Rossi, *Astonish* 34). J. L. Styan sees it as a defining moment in the development of the open stage. "With the audience seated almost round the players," he writes, "the weaknesses of the proscenium stage were sharply revealed." Placed in intimate proximity to the playing area, "the Danish audience recovered its primary function, itself becoming part of the play" (Styan, "Elizabethan" 218). Guthrie similarly felt that this *Hamlet* connected to its public in a "more logical, satisfactory and effective way than ever can be achieved in a theatre of what is still regarded as orthodox design" (*Life* 192). When asked decades later if he thought the ballroom experience had been significant, Olivier responded, "Oh, for everybody, for the world" (quoted in Rossi, *Astonish* 96).

As in the case of many legends, some of the facts regarding the Elsinore *Hamlet* have been massaged to conform to a desired mythology. Shaughnessy refers to "compression on Guthrie's part for the sake of melodramatic effect" (*Shakespeare* 113) in the director's description of these events from *A Life in the Theater*. Other contemporary accounts establish that the outdoor performance had been cancelled by the early afternoon. The decision to move indoors was therefore not as last-minute as Guthrie suggests. The ballroom also wasn't a completely bare and non-theatrical space. There was already a small cabaret stage at one end of this hall, on which cane chairs were placed to serve as thrones for Gertrude and Claudius. This stage and the floor in front of it defined a playing area, and the audience was placed on three sides. Spectators therefore did not sit "all around," as Guthrie claims. Shaughnessy believes that Guthrie distorts his account in order to not "compromise the simplicity of the opposition between the claustrophobic frontality of the picture frame and the radical spontaneity of a mode of performance so early in its infancy that it yet lacked a name" (*Shakespeare* 113). Guthrie's definition of the Marienlyst arrangement as "theatre in the round" (*Life* 190) also betrays his preference for a more circular configuration than is normally associated with Elizabethan staging, a predisposition that would later manifest itself in the 240° arc of the Stratford Festival tent.

The first night of *Hamlet* was not universally hailed as a success, and it was largely with the passage of time that the evening acquired mythic status. The *Times* reported the next day that "it would be absurd to offer a serious criticism of the performance." While the premiere "was a very gallant and much appreciated act on the part of a hard-worked Old Vic company," the reviewer looked forward to seeing the production outdoors "in all its glory" the following evening ("Weather Unkind to British Players" 12). Guthrie himself candidly analyzed the shortcomings of the ballroom presentation. "*Hamlet* is a very long play," he wrote. "After two hours of improvisation the actors became exhausted and a little flustered. The finale was a shambles, but not quite in the way the author intended" (*Life* 190). Ivor Brown, however, in a 1937 article for *Theatre Arts Monthly*, saw in the opening night at Elsinore the same kind of ground-breaking achievement later attributed to this event by critics like Styan. "That performance in a room in the Marienlyst Hotel," Brown wrote, "made me wonder more than ever why we make such a fuss about lights and atmosphere and all the rest of it when presenting Shakespeare." Brown believed the ballroom performance to be far superior to the production staged outdoors as originally planned the following night. The intrusive elaborateness of that second evening's scenography outweighed any advantage in its geographical setting, so that "*Hamlet* 'on the spot'" became "very like *Hamlet* in a modern theater, whereas *Hamlet* in a ballroom had been strange and different and perhaps more truly Elizabethan." The lesson of Elsinore was that if "we sit close, if we sit all round him, like the audience in his own Globe" then "Shakespeare will not fail us for a moment" (Brown, "Very Spot" 877).

Robert Shaughnessy, who deflates some of the hyperbole traditionally associated with this event, nevertheless describes the Kronborg adventure as "the pivotal event which, by his own account, led to Guthrie's eventual repudiation of the picture-frame stage" (*Shakespeare* 108). "Eventual" is, however, a key word in Shaughnessy's formulation. Elsinore was not for Guthrie the theatrical equivalent of Saint Paul falling off a horse on the road to Damascus. It would be many years before he would seriously attempt to replicate the open-stage configuration he had discovered in that hotel ballroom. Yet one detail of Guthrie's reaction to that first performance suggests that he was deeply moved. According to Olivier, Guthrie said immediately afterwards that *Hamlet* had "flowed through the ballroom like warm strawberry jam" (quoted in Olivier 88). The metaphor was significant for Guthrie. Jam was one of few indigenous products in County Monaghan, the location of Guthrie's estate. In the last years of his life, Guthrie became involved in a plan to locally manufacture "bramble jelly and rhubarb-ginger and violet plum jams" as a means of encouraging young Irish workers to remain in their rural homes and not emigrate to foreign cities (Shepard 19). Guthrie wrote that he deplored "the centripetal tendency of modern civilization, the remorseless devouring of her children by metropolis" (*Theatre Prospect* 29). Homemade confiture symbolized for him the potential triumph of manual craftsmanship over mass-production and of human community over industrial anonymity. Guthrie's reference to "warm strawberry jam" in describing the Elsinore *Hamlet* suggests that this production's intimate embrace of its audience inspired similar aspirations.

The Old Vic after Elsinore

Back at the Old Vic in the fall of 1937, Guthrie made a minor architectural adjustment possibly inspired by his Elsinore experience. The *Times* reported shortly before the 1937–8 season began that the "pit-stalls have been reseated" so that "the orchestra pit, when there is no music in production, can now be filled in and additional stalls provided" ("Improvements at the Old Vic" 10). Besides increasing potential revenue by adding seats, this change also allowed Guthrie to more closely approximate a thrust configuration by bringing the audience closer to the forestage. In spite of this gesture toward Elizabethan intimacy, Guthrie's Old Vic productions after Elsinore did not consistently employ the scenic minimalism of his later open-stage efforts.

A Midsummer Night's Dream, which opened on Boxing Day 1937, was a deliberate throwback to the pictorial tradition of the nineteenth century. It was "an album of Victoriana with full score" (Trewin 174) designed by Oliver Messel as "a land of insects' wings and moonlight, cobwebs and flowers," which expressed "a Grecian Classicism" (Williamson, *Old Vic Drama* 78–9). Dancers were rigged to soar about the stage, and these "flying fairies" were the highlight of the production. Although William Poel would have winced, this *Midsummer* was immensely successful with both audiences and critics. It was, according to George Rowell, "the most universally popular production of Guthrie's term of office" and was therefore "chosen for the princesses Elizabeth's and Margaret's first visit to the theatre" (126).

Unlike this elaborate *Midsummer*, Guthrie's 1938 *Hamlet* starring Alec Guinness reflected in its design an echo of the simplicity that the director had discovered at Elsinore. It used an austere permanent setting centered around two classical pillars. While there were steps and platforms as in the 1937 London *Hamlet*, this was a far simpler configuration than the range of "Alpine peaks" which Guthrie had employed at that time. This production is notable as Guthrie's first major foray into modern costuming. In 1933 he had proclaimed, "Modern dress I do not greatly care for" (quoted in Trewin 177). Guthrie chose to pursue this style only after his Elsinore epiphany and at a time when, at least in this production, he appears to have been moving toward early modern principles. This raises the general question of the relationship between modern dress and the Elizabethan movement.

"Shakespeare in plus-fours" (Trewin 95) had been widely viewed as a notorious gimmick when Barry Jackson first used modern dress at the Birmingham Repertory Company in the early 1920s. Today a common practice, costuming Shakespeare's plays in twentieth-century garb provoked widespread outrage as recently as the 1960s. "Reason hardly enters into this matter," Guthrie complained of negative reaction to the 1963 modern-dress *Hamlet* at his namesake theater in Minneapolis (*New Theatre* 104). Some practitioners, however, interpret modern dress not as an assault on tradition but as a return to early modern practices. Ralph Alan Cohen, founder of the American Shakespeare Center at the reconstructed Blackfriars playhouse, writes, "Since Shakespeare presented his plays largely in an anachronistic present, we argue that in dressing our plays in contemporary dress or in some melange, we are operating in the same spirit" ("Keeping" 8). Guthrie similarly asserted that "the assumption that Shakespeare 'saw' his characters in Elizabethan dress can also mean that he 'saw' them dressed not in Elizabethan but in contemporary style" ("*Hamlet*" 74). Both twentieth-century and early modern costumes were therefore valid for Guthrie. "Failing Elizabethan dress," he wrote, "it seems to me that modern clothes are the next most logical choice" (*New Theatre* 102).

Guthrie believed that when Shakespeare's characters are presented in contemporary costumes, audiences can better identify their status. "Almost instantaneously and with barely any conscious effort," he writes, "we can place them as high or low, rich or poor, solider or civilian" ("*Hamlet*" 75). Such a theatrical wardrobe therefore "brings the tragedy back from the remoteness of a long-bygone era, and from the vague territory of theatrical, quasi-operatic Romance, and compels us to regard the characters as men and women subject to the same passions, the same confusions and perplexities, as ourselves" (76). This is particularly important for progressive practitioners exploring Elizabethan conventions. Modern dress provides a means, as Cohen describes, for a company that is interested in early modern practice to avoid the taint of "museum theatre" ("Keeping" 9). Guthrie expressed a similar concern when he wrote of his 1963 *Hamlet*, "We wish to stress the modernity of the play, not to exhibit it as an antique" (*"Hamlet"* 74).

Besides modern dress, the 1938 *Hamlet* featured another costume motif which would become common in Guthrie's work. Trewin notes that the production "held to a formality of uniforms and court costume for the men, and long dresses for the women: the atmosphere of some Ruritanian palace levee" (177). "Ruritania" comes from Anthony Hope's novel *The Prisoner of Zenda* and refers to an imagined country, what Shaughnessy calls a "fictitious late nineteenth-century Middle-European social world" that serves as "a synonym for the comically self-important but politically impotent nation state" (*Shakespeare* 139). In the 1930s, films like *Duck Soup* used this kind of fictional European locality to mock the chauvinistic nationalism that had led to World War I. After the next war Guthrie regularly returned to this costume pattern. Observers identified Ruritania as a setting for Guthrie's modern-dress productions of *All's Well That Ends Well* at both Ontario (1953) and Stratford-on-Avon (1959); *Troilus and Cressida* at the Old Vic (1956); and *Hamlet* at Minneapolis (1963). Critics frequently tied Guthrie's application of this concept to a perceived anti-militarist agenda. Norman Marshall writes of *Troilus*, for instance, that by "dressing his production in this way Guthrie accentuated the most contemporary aspect of the play, Shakespeare's anti-heroic attitude to war" ("Guthrie" 101). Guthrie used this setting to mock jingoistic bellicosity and advance his agenda of eliminating political borders, an objective which Shaughnessy links ideologically to the director's desire to abolish the proscenium (*Shakespeare* 93–4; 135).

Shortly before the end of the 1938–9 season, Guthrie was officially appointed administrative director of both the Old Vic and Sadler's Wells. "Because of duties of organization," Audrey Williamson writes, "he therefore relinquished, for the time being, his position as active producer of the Old Vic Drama Company" (*Old Vic Drama* 122). Guthrie's artistic endeavors were further impeded by the start of World War II. All theaters shut down at the beginning of the conflict. The Old Vic reopened briefly in the spring of 1940, at which time Guthrie collaborated with Lewis Casson and Harley Granville Barker on *King Lear*. The theater then closed again for the duration, and was heavily damaged by the blitz.

During the conflict, the Old Vic's endeavors were restricted primarily to small-budget touring productions, with only occasional London engagements at the New Theatre. "The presiding genius of these tours was Tyrone Guthrie," Williamson writes, "and it was his resourcefulness that adapted both drama and opera to the conditions under which the companies had to work" (*Old Vic Drama* 213). Typical of these efforts was a "portable *Macbeth*" which Sybil Thorndike and Lewis Casson toured to thirty-eight mining towns in Wales, performing "on stages that varied between an echoing cinema and the table-cloth of a Miners' Welfare Hall" (Trewin 189). Guthrie's 1941 *King John* was designed for such a schedule with a Spartan, non-realistic set. Yet this production nevertheless represented for Williamson "all the stylized yet picturesque imagination that distinguishes Guthrie's productions of what one might call the 'banner class' " (*Old Vic Drama* 147). The *Times* was effusive in its praise:

> The play calls for the stir of drum and trumpet and the flaunting of flags to give point and colour to political and dynastic argument which, without their aid, is apt to weary and confuse, and Mr. Tyrone Guthrie and Mr. Lewis Casson have brilliantly supplied them. The scenery is not elaborate; curtains with heraldic breasts and devices supply the background, but by an ingenious use of mime and the principles of ballet, by effects of grouping and lighting, by the sweep and fall of banners, by formalized attitude and gesture, by, indeed, using properties and protagonists as an artist uses colour and composition, the producers convey the full impression of the impact of great events and make the play throughout not only exciting but beautiful to watch. (review of *King John* 6)

Guthrie would later use similar devices to bring historical pageantry to other sparsely decorated platforms. In contrast to his 1941 *King John*, Guthrie's postwar productions of *Henry VIII* at Stratford-on-Avon, *Richard III* at the Canadian Stratford, and *Henry V* and *Richard III* in Minneapolis employed bare stages not by necessity but by design. Guthrie's war-time experience helped convince him, as Trewin writes, that the ideal stage for Shakespeare "should not be clenched by the picture-frame; that there should be no kind of realistic background" (184).

By the end of the war Guthrie was exhausted by administrative duties and desired to return full-time to artistic work. Late in 1944 Laurence Olivier, Ralph Richardson, and John Burrell took over leadership of the Old Vic from Guthrie as an administrative triumvirate. Guthrie stayed on to serve as a theatrical director but left in 1945 over a dispute with Olivier. He was to direct the actor in a production of *Oedipus Rex*, but Guthrie became enraged when Olivier improbably insisted on presenting this tragedy on a double bill with Sheridan's *The Critic* (Bate and Jackson 158). Guthrie exclaimed "over my dead body" and walked out in protest (quoted in Rowell 136). Away from the Vic, Guthrie was free to realize his dream of an open stage. He did so in an unconventional theatrical venue.

The Edinburgh Festival

THE Edinburgh International Festival of Music and Art began in 1947. The first year was a success, but the Festival's organizers felt that Scotland had been underrepresented in the category of drama. They therefore sought someone to stage an indigenous theatrical classic in 1948. Guthrie because of his paternal ancestry and previous experience with the Scottish Players was, Ivor Brown writes, "the obvious choice as commander of these operations" (*Satyre* 27). Locating a masterpiece of Scottish drama was not easy, however, as there were few works to choose from. Guthrie finally found Sir David Lindsay's *Ane Satyre of the Thrie Estaits*. This play, written around 1540, is an allegory of the Reformation, which originally required six or seven hours to perform. Guthrie engaged the Scottish playwright Robert Kemp to edit the *Thrie Estaits* down to a manageable running time of two and a half hours. Kemp also somewhat modernized the play's language, although the published script remains as difficult to read as Chaucer's Middle English. Besides featuring an archaic style, the play's idiom proclaims its regional origins. In a *New York Times* review, W. A. Darlington described the *Thrie Estaits* as "written in a dialect so Scottish that parts of it deprived the English or American visitor of any advantage over other foreigners in the matter of language" ("Visit to Scotland" X3). Yet this obscure work, unperformed for centuries, became the surprise hit of the Edinburgh Festival. "After opening night there was a rampage for tickets," recalls Stanley Baxter, who performed in this inaugural production. "It was a success such as one dreams of in our business" (quoted in Rossi, *Astonish* 126). Guthrie's daring and original approach to staging was largely responsible for this unexpected triumph. Eleven years after Elsinore, the director finally found an opportunity to explore the configuration he had discovered in a Danish hotel ballroom.

In preparation for the *Thrie Estaits*, Guthrie and his associates searched Edinburgh for a performance space. They finally came upon the Assembly Hall of the Kirk of Scotland. Guthrie's great-grandfather had once served in this building as "Moderator General": the head of the Scottish Church and a kind of "nonconformist pope" (Stanley Baxter quoted in Rossi, *Astonish* 124). Upon entering the building, Guthrie immediately knew that he had found his venue. "The sole credit I take in connection with the whole business," Guthrie claimed, "is that, when we came to the Kirk Assembly Hall, I knew we were home" (quoted in Brown, *Satyre* 28). It was an odd choice, as the Hall had never been used for secular purposes. But it made sense for Guthrie, who could not resist the temptation to work, as Robert Speaight writes, "Under the disapproving statue of John Knox himself" (*Shakespeare* 235).

The Edinburgh Festival provided Guthrie with the opportunity to experiment with early modern conventions outside the limitations of a proscenium theater. Photographs (Figure 11) show that Guthrie's Assembly Hall configuration featured the major structural attributes of the early modern stage, along with some ahistorical adjuncts. There was a balcony over a curtained area which served as a discovery space. There were also dog-legged staircases on either side of the balcony, leading to the stage below. Guthrie would integrate similar units into his design for the Stratford Festival. The historical accuracy of this scenic element is open to question (Binnie 91 and throughout), but such staircases unquestionably improve a director's ability to move action seamlessly between the two levels of a permanent set. In front of the *frons scenae* was "a fifteen foot wide 'peninsular' platform which Guthrie built to project twenty-five feet into the auditorium" (Styan, *Shakespeare Revolution* 187). Brown describes this area as "lower than the Elizabethan platform-stage, being reached from the auditorium by a few easy steps." This meant that it was "approachable in a way that Shakespeare's loftier stage was not. The characters could enter down the aisles and through the rows of spectators and go off in the same way" (Brown, *Satyre* 29). In Ontario, Guthrie would later use the house for entrances and exits in this same manner. There is even less historical warrant for these "vomitoria"-style entryways than for Guthrie's onstage stair units, but they greatly increase the available patterns of stage movement. The most significant feature of the *Thrie Estaits* was its relationship to the audience. Guthrie wrote that the public in the Assembly Hall "focused upon the actors in the brightly lit acting area, but the background was of the dimly lit rows of people similarly focused on the actors" (*Life* 311). This created a sense of community and ritual participation which for Guthrie was an essential component of early modern staging.

One governing precept of Guthrie's work on the open stage was his doctrine of constant motion. He believed that because spectators could not always see each performer's face, the actors had to continually shift position in order to share their expressions equally with all members of the audience. Baxter recalls that in the Assembly Hall "the rule was simply to keep turning in circles and never to go to one part of the hall for too long" (quoted in Rossi, *Astonish* 125). Nathan Cohen, writing of Guthrie's work in Canada, derisively describes this practice as the "actor circumnavigating the stage from right to left, turning his back first on this group, then that, and then going to the reverse directions, thereby ensuring each section of the audience a fair opportunity to be deprived" ("Stratford" 269).

Guthrie's admonition to the Edinburgh cast that they needed to be "turning really all the time through 220 degrees" (quoted in Rossi, *Astonish* 125) seems odd, given that the Assembly Hall audience did not extend behind

11 Tyrone Guthrie's *The Thrie Estaites* in the Assembly Hall, Edinburgh, 1948

the *frons scenae*. Constant motion is only necessary in a theater where the arc of the audience is greater than 180°, as is the case at the Stratford Festival. In a seating configuration that does not extend behind the tiring-house façade, significant portions of the upper and lower stage allow an actor to be equally visible from all parts of the house. Directors at key moments can therefore place stationary performers in these strong positions. Such was the case in the Staunton Blackfriars' 2005 production of *The Comedy of Errors*, in which David Loar delivered an arresting version of Egeon's long speech in the first scene of this play while remaining completely still. Thrust staging always involves a careful balancing of sight lines. Directors must take care, for instance, that no section of the house views only the back of Hamlet's head during the course of an entire evening. But this does not mean that all of the performers need to be moving all of the time. Guthrie, breaking new ground in an era when there was no modern tradition of non-proscenium staging, overcompensated at Edinburgh in his desire to provide equal visual satisfaction to all three sides of the audience.

Guthrie's Assembly Hall configuration gained fame as what Norman Marshall calls the "most interesting and successful example of an open platform stage" (*Producer* 218). It became the city's "principal theatrical venue" (Cushman 15) and was used for Old Vic stagings of Shakespeare and Jonson at future Edinburgh Festivals. The *Thrie Estaits* was, like the Elsinore *Hamlet*, a defining moment in Guthrie's theatrical journey. Marshall concludes that Guthrie's Edinburgh experience made him "a fervent believer in the principles of open staging, so that when he became director of the Shakespeare Festival at Stratford, Ontario, he designed for it a stage on much the same lines as the one built for the Assembly Hall" (*Producer* 219). Before he would have the opportunity to build a theater on this model, however, Guthrie experienced the frustration of trying to employ early modern practices in a traditional proscenium format.

Henry VIII

In 1949, Anthony Quayle, then in charge of the Shakespeare Memorial Theatre, invited Guthrie to stage *Henry VIII*. Tanya Moiseiwitsch designed the production, but Guthrie was deeply involved in this process. The goal was to recreate as much as possible the Elizabethan freedom of the *Thrie Estaits*. Guthrie "designed the ground plan," Moiseiwitsch recalls, which "showed an asymmetrical setting of stairs going up to a platform above with alcoves below" (quoted in Rossi, *Astonish* 31). The set was non-representational. Moiseiwitsch and Guthrie intended it to serve equally well for any of the play's locales, whether royal chamber, street, or private home. In his staging, Guthrie made "extensive use of an apron stage" in a partial effort to transcend the limitations of the proscenium arch (Richmond, *King Henry VIII* 80). This production employed a device later common at the new Globe, when Buckingham's address to the crowd was "spoken to the audience from an empty stage" (Marshall, *Producer* 143).

Henry VIII also represented Guthrie's greatest attempt to reduce the intrusion of electronic lighting. The production was, according to Robert Cushman, "staged in unvarying light" (15). Muriel St Clare Byrne mitigates this slightly, writing that the illumination "remained unaltered throughout, except when imperceptible light cues varied the emphasis" ("Stratford" 120). Other than these "imperceptible" touches, Guthrie apparently sought to reproduce the original Globe's convention of universal lighting, in which both stage and audience were lit uniformly by sunlight from above. This effect was largely wasted at Stratford-on-Avon, where the frontal configuration did not allow light from the stage to spill onto the public. While it would have been possible to leave the house lights up, decades of tradition argued against such a choice, and the audience was left in the dark. Even if the spectators had been illuminated, the great distance between stage and public would have lessened the sense of shared experience and active participation that audiences had felt at Elsinore and Edinburgh.

While R. A. Foakes (present in 1949) has praised "the revolutionary nature" of this production, which brought "something of a thrust stage" to audiences who "were used to a proscenium arch" (quoted in Richmond, *King Henry VIII* 90–1), Guthrie nevertheless felt frustrated by the architectural limitations of the Shakespeare Memorial Theatre. His situation was not unlike that of Ben Iden Payne, who had sought to introduce Elizabethan costumes and staging to Stratford-on-Avon in 1934. Trapped within the confines of the picture-frame, these efforts took on the feel of historical re-enactments in the nostalgic spirit of "merrie-Englandism" (Howard 146). A similar fate befell Tanya Moiseiwitsch when she attempted an Elizabethan design for Anthony Quayle's 1951 production of the Henriad. As Dennis Kennedy observes, "for all her good intentions, in essential ways Moiseiwitsch's unit set in 1951 was little different from Poel's 'four-poster' set for *Measure for Measure* in 1893. Both were pictures of an Elizabethan stage rather than the thing itself" (*Looking* 157). To achieve "the thing itself" would require an architectural solution.

Around the time of *Henry VIII*, Quayle offered Guthrie a co-directorship, but Guthrie would only consider this if he were allowed to build a new theater (Bate and Jackson 149). When Quayle asked what he should then do with the existing structure Guthrie replied, "Who cares? It's a dreadfully old-fashioned theatre. You can only do old-fashioned work there. Push it into the Avon!" (quoted in Rossi, *Astonish* 26). Guthrie was not alone in his dislike for the Shakespeare Memorial Theatre. George Bernard Shaw called the original edifice, built in 1879, "the worst building in the world for the performance of Shakespeare's plays." When it burned down in 1926 Shaw announced, "I am extremely glad to hear the news, Stratford-upon-Avon is to be *congratulated*" (quoted in Pettigrew and Portman 72). But the replacement structure, built in 1932, offered little improvement. According to Tony Howard, it "blighted British Shakespeare" into the new millennium (145). Renovations announced in 2006 finally provided a way forward. V. V. Montreux, writing in 2008, describes "an empty space, a ghostly rubble where once stood the RST auditorium" (66). Meanwhile the facility's new Courtyard Theatre, which offers "thrust staging" wherein the "audience is highly visible throughout" due to "lighting spill" (68), enables precisely the effect that eluded

Guthrie in his 1949 *Henry VIII*. Guthrie, however, could not afford to wait half a century for Stratford-on-Avon to attain the "Globe-like performativity" Montreux describes (69). He understood that, as John Pettigrew and Jamie Portman write, progress in the twentieth century had been limited because "its theatres were still nineteenth-century buildings, and the proscenium continued to impose its inevitable demands even on those who wished to escape them" (73). To advance his vision Guthrie needed to design and build a new kind of performance space. He soon had this opportunity in another Stratford half a world away.

The Founding of the Stratford Festival

S EVERAL related ideological concerns motivated Tyrone Guthrie in his 1953 founding of the Stratford Shakespearean Festival. Foremost among these was his belief in the function of theater as a spiritual and, in a broad sense, "religious ritual" (Guthrie, *In Various Directions* 29). Modern theaters were not amenable to this mystic function, and the opportunity to devise an alternative configuration in which the audience would nearly surround the actors as in ancient times was a major factor in Guthrie's decision to come to Ontario. He also conceived of theater as a means of preserving community in a society increasingly alienated by mechanization, where "each year machines [do] more of the work which was formerly done by humans" (*New Theatre* 165). He saw the possibility of a genuinely shared experience between performers and public as theater's unique advantage over film and as the primary justification for the live stage's continued existence in the cinematic age. The intimate relationship between actor and audience required for this survival was not possible in a proscenium theater, and the open stage at Stratford offered Guthrie the chance to create a theatrical model that could compete with cinema and television. Under these more favorable circumstances, he believed "that a Theatre, where live actors perform plays to an audience which is there in the flesh before them" could "survive all threats from powerfully organized industries, which pump prefabricated drama out of cans and blowers and contraptions of one kind and another" ("Long View" 191).

Guthrie also sought to bridge the "social chasm" (*Life* 197) which he believed had come to separate actors from audience since the rise of the proscenium stage. Theater practitioners, he felt, were often treated as "the lower classes" by their affluent public ("Theatre at Minneapolis" 32). He designed his thrust stage to break down this social barrier as it abolished the physical partition of the proscenium wall. Another egalitarian goal of his was to expand the demographic of the audience. Theater should not, he felt, "be aimed at a cultural minority" (*New Theatre* 177) because "everyone, literally everyone, is part of human culture" (171). This program of inclusion led Guthrie to champion theatrical development in Canada, a nation which in 1953 had little dramatic tradition. He hoped that at Stratford classical plays would be "interpreted into a Canadian idiom" and "given a Canadian style" (172), thereby expanding access to theater for both audience and artists.

Guthrie's stated goals in founding the Stratford Festival contrast sharply with the interpretation of this event developed in recent decades by critics like Richard Paul Knowles and Dennis Salter. While Guthrie saw himself as an anti-authoritarian rebel breaking down barriers of class and geography, these later scholars portray him as a cultural imperialist serving an elitist and reactionary agenda. This more recent view perceives the establishment of the Stratford Festival as "discursively constructed as the founding of a Shakespearean National Theatre in Canada after the British (imperialist) Model, in which Shakespeare was used to serve the interests of cultural colonization by a dominant – and on occasion explicitly capitalist (or anti-communist) – elite" (Knowles, "Nationalist to Multinational" 26). Rather than breaking down social barriers and expanding access, the Stratford Festival offered a "product presented for the pleasure of a privileged and culturally dominant group of consumers" (Knowles, "Shakespeare, 1993" 215). Instead of enabling Canadian practitioners to find an indigenous means of expression through classical texts, Guthrie's efforts, in this interpretation, led these "postcolonial actors" to "disavow their particular historical conditions" (Salter 114). This left these performers with a sense of "divided identity" (122) which prevented them from achieving artistic or political independence.

The discrepancy between Guthrie's expressed intent and the opinion of his efforts held by his detractors originates in contrasting interpretations of the Elizabethan movement's ideological significance. These scholars perceive reconstructed early modern practices as separating Shakespeare from the material circumstances of contemporary audiences. Salter succinctly expresses this view when he writes that "the Stratford stage has sought to transport Canadian theatre – and the culture it represents – backwards in time to the very spirit of the Elizabethan age. It has often provided Canadians with the comforting illusion that they have secured unique access to Shakespeare himself" (121). This kind of escapism, however, was never the Elizabethanists' main objective. William Poel, Nugent Monck, and Tyrone Guthrie did not seek to turn their theaters into the kind of historically accurate amusement park derided by W. Bridges-Adams as "Ye Olde Oake Shakespeare Bunne Shoppe" (Bridges-Adams, *Letter Book* 29). This was particularly true at Stratford where there was no attempt at an "Elizabethan pseudo-antique style" (Guthrie, "Shakespeare at Stratford" 128). Guthrie notes, "We were determined to eschew *Ye Olde*" (*Life* 319). Instead Guthrie, like Poel and Monck before him, sought a contemporary response to the immediate challenges facing theater in the twentieth century.

"Ritual," J. L. Styan writes, was "Guthrie's favorite word" (*Shakespeare Revolution* 205). Indeed, Guthrie's writings reveal an almost obsessive concern with spiritual rites. He believed that theater "is the direct descendant of Fertility Rites, War Dance, and all the corporate ritual expressions by means of which our primitive ancestors, often wiser than their progeny, sought to relate themselves to God, or the gods" ("Long View" 193). He was religious but far from orthodox. His vision incorporated Christianity, as when he wrote of the "priest in Holy Communion" as "an actor impersonating Christ in a very solemn drama" ("Long View" 192), but he also expressed dissatisfaction with modern religion. "Christian culture," he lamented, "has taken over many of the ideas underlying dionysiac and other more primitive rites of spring. We have purified them, or it could equally be said, emasculated them, by the elimination of much grossness and sexuality" (*In Various Directions* 31). Guthrie looked back to ancient Greece for more meaningful religious celebrations. He saw a common origin for Greek religion and Christianity, and for Greek and modern drama as well, in prehistoric rituals. These were originally celebrated with human and then later animal sacrifices until finally, "Instead of an actual sacrifice, the offering took symbolic form. A *story* of sacrifice was enacted in honor of the God in a tragedy." Guthrie believed that Macbeth, Hamlet, and "even Willy Loman" were all "like the protagonists of Greek tragedy, victims at a ceremony of sacrifice" (33). When Guthrie's *Oedipus Rex* proved the most successful production in the Stratford Festival's second season, Brooks Atkinson wrote that "it would be ironic if Sophocles emerged as the godfather of a Shakespeare festival" ("Bard in Canada" X1). In fact it was hardly "ironic," considering Guthrie's emphasis on the ritual quality of theater and on the unbroken continuity he perceived between primitive rites of sacrifice and modern tragedy.

Guthrie saw the thrust stage as essential to recovering theater's sacred aspects. Such a configuration stressed "the ritual as opposed to the illusionary quality of performance" ("Shakespeare at Stratford" 131). The presence of audience members on three sides, where "spectators can see one another around, and beyond, the more brightly lighted stage" (*New Theatre* 69), increased the sense of community and participation so vital to Guthrie. He had discovered at the 1948 Edinburgh Festival that an open stage allowed the audience to "assist in" the performance instead of merely observing it, and he was determined to build a permanent monument to this precept in Ontario.

Tyrone Guthrie believed that interactive ritual was especially important to a modern society in which people had been alienated by technology. Like the Pre-Raphaelites before him, he bemoaned the industrial transition from "handcraft to mechanical processes" with its accompanying shift in emphasis "from quality to quantity." He feared that, because of this assembly-line mentality, "the joy will be taken out of work" and "a deadly standardization will be imposed, not just upon commodities, but on ideas" (*Life* 324). This anti-industrial bias partly explains his obsessive behavior in the early years of the Stratford Festival, when he sometimes seemed perversely determined to spend as much money and effort as possible on props and costumes. Such was the case in 1953's "incident of the shoes," an episode of Festival lore so famous as to be chronicled in the business magazine *Industrial Canada* (House 63).

In two different accounts of the Festival's founding, from *A Life in the Theater* and *Renown at Stratford*, Guthrie describes at length the problem of securing adequate footwear for performers. This challenge is also addressed by his designer Tanya Moiseiwitsch, who rejects the traditional theatrical notion that such apparel is relatively unimportant. This conventional wisdom, she insists, is "a fallacy on the open stage" because, in a theatre like Stratford's, "shoes can let down the whole effect" (Moiseiwitsch 114). Moiseiwitsch may be partly right, but Guthrie's insistence that for *Richard III* he "required shoes of a shape, and in materials and colors, which bore no resemblance to the shoes mass produced for the public" (*Life* 323) seems excessive.

The real significance of the shoes for Guthrie lay in his rejection of industrialism. He lamented that "Canada, like the United States, is organized for mass-production" and that it was "almost impossible to get people to bother to make something for which there is no mass-demand, for which no blueprint exists, which requires craftsmanship." Finally he found "an aged Jewish craftsman," who was "delighted to feel that his skill was valued again," to make shoes for *Richard III*. "Too old for the rush and flurry of competitive mass-production," Guthrie moralizes, "he was still a first-rate tradesman" ("First Shakespeare" 14). A similar "little bootmaker" (*Life* 325) was found to provide footwear for *All's Well That Ends Well*. For Guthrie the difference between the labors of these elderly cobblers and the industrial output of modern shoe factories had a parallel in the performing arts. Live theater was "the source of the custom-made drama," whereas film and television only created "the sort of drama produced for cheap mass-distribution," which "cheapened the art of acting by making it over-familiar" ("First Shakespeare" 31). Guthrie's comments anticipate more recent scholarship that sees theater as resistant to the globalizing pressures of late capitalism. "In a world of mechanical reproduction and high-speed global communication," Dennis Kennedy writes, "theatre remains by its very nature extraordinarily labor-intensive and local." Guthrie's fixation with quality and authenticity in props and costumes emphasized what Kennedy calls the "indigenous, place-bound, and indivisible" attributes of the theatrical medium ("Shakespeare" 50).

Guthrie understood that from a practical point of view theater had to change if it was to prosper in the cinematic age. "We have all been spoilt by movies," he wrote. Guthrie then elaborated:

> Perhaps our eyes have been opened by the movies and television. We expect to see the actors, we expect to hear them, so spoilt are we. And if you are sitting at the back of a theatre that holds 3,000 people you don't see the actors at all, and you only hear them if they are relayed by a loudspeaker. It is a disappointing and dreary experience which people simply do not support. ("Theatre at Minneapolis" 34)

As opposed to a "dreary" experience in the cheap seats of a large proscenium auditorium, the thrust stage offered the kind of "close-up" perspective which the film-going public had come to expect. Guthrie believed (as had Nugent Monck) that the open stage's lack of scenic illusion spared the theater from having to compete with film in terms of verisimilitude. "Most thoughtful people," he claims, "realized the moment the movies had passed the bioscope stage, that the death-knell was ringing for theatrical realism" ("Theatre in Minneapolis" 46). A non-scenic approach, however, was impossible in traditional theaters "because of the architecture of the buildings." A proscenium audience is "placed all on one side" while "looking at a picture frame" and is therefore "conditioned by the shape of the auditorium and 10 generations of playgoing to expect a picture" (Guthrie quoted in "A Regisseur Reflects" 14). These visual expectations increased once audiences began to regularly frequent movie houses. The open stage shifted this paradigm of perception, and allowed the public to judge live drama on its own terms without unfavorable comparisons to cinema.

Guthrie believed that theater needed to offer the public something film could not by giving spectators the chance to impact the quality of performance through their "assistance" and response. "Unlike the audience for movies or television," he wrote, theater-goers have "an active part to play" and can therefore "make or mar the occasion" (*New Theatre* 70). The power of the public in this regard is greatly increased by the intimacy of the thrust configuration. Knowles is correct when he writes that at Stratford the stage and the building "are, to a large extent, themselves the message." I disagree, however, with what he takes this message to be. While Knowles believes that this "stage and its auditorium impose physical conditions that once again construct audiences as passive consumers of the production-as-product and that support the replication of capitalist and patriarchal structures" ("Shakespeare, 1993" 219), this interpretation overlooks the real sense of empowerment through active engagement which Guthrie's open stage affords its public. The "spirit of egalitarianism and democratic inclusiveness" that Robert Shaughnessy identifies as the ideological motivation behind Guthrie's configuration (*Shakespeare* 135) enables a participatory effect that is not provided by cinema or proscenium theater – modes of performance which tend far more to "construct audiences as passive consumers" in the service of "capitalist and patriarchal structures" than does the Festival stage at Stratford.

In dealing with his Canadian collaborators, Guthrie was not above using his position as a "looming patriarch of British Theatre" (Salter 120) to exert authority over these former subjects of the English crown. Yet Knowles's interpretation of the Festival's creation as "the solidification of a delayed colonial celebration of a 19th-century brand of Canadian nationalism configured on an imperialist British model" ("Nationalist to Multinational" 20) should be at least partly mitigated by Guthrie's expressed notions regarding Canadian identity, sentiments which reflect his broader attitude toward colonialism in general. Guthrie strove to make the Stratford project as much as possible "an effort for and by Canadians" ("Shakespeare at Stratford" 127). "It was Dr. Guthrie," Herbert Whittaker wrote in 1958, "who established the Festival's particular flavor of Canadianism," a characteristic which "was more responsible for the success of the Stratford Shakespearean Festival than any other factor" (xxiii). Guthrie's writings display sensitivity on the topic of cultural hegemony. He hoped that the Stratford Festival would provide "Canadian artists" with a means to "express what the Canadian climate, the Canadian soil and their fellow Canadians have made of them" ("Long View" 171).

Some critics have dismissed Guthrie's "drive for a Canadian character" as "so much rubbish" (Cohen, Nathan "Theatre" 236). Dennis Salter, for instance, cites Michael Langham's 1982 observation that "there was never anything Canadian about Stratford ... that was a diplomatic thing Guthrie cooked up" (Salter's ellipsis) as proof of the founding director's insincerity (quoted in Salter 121). Langham, however, did not work in Stratford until 1955, when he directed *Julius Caesar* before taking charge of the entire Festival from Guthrie.

He therefore could have had only limited knowledge of what transpired during the first two seasons, which was the time of Guthrie's greatest involvement. Knowles suggests that Guthrie quickly abandoned any aspirations of promoting Canadian nationalism. "As early as 1954," he observes, "Guthrie admitted, 'I don't know how far it may be possible to interpret a classical play in a distinctively Canadian way'" ("Nationalist to Multinational" 24). This quotation of Guthrie is from "A Long View of the Stratford Festival" published in *Twice Have the Trumpets Sounded*. The perceived defeatist attitude is, however, called into question by the director's suggestion, immediately preceding the passage cited by Knowles, that "a Festival's claim to be a Canadian institution might be based upon the fact that the company of actors was overwhelmingly Canadian" ("Long View" 166). Personnel decisions at Stratford consistently moved toward this ideal. Guthrie acknowledged that in "the first year, although there were only four British actors, the weight they pulled was out of all proportion to their numbers." But he pointed to greater equity in 1954, when in *Measure for Measure* "two of the three chief characters were played by Canadian actors" and in "*The Taming of the Shrew* both the leading players were Canadian" ("Long View" 145). Brooks Atkinson acknowledged Guthrie's attempts to use local talent, writing in 1953, "Most of the actors – and very good ones too – are Canadian professionals" ("Canada's Stratford" X1).

Guthrie rejected the notion that Canadian performers should eliminate regionalisms from their speech. This is significant in terms of Knowles's critique of the Stratford Festival's colonialist leanings. In "Shakespeare, Voice, and Ideology: Interrogating the Natural Voice," Knowles claims that voice training which advocates so-called "neutral" speech "clearly reinforce[s] North American Anglophilia as embodied in 'ye olde' Shakespeare Festivals across the continent, in imitation of British voice and other training" and therefore betrays its "ideological underpinnings" as a means of cultural repression (103). Guthrie agrees. He not only claims that "it would be quite wrong for Canadian actors to try to pronounce the words of a classical play in an assumed 'English' accent" ("Long View" 185), but goes further, suggesting that "the plays of Shakespeare should be presented by Canadian actors speaking in a recognizably Canadian manner." He prefers this indigenous vocalization to either British accents or "the *macedoine* of dialects which passes for English on the rare occasions when Shakespeare's heard on Broadway" (175). Guthrie's advocacy of regional Canadian speech is therefore, by the terms of Knowles's own analysis regarding the ideology of voice on the stage, progressive rather than reactionary.

Guthrie's praise of Canadian speech and of Canada in general may have been, as Cohen and Salter assert, no more than public relations. If Guthrie was insincere, however, he was at least consistent. A decade later he expressed similar concerns regarding cultural imperialism when planning his namesake theater in Minneapolis. "We certainly did not want it to appear," he wrote of this venture, "as if once again Britain were trying to instruct the colonists"(*New Theatre* 43). Elsewhere during this same period Guthrie explained:

> Just because I come from Britain it is extremely important that I don't
> seem to be shoving British products down their throats. The Ameri-
> can theatre is always being grand-mothered by us. We come over and
> say "Old darlings, you really don't know anything about it! We have
> been at it for five centuries. Let me show you!" And it doesn't do. These
> are grown-up people who are developing their own theatre. If you
> are working in the Middle West this must be … an expression of the
> Middle West. ("Theatre in Minneapolis" 40)

Guthrie's comments on his work in the United States, along with his earlier
hope that Canadians at Stratford would be able "to assimilate classical works
of art as part of their own heritage, not just regard them as imports, acquired
at second-hand from overseas" ("Long View" 167), suggest greater enlightenment on Guthrie's part toward issues of national identity than his critics have
acknowledged.

Elements of Guthrie's own biography attuned him to the complications
of cross-cultural collaboration. Robert Shaughnessy suggests that Guthrie's
"Anglo-Irishness" and his awareness of "Ireland's troubled passage towards a
post-colonial national identity" made him particularly sensitive to issues of
imperialism (*Shakespeare* 91). Guthrie's views on the Irish question were pas-
sionate. His Protestant family's life had been turned upside down when their
county was awarded in 1922 to the Irish Free State rather than to the British-
ruled North. Guthrie compared the inequitable sectarian divide in Northern
Ireland with racial segregation in the Jim Crow South and frequently argued
for Irish unification. This personal connection to the Irish troubles helped
make Guthrie throughout his career a champion of local empowerment
and expression. He wrote of his early theatrical experiences in Belfast and
Glasgow, "While I was in Ireland and Scotland I believed that indigenous
drama was a valuable element in both national development and international understanding" (*Life* 347). Guthrie acted on his principles in 1926
when he resigned from a secure job with the BBC to produce low-budget
tours for the nationalist Scottish Players. Later in his career, Guthrie continued to champion local artistic expression while working in Australia, Canada,
and the United States.

It may be impossible for any representative of a dominant culture to completely rid himself of hegemonic impulses, particularly when dealing with that
culture's former colonial subjects. This aspect of Guthrie's work at Stratford
has, however, been over-emphasized by critics like Dennis Salter and Richard
Paul Knowles. Recently, Knowles has courageously confronted the possibility that he may have gone too far in his long-held emphasis on the imperialist
uses of Shakespeare. In an article subtitled "How I Learned to Stop Worrying and Love the Bard," Knowles acknowledges that his "tendency to focus,
post-new historically and post-colonially, on 'Shakespeare' as agent of the
colonial project" has sometimes "blinded [him] to the potential practical use
of Shakespeare" as a means for the colonized to develop a distinct cultural
identity ("*Death*" 62). The ideological context of the founding of the Stratford Festival, which has long been seen by Knowles and like-minded critics

as a prime example of Shakespeare's imperialist function, should be similarly re-examined. The positive ideological significance of Guthrie's agenda far outweighs any taint of cultural colonialism that clings to his efforts.

The Stratford Stage

Tyrone Guthrie came to believe that the possibilities of any theatrical endeavor are determined by the architecture in which it is performed. He was attracted to the Stratford project principally because there was no existing theater on the site. Guthrie could therefore start from scratch and engineer a radical departure from traditional performance spaces. His plan was to incorporate elements of early modern practice (and of Greek theater and the prehistoric rituals which preceded it) in an effort to create a new kind of venue that would serve the needs of the postmodern age. Margaret Groome has accused the Stratford Festival of contradiction in simultaneously portraying itself "as in direct descent from the best of the classical tradition and as a progressive enterprise" ("Stratford" 128). But for Guthrie and his supporters this was precisely the point. By embracing the past, the Festival would become "the theatre of the future" (Davies, "Ritual" 7).

In my discussions of the Stratford stage, I will generally use the present tense to refer to those features implemented at the time of the Festival's founding. Where discrepancies exist, I will make distinctions between the original 1953 tent configuration and the permanent Festival Theatre which opened in 1958. Later architectural adjustments at Stratford are beyond the scope of this study. The main acting area at Stratford is a five-sided platform which rises "out of a semi-circle of concrete called 'the gutter'" (Pettigrew and Portman 78). This platform is connected to the concrete floor by three steps. The top two of these are 18 inches wide, while the bottom one has a breadth of 3 feet. These steps run around the entire circumference of the platform, and are therefore more like continuous levels than stairs. John Pettigrew and Jamie Portman describe the resulting playing area as "surprisingly small, being about eleven feet deep and eighteen feet wide" (78). Cecil Clarke, however, suggests that the broad steps or levels leading up to the platform are in fact part of the playing area, and should be calculated when figuring the dimensions of the stage. He therefore measures the "total width of the stage, including the three levels" as 30 feet and the "total overall depth for acting" as 39 feet (Clarke 46–7). Photographs (Figure 12) show that the lowest and broadest of these steps leading up to the platform is spacious enough to serve as an acting area in its own right, and that the other two can effectively be employed for the placing of actors on staggered levels.

Although Guthrie describes the Stratford stage as having been "based on Shakespeare" ("Theatre at Minneapolis" 43), he cared more about the space's practicality than about how well it reproduced Elizabethan practices. Pettigrew and Portman write that Guthrie "was influenced by the football stadium" to include "two tunnels, or vomitoria, which allow actors access to the side and the front of the stage from the underworld beneath it" (78). This expanded on the practice of actors entering and exiting through the house that Guthrie had discovered in Edinburgh. He considered these vomitoria "vitally important" ("Theatre at Minneapolis" 44), and did not hesitate to incorporate this architectural element which has no apparent precedent in early modern theaters.

While not a slavish reconstruction, the Stratford stage does have Elizabethan attributes. Like the Globe and Blackfriars, the Festival Theatre has an onstage balcony, a trap door, and multiple upstage portals for entrances and exits. These elements, however, are orchestrated at Stratford in a unique manner which derives from the stage's relationship to its auditorium. The audience originally wrapped around 240° of the space, an arc reduced to 220° with the construction of the permanent building in 1958. This meant that a *frons scenae* placed parallel to the downstage border of the platform, as is the case at the reconstructed Globe and Blackfriars, would seriously obstruct the vision of a large number of spectators. To address this challenge, the onstage balcony does not rest on an even horizontal line but instead points toward the center of the auditorium "rather like the prow of a ship" (Pettigrew and Portman 7). This unit is supported by seven pillars which mirror its V shape, one of which rests at the downstage apex. The best description of this configuration comes from Robertson Davies, who writes that the "plan of the theatre is like a large deep-dish pie, from which all but one large slice has been removed; this slice, projecting to the center of the amphitheatre, is the stage area" ("Director" 119). This irregular design means that the Stratford stage does not have a traditional discovery space such as Guthrie had employed at Edinburgh. The position of the audience and the triangular structure of the

12 The Festival Stage in Stratford, Ontario

balcony mean that the area beneath cannot be closed off with curtains and used to reveal key theatrical images, as has been common practice in Elizabethan-style theaters from the time of Monck's Maddermarket.

Guthrie credited the Stratford Festival's success largely to the structure of its stage, writing that productions there "seemed livelier and fresher because of the design of the theatre" (*Life* 336). This architectural triumph was widely hailed by contemporary observers. Henry Hewes, writing in 1955, proclaimed that the mere development of this "functionally Elizabethan stage" had justified the Festival's existence (26); and Walter Kerr announced in 1957 that Guthrie and his collaborators had "given us the only really new stage and the only new actor–audience experience of the last hundred years on this continent" (quoted in Edinborough 511). Many later scholars also consider the Stratford stage a tremendous success. Dennis Kennedy asserts, "Until the creation of the Stratford Shakespearean Festival in Ontario the Elizabethan stage movement had been more notable for its failures than its successes" (*Looking* 152). Kennedy favorably contrasts the modernism of the Stratford stage with what he perceives as the archaism of early modern reconstructions in Oregon and San Diego, the "Elizabethan tiring-house facades" of which have "'Ye Olde Oake Shakespeare Bunne Shoppe' inscribed within the architecture" (153).

From the beginning, however, the Stratford stage has had its detractors. Nathan Cohen was the most persistent of these during the Festival's early decades. He contended that the "open stage had its tyrannies no less repressive to Shakespeare than the proscenium arch." Cohen believed that Guthrie's model necessitated "a 'go, go, go' treatment" ("Theatre" 235) marked by excessive movement, and that this peripatetic staging too often distracted the public from the business of a play. Open staging indeed poses challenges not encountered in a proscenium theater. A director must work in three dimensions rather than two because of the perceptions of the side audience. Many theater artists accustomed to the picture-frame are not up to this challenge. Knowles observes that at Stratford in recent years many "directors, some of them very prominent ones, simply give up and direct shows to the theatre's central aisle, treating the stage as they would any other" ("Legacy" 43). Pettigrew and Portman similarly acknowledge that directors at Stratford have often "failed to cope" with the complexities of the Festival Theatre (83). One can therefore reasonably ask whether the advantages of open staging outweigh these increased difficulties. A primary justification offered for the thrust stage by Guthrie and his supporters was the greater intimacy possible in this format, a goal clearly achieved at Stratford. The front row of the audience in 1955 was between 4 and 6 feet from the stage, depending on where one sat within the configuration (Clarke 46). The challenge has been to stage shows in accordance with the theater's sight lines so that the benefit of this increased proximity is not overshadowed by poor visibility or by the distraction of excessive motion designed to share an actor's face equally with all parts of the house. This task remains harder at Stratford today than in other thrust venues because of the Festival Theatre's 220° configuration.

Nathan Cohen's most serious indictment of the Festival stage was that it compromised reception of the text. "Speech is the heartbeat of Shakespeare's grandeur," Cohen wrote. "We do not come to 'see' Shakespeare, but to 'hear' him. And 'hear' him is precisely what is such a problem in the Festival Theatre" ("Stratford" 269). Partly, the cause of this defect is once again the extreme audience arc of the Stratford stage. Problems with audibility are necessarily more frequent if actors must regularly turn upstage to address spectators sitting behind the onstage balcony. But this accusation of aural deficiency also derives from the director's reliance on "Guthrionics" (Pettigrew and Portman 30), outrageous *coups de theatre* that often came at the expense of a play's language. An example was Guthrie's use of "a mighty sneeze" by a minor character to upstage Cranmer's baptismal oration in the 1949 *Henry VIII*. Trewin's explanation for this moment epitomizes the director's juvenile impatience with dramatic verse. Guthrie was "bored again, and expecting the house to agree" (Trewin 212). As Harold Clurman notes, in Guthrie's productions it often seemed that "the text as meaning (and as poetry with a life of its own) hardly exists" (99).

While this was a flaw in Guthrie's personal approach, some critics have extrapolated it to mean that thrust staging is inherently hostile to textual transmission. Kenneth Tynan concluded from Guthrie's example, "Only those forms of theatre in which words are secondary – such as musicals, dance drama, and commedia dell'arte – have much to gain from the three-sided stage" (quoted in Pettigrew and Portman 84); and Claudia Cassidy wrote of Guthrie's "outthrust stage" in Minneapolis that it was "more suited to the theater of movement than to the theater of the mind" (rpt. in Guthrie, *New Theatre* 121). This linguistic shortfall, however, is not representative of open staging in general. Because of the public's closeness to the playing area and the style of direct address which this format encourages, audiences in thrust venues like Chicago Shakespeare and the Staunton Blackfriars often hear and understand much better than they would in a proscenium theater, as evidenced by the ability of these spaces to avoid amplification. Most picture-frame houses of similar size find it necessary to mike their actors.

Guthrie's Stratford Productions

TYRONE Guthrie's Shakespeare productions at the Stratford Festival showcased both the strengths and the weaknesses of his directorial approach. The Festival's inaugural *Richard III* in 1953 "was in a processional style to which the stage seemed ideally suited." Robert Cushman describes this premiere as "the first of many great evenings for the flourishing of banners" (20). Guthrie signaled the importance of his novel architecture by having Alec Guinness deliver the opening soliloquy while sitting astride the balcony, then sprint down a staircase in view of the audience to join the funeral procession. The director creatively exploited the set's upper level throughout the evening. A soldier fell from the balcony during a battle scene, and Richmond was lifted in triumph to this structure at the play's finale. Guthrie disposed of two of Richard's victims through the trapdoor, another of the theater's Elizabethan accessories. Throughout *Richard III*, Guthrie's penchant for pageantry was matched by his desire to shock the audience. Robertson Davies suggests that Guthrie sought a deliberate parallel between the behavior of Richard's henchmen and the activities in a "Nazi torture chamber" or "the interrogation offices of the Third Reich" ("Director" 92). The "audience cringed" when for "a slight show of defiance Vaughan was flung to the ground and kicked in the groin" (90). The premiere was a great success. Even Nathan Cohen recalled in 1966, "The first night at Stratford was the most memorable single experience I ever had in the theatre" ("Great First Night" 25).

All's Well That Ends Well followed *Richard III* in 1953 and was, according to *Time* magazine, the "real hit" of the first Festival season (review of *Richard III* and *All's Well That Ends Well* 32). Joseph Price, in his stage history of the play, writes that Guthrie's production was the "first significant performance of *All's Well* in America" (65). The director chose the play partly because of his sympathy for Shakespeare's comic heroine, a compassion which suggests a feminist viewpoint. Guthrie wrote in 1964 that "because she intelligently and energetically pursues the man of her choice and finally captures him," Helena was traditionally thought "to be a forward and artful article. This view will always prevail where it is believed that the female's duty is to be no more than a submissive adjunct to the physically stronger and more intelligent male" ("10 Favorites from Shakespeare" 18). Price sees a connection between Guthrie's treatment of the play and William Poel's in 1920. The contemporary relevance in Poel's era hinged on the changing role of women in society following World War I. Guthrie, directing the play in the aftermath of a second global conflict during which women had been even further integrated into the commercial workforce, was similarly responsive to issues of gender equity. His production implicitly condemned the societal pressures put on working women during this era to return to the home. Price sees Guthrie's use of twentieth-century costumes in this production as an effort to connect Helena's plight with that of postwar women. "The fantastic turns of the plot, of Helena's traps," Price suggests, "became much more acceptable in modern dress to a contemporary audience which had been saturated with aggressive heroines, often 'career women' who had won reluctant males in innumerable romantic comedy films during the 1930s and 1940s" (52). Poel used contemporary costuming to analogous ends in 1920, and both Poel and Guthrie placed the King of France in a wheelchair, illustrating this ineffectual monarch's dependence on strong female characters.

As in the case of *Richard III*, Guthrie cleverly utilized his neo-Elizabethan stage for *All's Well*. The gulling of Parolles in Act IV, scene 1 demonstrated the imaginative possibilities of this non-scenic alternative. With no scenery or light cues, the performers established the darkness and danger of a "no man's land" between the trenches by miming their way through imaginary barbed wire among the stage's seven pillars. Neil Carson notes "the way in which the 'scenery' on a permanent, non-localized stage can be said to materialize and then melt away in the imagination of the spectators" (56). For Robert Shaughnessy, this theatrical freedom was tied to Guthrie's quest for social and sexual liberation. The 1953 *All's Well*, Shaughnessy writes, was "conceived as an uncertain movement from repression to liberalization and enlightenment"

(*Shakespeare* 138). He sees Guthrie's rediscovery of the comedy in its first American production as tied to the director's mission to free Shakespeare from the vestiges of a nineteenth-century pictorial tradition:

> In one way, the simultaneous rediscovery of *All's Well* and non-illusion-ist staging at Stratford offers itself to be read as a demonstration of a quasi-Foucauldian scheme of repression and liberation: Guthrie's pro-duction liberated the play which had been closeted and repressed by Victorian prudery, in a dynamic movement from shame and conceal-ment to frankness, openness and visibility. (137)

Shaughnessy's thesis may seem at first over-theorized, but he supports it with substantive examples from Guthrie's staging. Helena and the invalid King represent "the principal thematic antitheses of the production: male and female, youth and age, authority and integrity, and, above all, the paralysis of illusionism and the mobility of the open stage" (145). Their celebratory dance after the monarch is healed manifests for Shaughnessy "a rare vision of optimism and hope, and a testament to performance's capacity to escape the disciplinary strictures of text, production and stage." Guthrie's 1953 *All's Well* therefore presaged "a new, and as yet unrealized, era of theatrical health, happiness and liberty" (146).

If *All's Well That Ends Well* represented the zenith of Guthrie's directing career at Stratford, then 1954's *The Taming of the Shrew* was its nadir. William Hutt, who played Hortensio, believed that "Tony thought less of the play than he actually should have" and that the director "sometimes tended to be lightly frivolous if he thought a play was not as good as it should be" (quoted in Rossi, *Astonish* 182). Guthrie set out to reverse the traditional interpreta-tion. Rather than a bold and brash suitor, Petruchio was portrayed "as a shy, bespectacled young man with severe doubts about his prowess at shrew-taming" (Cushman 24). Katharina was equally timid. Cushman notes that this "interpretation might charitably be described as unorthodox" (24). For Davies, it was an unfortunate example of Guthrie's "playing against the lines" ("Taming" 39).

Besides being burdened with Guthrie's deliberate contrariness, the pro-duction suffered from an excess of comic gags. This *Shrew* was set in Califor-nia around 1900, and Norman Marshall writes that "Petruchio was a yahoo cowboy with a ten-gallon hat and a six-shooter, but bespectacled like Harold Lloyd" (*Producer* 182). Numerous observers made similar connections to the silent screen. Brooks Atkinson compared the style to that of "a Mack Sennett cartoon," but this critic was not amused. "Never have so many actors worked so hard for so long to produce such a sophomoric prank," Atkinson asserted. He believed that since Guthrie "has tossed most of the dialogue away in the frenzy of a hokum performance, logic suggests that he should also rid himself of the play and get a new author." In frustration Atkinson asked, "Why dedi-cate a theatre to Shakespeare if you have to discard him in order to entertain the groundlings?" (review of *Taming of the Shrew* 22). Guthrie's interpreta-tion for *The Taming of the Shrew* was wrong-headed, his Wild-West setting puzzling, and his excess of comic shtick ill-advised. All of these elements nevertheless demonstrate that Guthrie did not feel bound by theatrical tradition and had no holy reverence for Shakespeare's authorial intent. No one could accuse this *Shrew* of being "museum theater."

Guthrie's next Shakespeare at the Stratford Festival was 1955's *The Merchant of Venice*. Guthrie cast Frederick Valk, a Jewish refugee who had fled the Nazi terror, as Shylock. In spite of this topical relevance, the director chose not to highlight the play's anti-Semitic aspects. Instead, Guthrie pursued what Davies called "the adult's fairy-tale conception of the play" which made it "like a story from Bandello or Boccaccio richly brought to life" ("Merchant" 56). There were broad characterizations of a "scimitar-flourishing Moor" and "a Prince of Aragon who seemed to be the most obscure and most hemophilic of all the Hapsburgs" (58). A comic pageant ensued when the caskets were borne on stage by young women dressed in corresponding colors of gold, lead, and silver. The joke was that the lead casket weighed so much that the poor girl kept dropping it and had to be assisted by Portia's servant Balthazar. While it was more successful than 1954's *Taming of the Shrew*, some found this *Merchant* insipid. Nathan Cohen complained that it contained "no hint, aside from the intrinsic racism, of the play's virtues and agitations" ("Tyrone Guthrie" 425). For students of popular culture, the production is most memorable for the presence in the cast of a young William Shatner who, Davies wrote, "played Gratiano as a bore, with a ready and rattling laugh." He was, however, "a young bore, to whom all may be forgiven for his gaiety." "What such a man would be at forty," Davies opined, "we are not obliged to enquire" ("Merchant" 66). Future generations of American television viewers would unfortunately witness this very phenomenon.

1955 was Guthrie's last year in charge of the Stratford Festival. In 1957, the final season in a tent, he returned as a guest director. His production of *Twelfth Night* indulged in the same kind of heavy-handed comic business which had marred 1954's *Taming of the Shrew*. "Mr. Guthrie does go on endlessly," Brooks Atkinson lamented. "Don't expect much from the romantic scenes," he warned his readers. The director had "lost his heart to the … clowns," which resulted in a *Twelfth Night* that was "funny but also formless, over-extended and tone-deaf" (review of *Twelfth Night* 16). This was Guthrie's final Shakespeare at Stratford. He would return in later years to direct Operettas in the Festival's Avon Theatre but never again worked on the open stage which had revolutionized Shakespearean production.

Minneapolis

Until his death in 1971, Guthrie continued his career as a freelance director in Britain, America, and elsewhere. He also searched constantly for opportunities to build new theaters on the open-stage model in what Nathan Cohen calls an "obsessive quest for another Stratford 'miracle'" ("Stratford" 276). In 1963, he opened the Tyrone Guthrie Theater in Minneapolis. While the Minnesota playhouse bears the director's name, it does not represent his architectural vision as fully as had the performance space at Stratford. Shakespeare was not to be the principal focus in Minneapolis. "The Theatre in the Twin cities must attempt to cope with a more varied repertoire," Guthrie wrote, adding that it therefore "must aim to be more flexible." A permanent set was deemed unsuitable for this broader catalogue of drama. Guthrie and Moiseiwitsch instead developed a design "of two immense sliding doors or screens, which, when closed, formed a sort of corrugated wall. They were on wheels and could slide apart." Guthrie, wary of imitating a proscenium, insisted that these doors would not "disclose a picture" but would rather "open merely to permit wagons, previously set with furniture and properties as required, to be pushed out onto the stage" (*New Theatre* 74). This compromise with the pictorial tradition increased in 1980, when Artistic Director Liviu Ciulei redesigned the performance area, making its "size, shape, and height" adjustable by means of "accordion walls" and "interchangeable floor panels." The goal of this remodeling was to give "stage designers greater freedom" ("Guthrie Theater"). There had been no need for production-specific "stage designers" at Stratford, where the permanent set provided an unchanging functional background for all Festival endeavors.

Guthrie was hindered in his work at Minneapolis by disagreements with the project's architect, Ralph Rapson, who opposed the director's plan for close proximity between actors and audience. Rapson visited the Stratford Festival but came away unimpressed. According to Guthrie, the architect exclaimed, "All those *people* all *around* me" in a fit of claustrophobic panic (quoted in Guthrie, *New Theatre* 73). Guthrie had hoped to steeply rake the Minnesota auditorium in approximation of the stacked gallery configuration which Franklin J. Hildy considers an essential component of early modern playhouses ("Reconstructing" 13). The disagreement with Rapson led instead to an odd compromise in the auditorium's design. *The New York Times* reported in 1962, "While seats to the left of the stage will be arranged with the conventional orchestra and balcony separation, those to the far right will rise in steep, continuous inclines from the foot of the stage to the top of the theatre" ("Guthrie Inspects" 28). Guthrie was thus prevented from completely achieving the intimacy he had desired in Minneapolis.

Whether because of deficiencies in design, poor quality of performance, or simple bad luck, the inauguration of the Guthrie Theater with *Hamlet* in 1963 was not the kind of success the Stratford premiere had been a decade earlier. Guthrie blamed the opening night house, which was "a 'fashionable' audience, drawn by the occasion, not by any desire to see a great tragedy." Guthrie recalls ruefully, "After six minutes, some of the sillier Society Ladies began fidgeting with their scarves and admiring their own rings and necklaces; after ten, the coughing began; after twenty, it was clear that the excitement had evaporated and the battle to win the attention which the play demands had been lost." This same type of public had attended the first night at Stratford but the play in that case had been *Richard III*, which Guthrie staged as a highly accessible melodramatic pageant. Guthrie writes that as the evening began in Minneapolis, "I realized with painful clarity just what a risk we had taken by opening with *Hamlet*" (*New Theatre* 109).

Critics blamed not the audience but the production. Claudia Cassidy wrote in the Chicago *Sunday Tribune* that Guthrie's *Hamlet* was "amateurishly acted and clumsily directed, with little indication of the freedom within disciplined form that is the basic classic style" (rpt. in Guthrie, *New Theatre* 120). In a common criticism of Guthrie's work, she noted "incessant, often meaningless movement, distracting stage business, and highly personal interpretations by the director" which "made *Hamlet* interminable" (122). She concluded that "the Minneapolis *Hamlet* obscures and destroys a great play. It is drab and misleading" (123). Most other critics were more positive, although all expressed some qualms. Herbert Whittaker in the Toronto *Globe and Mail* hailed Guthrie's "rare and unusual creativity as a stage director" (rpt. in Rossi, *Minneapolis* 79) and generally approved of the production's "parade of fine theatrical tricks" (80). But Whittaker also noted that "good speech" was "not yet a matter of full accomplishment by the Minneapolis company" and claimed that Guthrie's use of a full text was "hard on them – and often on their audience" (80).

The response to the inaugural *Hamlet* was typical of Guthrie's experience in Minneapolis. He never quite captured the magic he had found in Ontario. Michael Langham, who served as Artistic Director at both theaters, observed that Guthrie "made far less impact in Minneapolis than he had in Stratford." Langham "was quite shocked to find how mildly he was revered locally. It wasn't as if a great man had come to Minneapolis and made something fantastic happen, which is what I'd felt at Stratford" (quoted in Rossi, *Astonish* 284). Guthrie's one major success in Minnesota was an adaptation of the *Orestia* titled *The House of Atreus*, which opened in 1967 to popular and critical acclaim. Predictably, however, *The House of Atreus* failed to survive transplant to a proscenium house on Broadway. Guthrie resisted this relocation but finally consented against his better judgment because, late in life, he was exhausted by poor health. *Atreus* on Broadway turned out to be a great mistake. As Guthrie had feared, the "production did not suit the theatre" (Forsyth 301).

I N his final years Guthrie's writings and theatrical endeavors frequently show signs of being hastily produced in order to secure what James Forsyth calls "money for jam" (284) – his ill-conceived plan to manufacture traditional jams in an attempt to revive the local economy near his Irish estate of Annagh-ma-Kerrig. Guthrie died on 15 May 1971. In announcing his death the estate's steward, Seamus McGorman, proclaimed, "A great tree has fallen out the sky" (quoted in Rossi, *Astonish* 150). When Guthrie's theatrical associates assembled in June for a memorial service at St Paul's, Covent Garden, they noticed while entering the church that, indeed, "a tree that had stood for many years by its door had fallen down" (Forsyth 343). As this arboreal allegory suggests, Tyrone Guthrie was a towering figure in the history of Elizabethan staging. His legacy regarding the recovery of early modern theatrical practices is significant but complex.

While Nugent Monck's Maddermarket Theatre accommodated a few token spectators right and left of its platform, Guthrie built the first modern performance space that embraced the Elizabethan paradigm of an audience significantly distributed on three sides of the stage. His desire to emulate the circular sites of prehistoric rituals led Guthrie to design the Festival Stage at Stratford with seating that wrapped behind the stage, surpassing the 180° arc of the Globe or Blackfriars. This led to problems of sight lines and audibility which exceed those of more typical open-stage arrangements. Observers who have experienced thrust staging primarily through the Stratford Festival have therefore frequently been led to reject this configuration as inherently unfriendly to the delivery of text in performance. Guthrie's penchant for exotic pageantry convinced contemporary critics like Nathan Cohen that luxurious spectacle was a necessary component of Elizabethan staging. Some later scholars, most notably Margaret Groome and Richard Paul Knowles, have been similarly misled by the idiosyncrasies of Guthrie's personal aesthetic to view the open-stage movement as an adjunct of the visually dominated commercial paradigm rather than as an alternative to this theatrical status quo.

Because he was a British director who sought to stage the works of an English playwright "within the particular conditions of Canadian postcoloniality in the postwar years" (Shaughnessy, *Shakespeare* 123), Guthrie has been accused of artistic imperialism. While he did not consciously pursue an agenda of cultural hegemony, this notion has combined with the director's perceived bourgeois dependence on lavish production values to lead many critics to condemn his work as ideologically regressive. In much the same way, William Poel has been judged reactionary because of his alleged fetish for historical reconstruction. In both cases, theater practitioners who considered themselves radical reformers have been received as retrograde conservatives. Such misunderstandings may be the fate of all who seek new forms through the imperfect process of theatrical experimentation.

Any reader aspiring to objectivity will blush at Roberson Davies's claim that in "forming an estimate of the work of Tyrone Guthrie as a director, it is necessary to remember that he is a genius." But one can more easily accept Davies's accompanying conclusion that "both Guthrie's astonishing successes and his wrongheaded failures will defy explanation, for there is little ordinary reason in them" ("Genius" 29). Guthrie admitted that some of his efforts missed the mark. He professed in his defense, "I'd rather be hung for a good powerful, self-confident sheep than a wee half-hearted baa-lamb" ("Modern Producer" 83). While his restless style often led to questionable choices in performance, Guthrie's ever-changing inventiveness refutes the notion that he ever staged "museum" productions. Rather than advocating "timeless" presentations of early modern drama or interpretations frozen in a historical past, Guthrie believed, "If it's your job to put one of Shakespeare's plays upon the stage, my view is that you should think carefully and deeply what it means to you – here and now … and express that meaning as best you can, and as boldly as you can" ("Modern Producer" 83). More recent companies like Chicago Shakespeare and the American Shakespeare Center at the Blackfriars Playhouse have built on the foundation of Tyrone Guthrie's efforts. They have to a large extent achieved the promise of the open stage without falling prey to Guthrie's vices.

5 The New Globe

DISCUSSIONS of Elizabethan staging in the early twenty-first century inevitably center on "Shakespeare's Globe," the outdoor playhouse on the south bank of the Thames that W. B. Worthen calls "the most notorious theatre built in recent memory" (*Force* 28). This reconstruction was the brainchild of the late American actor Sam Wanamaker. According to legend, Wanamaker sought out the site of the original Globe during his first visit to London in 1949. When he discovered that the playhouse was only commemorated by a meager plaque, Wanamaker "made up his mind then and there to erect a proper monument – a full-scale, working replica of the theatre itself. And that is exactly what he did with the rest of his life" (Stasio 54).

This is a great creation myth, but it involves a good deal of oversimplification. Wanamaker did not set out to authentically reconstruct the Globe. His initial plan instead involved "a modern building which simply reflected the *form* of Shakespeare's Globe," a design composed of "a brick drum with galleries, a roof and stage lighting" (Day 32) as in the "Swan Theatre at Stratford" (126). This structure was to be part of a major redevelopment of the Bankside area, intended to gentrify and rejuvenate this neglected borough. Wanamaker encountered strong resistance to this idea and turned for support to the international academic community. With their involvement the reconstructed amphitheater at the center of the project took on ever-greater importance. Toward the end of his life Wanamaker "reduced his vision for the south bank from the incredible to the merely improbable" and decided to build only the Globe complex, abandoning the rest of his development scheme (126).

The scholars who determined how the playhouse would be built saw it as a "test-tube" that would provide "the basis for experiments" (Gurr, "Staging" 159). Their discourse frequently adopts a scientific vocabulary. For Alan Dessen, the Globe would be "a laboratory for investigating how the original scripts would or could have been staged" ("Globe" 195). Andrew Gurr suggests that Shakespeare's plays "might be seen as a form of software, designed to fit a particular machine or piece of hardware, and we need to reconstruct the hardware the plays were designed for so that we can see more clearly how these supremely rich and intricate programs were designed to work" ("Rebuilding" 11–12). Many scholars do not accept this rationale. Marion O'Connor mocks what she terms the "rhetorical stable of quasi-scientific terminology around 'Shakespeare's Globe' on Southwark" and rejects "even the notional possibility of testing anything in theatrical reconstructions" ("Useful 32). Even Paul Menzer, director of a graduate program at Mary Baldwin College that is affiliated with the American Shakespeare Center, cautions that "attempts to use the Blackfriars and Globe stages must always fall short of the empiricism promised in the word 'laboratory'" (223). For Menzer and O'Connor, an empirical approach is invalid for several reasons. Too little is known about the original Globe, and the project's designers are inevitably affected by the prejudices of their age and therefore unable to impartially recreate the past. Even if these difficulties could be overcome and an accurate Globe rebuilt, the public frequenting such a theater would be necessarily "inauthentic."

Proponents of reconstruction have long recognized the mindset of modern playgoers as the Achilles' heel of their endeavor. While writing in 1979 in support of a proposed Detroit Globe, John Russell Brown acknowledged that "a true Elizabethan audience is, needless to say, unobtainable." He suggested that this deficiency could be offset by recreating the broad-based spectator demographic which existed in Shakespeare's day. The "young and the poor – and also the addicted and the fearless" should be encouraged to "behave as they did in the Globe Theatre" (Brown, John Russell 20). Brown does not consider the extent to which the "addicted and the fearless" of Detroit would comport themselves differently than their early modern counterparts. Andrew Gurr proposed indoctrinating all visitors to the Bankside Globe with an extensive "exhibition displaying the life and times of sixteenth-century playgoers" (*Rebuilding* 25), through which spectators would have to pass as a "proper prelude to the experience" (161) before entering the amphitheater itself. Coaching an audience in this manner would likely skew the results of any performance experiment, and the new Globe's planners ultimately realize the limits of authenticity. "Everyone connected with the project," writes W. B. Worthen, "is well aware the Globe can only be a complex *contemporary* undertaking, one which evinces an understanding of the working of history that is fully our own" ("Reconstructing" 34). Yet supporters believe that, while inevitably compromised, the new Globe is still a valuable tool for understanding Shakespeare's plays and their original stagings. Menzer writes that while "the gap between then and now is too wide, the static of four hundred years too loud" for new Globe performances to be truly "indicative of early modern practice," scholars may still be able to "observe specific practice and extrapolate general trends" as they "watch actors themselves unlearn modern theatrical conventions as they adjust to the material conditions of early modern theaters" (228).

For many critics writing from an ideological perspective, however, this stated objective of studying the past actually masks the project's "covert, idolatrous agenda," which is to use Shakespeare's cultural authority in a reactionary quest to stifle social progress. The appeal to the Globe as a universal symbol of "essential" artistic excellence encourages people, in this view, to "forget about change and about the history and politics which produce it." Terrence Hawkes mocks what he sees as the Globe's comforting effect on conservatives. "Let Europe loom, the pound wilt," he exclaims, "Shakespeare's wooden O offers a peculiarly satisfying bulwark against change" (142). Anti-American sentiment directed at the Chicago-born Wanamaker compounds suspicion of the Bankside endeavor. "Naturally it would be an American who longs for this," writes Marjorie Garber. She compares Wanamaker's quest to "the Rockefellers rebuilding colonial Williamsburg or Disney reconstituting the psychic realms of fantasyland, frontierland, and tomorrowland in the conservative suburbs of Los Angeles" (246). Hawkes connects the reconstructed playhouse to the military and economic goals of Yankee imperialism. The

new Globe, he writes, "shares certain features of other rather more threat-
ening transatlantic missions periodically set up in our midst" and therefore
represents "the continuation of American foreign policy by other means"
(153). John Drakakis likewise considers the new amphitheater "as subtle
an example of the operation of a cultural imperialism as one could wish to
see" (39).

Ironically, the two sides in this debate share a common rationale. They
both defend their positions by rejecting essentialism and emphasizing the
particularity of discrete historical moments. Opponents of the new Globe see
the playhouse as seeking to deny cultural specificity through its function as
a "timeless" monument. Drakakis believes that Wanamaker's project partici-
pates in the "deification" of Shakespeare as "universal, transcendent, and eter-
nal" (25), and Hawkes similarly describes its attempt to "determine, establish
and reinforce essentials" (142). The new Globe, for these critics, denies "one
of the basic tenets of current literary theory: that there is irreducible difference between different societies and historical periods" (King 122). Many of
the project's proponents, however, justify their position in terms of this very
emphasis on the material uniqueness of specific cultural moments. Gabriel
Egan writes, "If it is found that playhouse design is an important determinant
of the drama then the reconstructed Globe may be defended as a historicist
tool which undermines the claim that Shakespeare's work transcends historical and cultural difference" (15). These scholars sometimes rebut criticism
from theater practitioners by appealing to this notion of temporal specificity.
Chastising performers for refusing to follow Elizabethan staging practices at
the Globe, Alan Dessen claims that "most actors are essentialists" because
they "regularly assume that various performance choices in Shakespeare's
time would be identical or, at the least, comparable to" similar choices today
("Globe" 195–6).

The tendency of both positions in this dispute to reject essentialism suggests some commonality between these two opposing camps. They share the
assumption that the playhouse's primary function is to look backward in an
effort to recover the past. Neither side was therefore prepared for what has
happened since 1997. The Globe today is neither an empirical laboratory of
historical experimentation nor a conservative monument to "Merrie Olde
England." Instead it is, as Bryan Appleyard writes, "the beating heart of theatrical London" (8). Recently, hard-won critical acclaim has supplemented
the popular and economic success that the playhouse has enjoyed since the
beginning. It is "the only classical theatre in Britain that is making money
rather than losing it" (King 123). The *Daily Telegraph* reported in early 2006
that the Globe "had made a pre-tax profit of about £1.5 million every year
since it opened a decade ago" and had "filled 85 percent of its 1,500 places
every year" ("Shakespeare's Globe Makes £1.5 Million" 9). This popularity
caught the project's backers by surprise. Andrew Gurr admits, "None of us
believed it would attract big crowds ("Preface" 29). For Gurr, this unexpected
theatrical viability is "probably the biggest discovery in Shakespeare in the
past 10 years; a real revelation" (quoted in McCormack 3).

Part of the Globe's success is due to the power and responsibility it grants its audience. The proximity and visibility of playgoers connects them to the performers in a way not possible in traditional venues; and the absence of lighting effects and elaborate sets means that no production can proceed without the consent and participation of the public. Because of its casual atmosphere which encourages vociferous audience reaction, the Globe appeals to a demographic otherwise more likely to attend a sporting event than a play. Forty-three percent of Globe playgoers are first-time visitors (Carson, Christie, "Democratising" 123), many of whom, according to founding Artistic Director Mark Rylance, are "taking a chance on their first Shakespeare play" ("Research" 113). Ninety-seven percent of all Globe audiences respond positively when asked if they find the playhouse "welcoming and accessible," which for Christie Carson indicates a "cultural accessibility" that distinguishes the Globe from more traditional theatrical venues ("Democratising" 123). The Bankside amphitheater may therefore help reverse a hundred-year trend in which performances of Shakespeare have gone from being celebrations of "carnivalesque popular culture" to bastions of "middle class respectability" (Shepherd and Womack 116). If so, it will fulfill the prophecy of its founder, Sam Wanamaker, who predicted that "the Globe will make the *theatre* (not only Shakespeare) once again popular, public and accessible" (quoted in Holderness, "Interview" 21). This supposed monument to the past may therefore actually be the playhouse of tomorrow. To measure its potential as a postmodern paradigm, I will consider the factors that have contributed to the Globe's success as well as those shortcomings which might profitably be avoided in future reconstructions.

The Quest for Authenticity

UPON reviewing the historical record for the first time, one is struck by how little evidence exists of the original Globe's size and appearance. Jean Wilson notes that even the archaeologists from the British Museum who in 1989 excavated the historical Globe site (a few hundred feet from the reconstructed amphitheater) assumed that more was known about this early modern structure than is actually the case. While these scientists shared an "unconscious assumption" that the Bankside reconstruction was based on a great deal of available data, in reality the new Globe relied "according to preferred definition, on rigorous scholarly inquiry into a variety of sources leading to informed deduction, or guesswork" (Wilson 166–7). Gurr acknowledges that the project utilized a "'best guess' technique" ("Shakespeare's Globe" 35). This kind of "guesswork," however, was far from haphazard and involved the rigorous efforts of dozens, if not hundreds, of scholars over many decades. The challenge was the quantity and quality of evidence surviving from the early modern era. Before the discovery of archaeological remains, experts based their understanding of the Globe on four contradictory illustrations of its exterior; one drawing of the interior of a different but roughly contemporary amphitheater; and the building contract for a third playhouse which makes frequent allusions to the Globe.

In 1790 Edmund Malone became the first major figure to postulate the

appearance of the original Globe, which he identified as a hexagonal structure. Malone had access to Philip Henslowe's papers documenting this
impresario's dealings at the Rose and Fortune theaters, but Gurr suggests that
this archive does not attest to a six-sided shape and that Malone's reasons for
embracing this model are unclear ("Shakespeare's Globe" 27). Malone may
have been influenced by Hester Thrale, a friend of Samuel Johnson's. Thrale
claimed to live on land that contained the ruins of the Globe, which were
exposed during an expansion of her husband's brewery. Malone wrote, in a
supplementary volume to the second edition of Shakespeare's plays edited
by Johnson, that "the *Globe,* though hexagonal at the outside, was probably a rotunda within" (quoted in Clout 43). This mirrors Thrale's assertion that the playhouse "tho' hexagonal in form *without,* was round *within*"
(quoted in Clout 36). Martin Clout believes that Malone's "reiteration of the
Globe's hexagonal form" was "most probably derived from Dr. Johnson" with
"Thrale's excavation as the source of that information" (44). Clout also suggests that there is "some evidence of an early archaeological intention" behind
the brewery dig (39).

Scholars have long rejected Mrs Thrale's theory. According to C. Walter
Hodges in 1953, she saw "not the ruin of the Globe, but of some old tene-
ments a little way off to the south of it, which were demolished in 1767"
(*Globe Restored* 20). Her cause is not helped by the fact that Thrale's current
champion, Martin Clout, operates on the fringes of the research community.
Barry Day describes him as a "self-proclaimed Shakespearean scholar and
historian – mainly because other academics d[o]n't consider him to be one
of their number" (152). Nevertheless, the 1989 discovery of Globe remains
on the site of Mrs Thrale's one-time property challenges the traditional view
of her account. "It may be," Wilson writes, "that generations of male theatre
historians owe one intelligent and well-educated eighteenth-century lady a
profound apology" (181). Even if Thrale did observe a portion of the Globe's
ruins, however, her description of them as six-sided remains doubtful. She
did not claim to have seen the entire shape of the structure, but only one
"angle of the outer gallery foundation and one or two angles of the inner gallery foundation." It was only by speculating what the Globe's shape would be
"if the angle of the outer gallery foundation was repeated around the theatre"
that she arrived at her hexagonal conclusion (Clout 41). The irregular shape
revealed by the Rose excavation makes any such attribution of regular foundation patterns to Elizabethan playhouses highly speculative.

Malone's six-sided Globe was replaced in nineteenth-century conceptions
by the circular amphitheater represented in a 1610 map by Joducus Hondius.
Hondius portrays the playhouse as a round building that either sits on top of
a giant foundation or has some kind of skirt around its lower story. This image
was the basis for William Poel's 1897 model of the Globe and for the 1912 Earl's
Court Globe designed by Edwin Lutyens, both of which incorporated a covered walk-way around their lower sections as a means of explaining the skirt
seen in Hondius. I. A. Shapiro, in a groundbreaking 1948 *Shakespeare Survey*
article which systematically analyzed the visual evidence from early modern
engravings, writes that Hondius's "emphatic representation of [the Globe] as

circular is contemporary evidence not to be brushed aside" (32). Other contemporary representations, however, do not include the odd protuberance at the amphitheater's base.

After the Folger Shakespeare Library opened in 1932, widespread reproduction of C. J. Visscher's 1616 "View of London," a copy of which was owned by the Folger, led to this engraving's supplanting the Hondius map in scholarly notions of the Globe (Figure 13). Visscher inspired, for instance, the theater John Cranford Adams designed as part of the Folger Library in Washington, DC along with Adams's plans for a reconstructed amphitheater. The engraving portrays the Globe as a six or eight-sided polygon. Slightly more than three sides are visible, and it is difficult to ascertain how many remain unseen. Gurr describes the Visscher playhouse as "a three-storeyed octagonal structure, as tall as it is broad, sloping inwards towards the top" (*Rebuilding* 35). Shapiro's article discredited Visscher as a source. It demonstrated that this engraving was not "an original work" and that "the reliability of all versions of Visscher's view is suspect" (Shapiro 27). "There are so many inaccuracies in its representation of Southwark," Shapiro wrote, "that it seems doubtful if Visscher was ever there, and in fact there seems to be no evidence that he either worked in or visited London" (27–8). Despite falling out of academic favor, the Visscher image continued to circulate. The cover illustration of C. Walter Hodge's 1953 *The Globe Restored* features a God-like hand holding the Visscher Globe in its palm.

According to Shapiro and later academic consensus, Visscher lifted his image of the Globe from *Civitas Londini*, a view of London composed in 1600 by John Norden. Yet, paradoxically, scholars soon embraced this source of

13 A detail from Claes Visscher's engraving of London, showing the Bear Garden and the Globe

Visscher's polygonal amphitheater as evidence that the Globe was circular. This was possible because Norden's work actually contains two images of the Globe. In a broader panorama the playhouse appears as polygonal, but in a smaller "inset map of London" it is round. Shapiro writes of the panorama that because it "shows all four theatres as polygonal its accuracy of detail must be immediately suspect" because "evidence of, at the very least, one 'round house' among the Bankside theatres is overwhelming" (29). The evidence to which Shapiro refers consists of the Hondius map and an undated engraving by Francisco Delaram which, because of the uncertain identity of the playhouse represented therein, suggests "that the Beargarden *or* the Rose *or* the Globe was cylindrical" (25). For Shapiro, the polygonal structures in the panorama of *Civitas Londini* are "purely conventional" and do not represent the actual appearance of the Bankside playhouses. The panorama itself, "or at least that part which depicts Southwark," is probably "by another hand" than Norden's (30). Shapiro takes the representation of the Globe in the inset map to be accurate because "apart from engravings whose authenticity is suspect, all the positive evidence confirms Norden's representation of these theatres as round" (28).

To a certain extent Shapiro's reasoning is, like the playhouse design he

14 A detail from Hollar's "Long View" of London, showing Southwark, including the Bear Garden and the Globe (captions reversed)

champions, circular. Visscher is wrong because he copied from Norden's panorama, which is wrong because it shares an image with Visscher. In reality, all of the contemporary images of the Globe discussed thus far have credibility problems. Andrew Gurr, collaborating with archaeologist Simon Blatherwick in an article for the journal *Antiquity*, writes that "pictorial evidence about the first Globe, by Norden, Visscher, Hondius, Delaram and others, is imprecise and unreliable, depicting it with equal unreliability as circular, hexagonal, or octagonal" (Blatherwick and Gurr 327–8). A more trustworthy source is Wenceslas Hollar's "Long View" of both shores of the Thames (Figure 14). A native of Prague, Hollar was a "Bohemian artist" in the geographical sense of the term. Before the Civil War, Hollar was "drawing master to the young prince, later King Charles II." During the conflict, he served for a short time in the same royalist garrison as "the aged architect Inigo Jones" (Hodges, *Shakespeare's Second Globe* 12). Hodges writes that Hollar's intention in his "Long View" was to "publish a faithfully executed panorama" of London. By combining etchings from seven large plates, Hollar created "one of the longest, most accurate, and most comprehensive portrait views of any great city ever made" (11). Future scholars have been grateful for his efforts, because the "Long View" is "the one and only image" of the Globe "from the hand of a reliable draughtsman which has survived" (14).

Yet problems exist even with this most credible of contemporary illustrations. Hollar did not move to England until 1637. The amphitheater pictured in his "Long View" is therefore the second Globe, built after the original was destroyed by fire in 1613. While contemporary building regulations and other documents suggest that this later structure was built upon the foundations of the first, there is no way of knowing exactly how much the second Globe differed from the playhouse constructed in 1599. Another complication is that Hollar's evidence actually consists of two distinct representations. The first is the original drawing the artist made in London "at a time near the beginning of the English Civil War" (Hodges, *Shakespeare's Second Globe* 11). The second is the 1647 etching Hollar made from this illustration in Antwerp. This latter depiction includes features not found in the primary sketch, which seem to have been added from a combination of memory and invention. Most notoriously, the Globe in Hollar's etching is topped by an onion-shaped cupola, which seems to owe more to the artist's "youth in Bohemia" than to anything he would have seen on Bankside (73). Hollar's etching labels two playhouses. One is called "The Globe" and the other, intended to represent the Hope Playhouse which also featured animal combats, carries the inscription "Beere bayting." The names of these amphitheaters were accidentally reversed by the artist in 1647. While experts have long dismissed this as a simple error of transposition, it is nonetheless unsettling. Because of the etching's comparative unreliability, Globe reconstructors have focused instead on Hollar's original drawing. This image too has provoked some controversy, because its original pencil lines have been partially inked over, leading scholars to disagree as to which lines should be used to estimate the amphitheater's dimensions. This would be a point of great contention during the final stage of the Wanamaker project.

While contemporary representations of the Globe's exterior are contradictory and confusing, there are at least several options to choose from. No
such luxury exists for reconstructing the playhouse's interior. As John Peter
writes, "We simply don't know what the Globe stage was like. There is no,
repeat no, actual evidence." All we have is a "drawing, not of the Globe but
of the Swan, by the Dutch traveler Johannes de Witt," which Peter describes
as "an extremely amateurish piece of work with muddled perspectives and
almost certainly done from memory" ("Dramatic" 14). The Swan was an
amphitheater built four years before the Globe in the same Bankside neighborhood. The drawing to which Peter refers (Figure 15) was drafted in 1596
by Aernout van Buchell from a sketch by de Witt. Copies were discovered in
1888 by Karl Theodore Gaedertz in the library of the University at Utrecht.
Graham Holderness notes that, while the new Globe's planners have been
wary of "Disneyfication," the "touristic component of the Shakespeare industry" in the late sixteenth century ironically provided much of what we now
know about English playhouses through the testimony of foreign "tourists"
like de Witt ("Bardolatry" 8).

The Swan drawing portrays what we have come to think of as an Elizabethan tiring-house façade, in front of which an elevated stage protrudes into
the yard of an amphitheatre. This stage is partially covered by a roof that is
supported by two large pillars. While the drawing's perspective is imperfect,
it clearly depicts these pillars as placed no more than half-way downstage.
At the new Globe these posts are much further forward, which creates significant sight-line challenges. There are two upstage doors in the *frons scenae*
depicted in the Swan drawing, but there is no central entrance or "discovery
space." The new Globe has such an alcove, but its existence is unsupported
by this sole extant representation of interior playhouse design. Problems
of visibility related to this feature in the current Globe have led Richard
Proudfoot to quip, "For those who are seated in the side galleries on all three
levels and in the Lords' Room above the stage, the discovery space might
more aptly be named 'concealment space,' as they can see nothing" revealed
in this opening (215). Tiffany Stern provides one possible solution to these
sight-line problems when she writes that "historically at the Globe members
of the audience had freedom of movement in the galleries as well as in the
yard" ("You that walk" 211), and that spectators could thereby shift position
to avoid visual obstacles. This behavior seems incredible today, but Ralph
Alan Cohen reports that during a 2002 production of *The Winter's Tale* at
the reconstructed Blackfriars Playhouse "audience members too far upstage
to have a view into the discovery space so wanted to see the statue Paulina
revealed that they stood and moved to a better vantage spot" ("Directing"
223). Cohen's description of these perambulators as "well-dressed people"
and "pillars of the community" (223) suggests that a less-inhibited audience
at the original Globe might have readily followed a similar course of action.
Cohen claims that Paulina's injunction, "Then all stand still" (5.3.95), spoken
immediately prior to the reanimation of Hermione, may have been originally
intended to still these wandering spectators (224).

Besides contemporary illustrations, scholars have long relied on a key

15 A drawing of the Swan playhouse, copied by Aernout von Buchell
from a sketch by his friend Johannes de Witt, who made
the original drawing in 1596 when he visited London

piece of documentary evidence. In 1600, Philip Henslowe hired Peter Streete (sometimes spelled Street) to build the Fortune playhouse. Streete had constructed the Globe in 1599, and Henslowe wanted him to build the Fortune largely in imitation of this amphitheater. The contract for this work has survived, and Franklin J. Hildy calls it "the Rosetta Stone of Shakespearean playhouse studies" ("Reconstructing" 3). Many scholars, however, express frustration with its contents. Jean Wilson laments that in the Fortune contract "the Globe is used as a point of reference and comparison, which is unfortunate, because instead of illuminating both theatres, this tends to cloud our knowledge of both. Except where specified, everything is to be 'like the Globe': but we have no idea what the Globe was like" (75). John Orrell similarly complains of the contract's "exasperating and repeated allusions" to the Globe, references which are largely meaningless without more knowledge of this earlier structure ("Designing" 52–3).

Because the Fortune contract tends to give "particular details only – or mostly – where the model of the Globe was to be departed from" (Orrell, "Designing" 53), it might today be easier to reconstruct the Fortune than the Globe. This is what the German scholars Ludwig Tieck and Gottfried Semper attempted in the 1830s. The details provided in the Fortune contract allowed them to successfully design the theater's exterior and auditorium. "It was when they came to the stage, however," Hildy writes, "that these two men ran into trouble" ("Reconstructing" 6). The preconceptions of their era led Tieck and Semper to "carry the stage across the full 55' width of the yard and into the side galleries, converting them into conventional *wing spaces*," a configuration which produced "an audience arrangement that was essentially frontal and – predictably – not significantly different from the arrangement to be found in the early nineteenth century" (8). Plans reproduced by Gurr for a proposed Elizabethan "Mermaid Theatre" in the 1930s show a similar design (*Rebuilding* 32). The power of the proscenium had apparently not lessened during the intervening century. As it was, lack of funding scuttled both projects. Neither Tieck's plan nor the Mermaid ever went beyond the drawing board.

After the discovery of the de Witt drawing in 1888, no significant new evidence of early modern playhouse design appeared for over a century. Scholars had to content themselves with reinterpreting the existing data, alternately favoring one model or another according to prevailing trends. Then in 1989 archaeological excavation began at the site of the Rose, followed shortly thereafter by a smaller dig at the Globe. Because the majority of its site lies beneath an occupied apartment house, progress at the Globe has been tantalizingly frustrating. "It reveals," complained Wanamaker's lead architect Theo Crosby, "just enough to be irritating" (quoted in Day 207). The excavation of the Rose, by contrast, produced data from two separate incarnations of this playhouse, the original 1587 construction and a 1592 remodeling, which challenged many elements of the scholarly consensus and gave new authority to discarded models. C. Walter Hodges, for instance, had long argued for rectangular stages in Elizabethan playhouses, and took these platforms to be the descendants of similar scaffolds used in medieval street performances. He therefore rejected the tapered stages advocated by John Cranford Adams. Yet Hodges noted with chagrin in 1990 that the Rose dig revealed this theater's stage to be "tapered, just as Adams showed it" ("What is Possible" 43). The overall shape of the excavated playhouse further restored Adams's prestige. Gabriel Egan observes that "the theoretical reconstruction to which the uncovered Rose bore closest resemblance was, to everyone's surprise, the discredited Globe of John Cranford Adams," which had been inspired by Visscher's polygonal image (11).

The down-sized Globe at the 1912 "Shakespeare's England" exhibition, which Gurr had derided as a "Lutyens fantasy" inspired by the whims of its architect ("Shakespeare's Globe" 46), also gained newfound credibility. Hildy notes that the Rose revealed by the excavations "turns out to be much closer in size to Lutyens's Globe than to any of the reconstructions proposed since" ("Reconstructing" 23). Sometimes evidence from the digs pointed away from the current consensus, but not toward any previous theoretical model. "Upon first glance the remains of the Rose controverted the most basic assumptions about playhouse design," Egan writes. "The groundplans of both phases were irregular polygons, and so chaos prevailed where order was expected" (10–11).

With so many flaws in the conventional wisdom revealed by just a small amount of archaeological evidence, one can reasonably ask whether the chimera of historical accuracy is worth pursuing. Andrew Gurr describes " 'authenticity' " in the aftermath of the excavations as "a concept which even now, or perhaps especially now, I have to quarantine in quotation marks" ("Shakespeare's Globe" 46). Hugh Richmond suggests that, rather than trying to rebuild the Globe authentically, it would be better to create a theater that merely captures the general qualities of an Elizabethan playhouse ("Techniques" 162). The problem with Richmond's logic is that there is no way of knowing which particular Elizabethan elements will significantly impact performance until they are recreated. Seemingly trivial attributes may ultimately prove important. Hildy asserts, for instance, that earlier twentieth-century theaters built on an Elizabethan model missed a tremendous opportunity by not stacking their public in layers ("Reconstructing" 13). Another unexpected discovery at the new Globe has been the formidable energy created by an audience standing in close proximity to the stage, an option not explored by Nugent Monck or Tyrone Guthrie. "No one believed," writes Hildy, "that five hundred to seven hundred people would pay to stand at every performance, but they do" ("Why Elizabethan" 117). The response of these "understanders" has been enthusiastic. "I was a groundling for all four plays," writes Lois Potter of the 1999 season, adding that this is "by far the best way to see them" (Potter, "Stage" 81). The "special acoustics" that John Russell Brown predicted would result from the use of authentic building materials (21), have also been a factor in the amphitheater's success. Even W. B. Worthen, suspicious of historical authenticity, acknowledges that "it would be difficult to reproduce the surprisingly clear yet rich acoustics of the Globe with harder materials" than the traditional timbers currently employed ("Reconstructing" 45).

No matter how hard it tries, however, the new Globe will never be truly

"authentic." One can view this fact harshly, or one can adopt the philosophical approach C. Walter Hodges arrived at after half a century spent trying
to rebuild Shakespeare's playhouse. Hodges was fond of drawing low railings
around his depictions of Elizabethan stages, and continued to do so even
after he had been convinced that this feature was historically inaccurate.
He explained that such anachronisms "form an unconscious pattern which
belongs to the period in which the work was created, and so eventually they
become interesting and valid in themselves." Any theatrical reconstruction
must, for Hodges, inevitably share the fate of Ludwig Tieck's attempt to recreate the Fortune, which if it had been built "would today stand as a splendid
example not so much of an Elizabethan London theatre, but of nineteenth-
century German Romanticism. It would be as it were two historic buildings
in one, and an excellent theatre besides" ("What is Possible" 48). I would
add that the true value of reconstruction lies not in finding out how specific
factors might have impacted early modern performance, but rather in dis-
covering how Elizabethan conventions can energize theatrical representation today. As Potter wrote in 1999, "However inauthentic a recreation of the
seventeenth-century experience, the Globe seems to me to offer a perfectly
authentic – and enjoyable – twentieth-century one" ("Stage" 81).

Earl's Court and the Chicago World's Fair

"Shakespeare's England"

William Poel began the modern quest for Elizabethan playhouse reconstruction in 1893 with his "Fortune fit-up." This structure attempted to recreate an
early modern stage within the confines of the proscenium theaters where Poel
staged his revivals. Marion O'Connor refers to the fit-up as a "flagrantly fake
Elizabethan stage" and a "tawdry specimen of low-budget Victorian stagecraft" ("Theatre of Empire" 71). Poel recognized its limitations and therefore
set out to design a more authentic early modern space. In 1897, exactly one
hundred years before Wanamaker's amphitheater opened on Bankside, Poel
drafted plans for a replica of the Globe based on the Hondius illustration.
The de Witt drawing also apparently influenced Poel's design, as its roof covered only half the stage. A model was built from these plans in 1902, and this
miniature Globe was used in promotional efforts by the London Shakespeare
Commemoration League to fund the reconstruction of a full-sized playhouse.

In 1900, Poel petitioned the London County Council for a grant of land
on which to build an outdoor amphitheater. Current regulations prohibited a
structure of this kind in London, so the League's campaign shifted toward the
erection of a "Shakespeare Temple" (a name that suggests literal bardolatry),
which would include a memorial statue. Tentative agreement was reached on
this plan in 1905. Poel then attempted to include within this memorial a scaled-
down theater he defined as "a building in which Shakespeare's plays could be
acted without scenery" (*Shakespeare in the Theatre* 231). This modest Elizabethan performance space was scuttled by the objections of Herbert Beerbohm Tree, and the "Shakespeare Temple" scheme eventually fizzled. In 1908,

Poel's idea for a reconstructed Globe merged with the developing notion of a National Theatre. This was the kiss of death, as Poel's vision became mired in the many bureaucratic disputes related to this venture. "It would be tedious to relate (except for purposes of satire)," Robert Speaight writes, "the subsequent activities of the National Theatre Committee" (*William Poel* 214). When this theatrical institution was finally formed after World War II, it no longer maintained any commitment to Elizabethan reconstruction.

Meanwhile, Poel's Globe caught the attention of Mrs George Cornwallis West, the former Lady Randolph Churchill and the American-born mother of the future Prime Minister. She engaged the services of the architect Edwin Lutyens to build an amphitheater from Poel's model for the 1912 "Shakespeare's England" exhibition at Earl's Court. Lutyens was known for recreating architectural styles from earlier eras, including the Tudor period. He was also a theatrical designer and planned the original sets for the 1904 premiere of J. M. Barrie's *Peter Pan*. According to Marion O'Connor, Lutyens was an elitist who used his architectural gifts to advance the interests of the British ruling class. The architect modeled the children's home in *Peter Pan* after his own family's dwelling, and O'Connor notes that he omitted any reference to the servants or their quarters. She sees similar "erasures" in Lutyens's efforts at "Shakespeare's England" ("Theatre of Empire" 76). For O'Connor, this exhibition served a reactionary agenda by representing only "one version of English history. It was a version that so emphasized one class as to exclude most of the nation and so emphasized continuity as to occlude change" (94).

Certain aspects of "Shakespeare's England" support O'Connor's thesis. She describes a courtly tournament held at the exhibition as an opportunity for "the ruling class of 1912" to confirm their status through a "display of expenditure and equestrian abilities" (93–4). By these means, "the celebration of the past" at Earl's Court was turned into "a justification of the present" (91). O'Connor's interpretation of Frank Benson's participation in this tournament is, however, simplistic. The *Times* announced on 3 July 1912 that Benson would serve as "the Herald and 'producer' (in theatrical parlance)" for this event ("Elizabethan Tourney" 11). O'Connor describes Benson as an "Oxford graduate whose Shakespearean touring company played at Cheltenham Ladies' College in morning dress" ("Theatre of Empire" 92), thereby implicating him in what she perceives as the tournament's function of solidifying class privilege. This reading overlooks Benson's status as a Socialist and follower of the Pre-Raphaelite revolutionary William Morris. Rather than a sycophantic endorsement of the ruling class, Benson's activities at "Shakespeare's England" reflect the complex ideological relationship of the Elizabethan movement to the status quo.

On the one hand, nostalgia for the early modern period suggests a longing for absolute monarchy. The presence of the royal family at "Shakespeare's England" in 1912 combines with the contemporary support of Prince Philip for the new Globe in Southwark to suggest that British royalty have sometimes used Elizabethan reconstruction to legitimize their status. The naïve sense of national community created by "Shakespeare's England" may qualify as what John Drakakis calls "the manufacture and periodic mobilization of a reactionary populism – usually in support of royal weddings and foreign quarrels – which, even at the relatively urbane level, works to obscure historical difference" (26). But the scientific-industrial complex, rather than the constitutional monarchy to which Benson paid playful homage at "Shakespeare's England," was the real center of power in the twentieth century. The Pre-Raphaelite brand of Socialism to which Benson, Poel, and Nugent Monck subscribed abhorred this hegemony of technological positivism and sought to subvert it. Elizabethanism cannot therefore simply be interpreted as the reactionary embrace of a feudal world picture. It was instead primarily a progressive attempt to find solutions to the injustices of the modern age.

The actor-manager Patrick Kirwan, who later headed the Shakespeare Memorial Theatre at Stratford-on-Avon, staged brief selections from Shakespeare's plays in the Globe replica at Earl's Court. The most notorious feature of these spectacles was the presence of costumed performers in the pit, who boisterously impersonated an Elizabethan audience. According to O'Connor, these ersatz orange-wenches and apprentices were "on display as objects of popular-audience identification." They emphasized "the merriment of the Elizabethan chapter in the national story" as "a matter of machismo, imperialism, and Shakespeare" ("Theatre of Empire" 91). An imperialist mindset did inform some aspects of "Shakespeare's England." A lake on the grounds, for instance, included a replica of Francis Drake's ship, the *Revenge*. Winston Churchill, then First Secretary of the Admiralty, used a re-enactment of Drake's sailing against the Spanish Armada as the occasion for a speech urging British naval expansion in the North Sea as part of the build-up to World War I. Yet while O'Connor describes "the Globe and the *Revenge*" as "the pair that dominated the visual display" (91) at Earl's Court, her connection of Kirwan's imitation groundlings to an imperialist agenda is tenuous. Their exuberant behavior hardly seems in the same league with Churchill's ode to militarism. Simon Shepherd and Peter Womack propose a subtler ideological function for the pseudo-audience at "Shakespeare's England."

Despite the oft-quoted passage from *Hamlet*, early modern references to "groundlings" are very rare. If used at all, the word generally referred to a kind of fish. It was not until the nineteenth century that the term came to commonly represent ill-behaving "understanders" in Elizabethan playhouses. The "groundling" is therefore "a class myth, whose structure has as much to do with the period of its formation (the nineteenth century) as with the period on to which it is projected (the sixteenth)" (Shepherd and Womack 112). The rise of the groundling in critical thought coincided with the demise of the theatrical "pit." This was the inexpensive, ground-level area directly in front of the stage, which had no reserved seats and offered only open spaces on backless benches. Beginning with the redesign of the Haymarket in 1880, this model gradually gave way to a modern paradigm in which the closest seats are the most expensive. Less affluent patrons were pushed back further from the stage and eventually out of the theaters all together. Shepherd and Womack suggest that the groundlings' "appearance in the accepted picture of Elizabethan theatres is an ideological reflex of their expulsion from Victorian ones" (115). By portraying poorer spectators as barbaric and ill-mannered in critical writings about the early modern era and in the reconstructed venue at Earl's Court, the theatrical and academic establishment marked the playhouse in general, and Shakespeare in particular, as the preserve of the upper classes. Working-class audiences got the message and largely stayed away from performances of Shakespeare for most of the twentieth century.

Poel's reaction to the reconstructed Globe at "Shakespeare's England" was not favorable. Lutyens made several changes to Poel's design, shrinking the size of the overall structure and reducing the depth of its platform stage. Poel demonstrated his commitment to thrust staging when he complained that Lutyens's structure "lacked the essential feature of an Elizabethan playhouse – that is, the projection of the platform into the middle of the arena" ("Shakespeare Memorial Theatre" 10). He reserved his sharpest criticism, however, for the performances at "Shakespeare's England" and, particularly, for "the costumed figures who are supposed to impersonate the 'groundlings'" (*Shakespeare in the Theatre* 208). O'Connor claims that Poel "took antiquarian offense" to this imitation audience ("Theatre of Empire" 88), but his objections were not archaist. Poel merely resisted the "theme park" atmosphere of the Earl's Court event, the very attribute which O'Connor elsewhere laments in connection to theatrical reconstructions ("Useful" 32). "The obsolete but picturesque phrase 'Ye Olde' has perhaps something fascinating in it to the modern aesthetic temperament," Poel wrote, but he rejected this fetishization of the antique. "To the Elizabethan the Globe was a new building; there was nothing 'Olde' about it" (*Shakespeare in the Theatre* 208).

"Shakespeare's England" was the closest Poel ever came to seeing the Globe rebuilt. He failed in his other efforts at reconstruction, and the resulting frustration led him to refuse a knighthood in 1929 as a protest against "those who were content to regard the building of a Shakespeare playhouse as being solely a business proposition" (quoted in Speaight, *William Poel* 254). Nor were later British attempts to erect an Elizabethan amphitheater successful. "More than half a century after Poel made his proposal," Speaight lamented in 1954, "the Globe Theatre remains a blue-print. Is it too much to hope that by the time the quarter-centenary of Shakespeare's birth is celebrated in 1964, the blue-print may have been converted into a building?" (*William Poel* 215). As it turns out, this was too much to hope, but the project would eventually be realized.

The Chicago World's Fair

In 1934, the same year William Poel died, Sam Wanamaker first encountered Shakespeare's Globe. British writers have sometimes exaggerated the hard-boiled dangers and privations of Wanamaker's upbringing. The actor was born in Chicago in 1919. Barry Day writes that this "was the era of Al Capone and prohibition. Gangster John Dillinger was shot outside the cinema Sam and [his brother] Bill used to frequent. You couldn't live in the ghetto and not be able to look after yourself" (45). The Biograph, where Dillinger met his demise, is actually located in a fashionable neighborhood near Lincoln Park, far from the "ghetto." While Day later notes that Sam lived "on the wrong side of town" from this fashionable Lakefront district (48), Wanamaker's ability to attend Drake University in Iowa and the Goodman Theatre School suggests that he was not a street urchin. This does not, of course, minimize the sacrifices Wanamaker's working-class parents made to send Sam and his brother to university, or the very real physical toughness that Wanamaker needed to fend off beatings from anti-Semitic schoolmates. He was, however, no Bugsy Siegel (although both men shared a passion for real-estate development).

The child of Ukrainian immigrants, Wanamaker had no interest in Shakespeare before he first encountered the playwright's work at the 1934 Chicago World's Fair, known as the Century of Progress Exhibition. Wanamaker was lured to the Fair by the promise of "free spectacle – English Morris-dancing and Queen Elizabeth and her courtiers" at the Exhibition's "Elizabethan Village" (Wanamaker quoted in Holderness, "Interview" 21). More salacious entertainment was also available in the form of "a sideshow in which Lady Godiva repeat[ed] her historic equestrian accomplishment hourly for Peeping Toms" (Martin X2). 1934 was the second year for the Century of Progress, and the previous Exhibition had been very different. The 1933 Fair embraced a relentless positivism through its celebration of modern technology. R. L. Duffus questioned the efficacy of extolling man's "too fanatical inventiveness" at a time when "a century of dazzling scientific advancement has culminated in unemployment and misery" (SM1), but the first Century of Progress Exhibition remained unapologetically futuristic. While Wanamaker visited a recreation of Elizabethan England in 1934, the previous year had been dominated by a very different European import.

On 15 July 1933 *The New York Times* reported, "More than 100,000 Chicagoans and World's Fair visitors, massed on and near the Navy Pier, roared a tremendous welcome late this afternoon to 100 gallant Italian airmen under the command of General Italo Balbo as they brought the first of their twenty-four huge seaplanes safely to rest on the waters of Lake Michigan" ("100,000 at Chicago" 1). Balbo's armada had been scheduled to coincide with the Century of Progress in order to demonstrate "Italy's technical development of modern aviation" and to "bring a message of friendship to the United States" in "the eleventh year of the Fascist revolution" (Balbo quoted in "Southern Route Safer" 15). For the first time since the sixteenth century, Italy represented the vanguard of modernity. President Roosevelt called Balbo and his companions "most welcome visitors" and expressed "great admiration for their achievement" (quoted in "Southern Route Safer" 15). Chicago embraced the Italian General, proclaiming 15 July "Italo Balbo Day" ("Chicago to Mark" 3) and re-christening a street in the South Loop after the aviator. Balbo Drive remains to this day probably the only avenue in America named for an Axis war hero. Wanamaker's unionist background and family history insulated him from fascist influence, but one nevertheless wonders what ideas a young man of Sam's energy and determination might have taken away from the World's Fair in 1933.

While the first Century of Progress Exhibition had been financially successful, organizers were somewhat alarmed by its excessive modernity and sought in 1934 to offer something more traditional. There was also a desire to raise the tone and "display more of the meritorious and less of the meretricious" (Duncan-Clark E7). A simulated "Belgian village" had been popular in 1933, and organizers expanded on this idea by presenting a variety of nationally themed exhibits, including one devoted to early modern England. The Fair's planners recruited Thomas Wood Stevens to build a Globe for inclusion in this Tudor attraction. Stevens was a pioneer in educational theater and had worked with Ben Iden Payne at the Carnegie Institute of Technology to advance the cause of Elizabethan staging. His Chicago Globe was, according to Franklin J. Hildy, "an odd combination of the Fortune contract and the then prevalent idea [from Visscher] that the Globe was eight-sided" ("Reconstructing" 27). The design was compromised by the arrangement of its audience. Spectators in the pit did not stand, but rather sat on benches. The third, highest gallery was for appearances only and not used for seating. For Hildy, these deficiencies "prevented the space from generating the kind of energy and excitement we know these buildings were capable of producing" ("Why Elizabethan" 109). But the Chicago Globe was nevertheless a great success. More than 400,000 people attended performances, and many of these developed a new appreciation for Shakespeare on the stage.

Similar Globes were built in San Diego in 1935 and Dallas the following year. By 1936 Wanamaker, who had become an admirer of Shakespeare at the Century of Progress Exhibition, was performing in one of Stevens's three companies of players at the Great Lakes Festival in Cleveland. These troupes, working in California, Texas, and Ohio as well as on national tours, staged five thousand performances of early modern plays for over two million spectators between 1934 and 1937. This spawned an "explosion of Elizabethan revival activities" which eventually led to the establishment of hundreds of Shakespeare Festivals throughout the United States (Hildy, "Why Elizabethan" 111). One of the most distinguished products of this movement, the Chicago Shakespeare Theater, today resides at Navy Pier, the very spot where Balbo triumphantly landed in 1933. When an alternative to futuristic authoritarianism was badly needed, the Elizabethan movement offered a humanistic option.

Building Wanamaker's Globe

SAM Wanamaker first came to England in 1949 to play the role of Geremio in the cinematic adaptation of Pietro di Donato's novel *Christ in Concrete*, released in Britain under the title *Give Us This Day*. This was a neo-realist saga about Italian immigrants working in the American construction industry. Geremio is forced by economic pressure to work on an unsafe, non-union job site. He is killed when the building collapses, drowning him in a pool of liquid concrete. Wanamaker may have recalled this experience of being crushed and devoured by a construction project during the tribulations of his decades-long quest to build the Globe, a process he described as an "epic journey through a sea of icebergs" (quoted in Day 34). *Give Us This Day* was a perfect fit with the actor's political sympathies. The film was shot in England because its director, Edward Dmytryk, had been blacklisted by

Hollywood red-hunters, as had other members of the cast. While he was film-ing in London, Wanamaker discovered that there was no fitting monument to Shakespeare and conceived the notion of reconstructing the Globe on or near its original location. Despite his passion for this project, it was placed on hold for the next twenty years.

During the 1950s, Wanamaker enjoyed great success on the London stage. He exemplified the American "Method," a style of acting which at the time constituted a great innovation. Kenneth Tynan described Wanamaker's tech-nique as "downright dangerous." "He enjoys smoldering," Tynan wrote, "and when smoldering is not enough, he throws things" (quoted in Day 51). Wana-maker played Iago to Paul Robeson's Othello at Stratford-on-Avon in 1959. The pairing of two Americans in these roles was too much for the English public, who vented their outrage at Sam. According to Barry Day, "words like 'Hollywood' and 'cowboy' were used freely" to describe his Iago (56). The *Times* description of Wanamaker's Iago as a "slick shyster" who "nobody could possibly trust" ("Miscasting" 14) hints at anti-Semitism as well as anti-Americanism, and the experience effectively ended Sam's British stage career. He never again played a leading role at Stratford or in the West End. Fortu-nately the McCarthy era was over, and Wanamaker felt comfortable returning to the United States. He spent the 1960s working internationally as a director and actor in both theater and film.

In 1969 Wanamaker began his campaign to build a Shakespearean theater as part of a broader Bankside development project. This plan was not driven by the considerations of monetary gain that inform most real-estate develop-ment. Although Wanamaker's critics characterized him as a "Shylock Ameri-can entrepreneur lining his pockets with the money he was coining from Britain's glorious cultural past" (Day 71), his actual goals were more altruis-tic. Some confusion regarding motivations is understandable because, while Wanamaker was articulate in his advocacy of the new Globe, he did not docu-ment the ideological underpinnings of his larger development plan. Architect Theo Crosby, a principal collaborator in both the Globe reconstruction and the proposed Bankside renewal, did describe a philosophy of urban planning, and his thoughts illuminate Wanamaker's project.

Crosby was highly critical of the "Modern movement," in which "to achieve the maximum benefits of technology" the "intellectual and creative elements in society must be bent to the service of the machine" (Crosby 8). Crosby believed that restoring "our feelings of continuity with the past" (87) could provide "a possible way out" (9) of this dilemma. He argued that it was necessary to preserve and, where necessary, recreate buildings from earlier eras because they were "enormous *examples* of an alternative mode of per-ception, of another set of priorities, an alternative to our accommodation to the industrial system" (9). Such "monuments carry a subversive message" because "they are reminders of our better selves, our communal responsibili-ties and of our present slavery to the requirements of the production process" (85). This philosophy links Crosby and Wanamaker to the Pre-Raphaelite sentiments of William Poel and Nugent Monck and to the suspicion of modernity expressed by Tyrone Guthrie.

Sam Wanamaker won Theo Crosby to his cause at a 1969 meeting of the Architectural Association when the actor presented a rather pathetic model for his proposed development which, according to Crosby, "seemed to consist of a lot of shoe boxes arranged all over the Thames" (quoted in Day 125). The architect saw past the defects of Wanamaker's presentation and grasped the sincerity and progressive intent behind his plan. Crosby signed on almost immediately, but few others were so readily convinced. The same anti-American sentiment which had plagued Wanamaker at Stratford bedeviled his efforts in the Bankside project. Suspicion that Sam was a carpetbagger merged with concerns that all of Southwark would be transformed into a kitschy theme park. The development scheme sought to distance itself from the specter of Disneyfication by enlisting the aid of leading academic experts in the construction of the playhouse at the project's center, thereby conferring an air of legitimacy on the entire endeavor. These authorities recommended that Wanamaker "build the most authentic reconstruction of Shakespeare's first Globe that modern scholarship was capable of producing" (Hildy, "Reconstructing" 29). From that point onward, historical accuracy became the *raison d'etre* of the Bankside movement. Authentic reconstruction, however, was no simple task.

In the early years, a number of different researchers took charge of the amphitheater's design. In 1970, Richard Southern initially led this effort and was followed briefly by Richard Hosley. The model produced by Southern and Hosley differs from the eventual reconstruction in its sixteen-sided form and in the fact that its "heavens" covered only the back of the stage, leaving the front section exposed to the elements. The Southern-Hosley Globe had a diameter of 100 feet, a figure determined by applying the 33-foot height established in the Fortune Contract to the image from Hollar's "Long View" and thereby deducing the structure's proportional width. John Orrell would eventually apply more complex calculations to Hollar's drawing to arrive at this same diameter.

C. Walter Hodges replaced Hosley, which led to a major philosophical argument. Hodges wanted to rebuild the second Globe, the one built in 1614. He reasoned that this was the structure represented in Hollar's drawing, which was the most reliable source of contemporary visual evidence. Hodges further believed that reconstructing the second Globe would allow the incorporation of advances in playhouse design which had occurred between 1599 and 1614. Chief among these was an improved building technique that allowed the roof over the stage to be supported without pillars. Hodges referred to the contract for the Hope playhouse, built at about the same time as the second Globe, which specified that "the Heavens all over the said stage [were] to be borne or carried without any posts or supporters to be fixed or set upon the said stage" (quoted in Hodges, *Shakespeare's Second Globe* 59). Such an arrangement would offer better sight lines than any configuration that included onstage pillars.

Wanamaker and his advisors rejected Hodges's plan because Shakespeare wrote no plays for the 1614 amphitheater. "By no stretch of the imagination," Day writes of this logic, "could you call the second Globe *Shakespeare's*

Globe" (81). Hodges countered that "the Second Globe has as much claim to be considered Shakespeare's theatre as had the first" because the playwright was still a shareholder during the 1614 reconstruction (*Shakespeare's Second Globe* 19). The dispute was irreconcilable, and Hodges left the Wanamaker team. He wrote in 1973, "In the summer of 1970 I was asked to advise in a project to build a full-size reconstruction of Shakespeare's Globe playhouse on or as near as possible to its historic site on Bankside." This endeavor, Hodges claims, "came to nothing – or at least declined into such a good imitation of coming to nothing that I am sure there cannot be any present offense in thinking so" (*Shakespeare's Second Globe* 7). After leaving Southwark, Hodges joined a similar project in Michigan. Despite Hodges's diagnosis, Wanamaker's amphitheater did not come "to nothing," but eventually rose on Bankside. The Detroit Globe, on the other hand, was never built.

As design went forward, the new Globe sought goodwill within the academic community. In 1971 the First International Shakespeare Conference in Vancouver, impressed by Wanamaker's audacious plan, issued a statement "that such a reconstruction would be of the greatest value to Shakespearean scholarship and to the history of the theatre, as well as of widespread interest to people and to education everywhere in the world" (quoted in Hodges, *Shakespeare's Second Globe* 7). Ten years later, however, at the Third International Shakespeare Conference in Stratford-on-Avon, the whole endeavor "was almost sand-bagged" by academics with ties to Stratford's Shakespeare industry. They feared "a rival Shakespearean venue not much more than a hundred miles to the south" and therefore refused to endorse the new Globe (Day 83). Following this conference, Andrew Gurr rallied support by circulating a letter among 200 Shakespeare scholars, asking them to sign in affirmation of the planned reconstruction. The only one to refuse was John Russell Brown, who had conflicts of interest as the academic advisor for the National Theater (located along the same riverfront as the proposed Southwark Globe) and as a supporter of the Detroit project. Gurr then met with Wanamaker and received a firm promise of "no compromise" regarding historical accuracy, although Gurr acknowledges that at this same meeting, "we had half an hour on whether to have a plastic roof" (quoted in Day 85). Rather than a first principle, "authenticity" was a philosophy Wanamaker accepted to win the support of academics.

Gurr skillfully built consensus by inviting scholarly experts to a series of planning seminars, hosted by Theo Crosby. These meetings were run "on the old Quaker principle of allowing people to argue until everyone agreed" (Day 87). John Orrell took over design duties, and in the early 1980s the project was moving forward. Then, in 1982, several leftist opponents of the new Globe were elected to the Southwark Council. They sought to renege on an earlier agreement which would have allowed Wanamaker to build on a lot currently used for the storage of trash-collection equipment. The Council wanted this proposed site to be used instead for housing. Wanamaker agreed that there should be housing nearby but asserted that these flats could be built elsewhere. The reconstructed playhouse, he insisted, would offer "a potential public amenity accessible to all" (quoted in Holderness, "Interview" 17).

A protracted court battle ensued. John Drakakis saw this as a clash between "Shakespeare and the Roadsweepers" (24) in which "the local inhabitants of the third poorest borough in England" (38) were "victim[s] of a cultural hegemony consisting of a power elite supported by an influential right-wing press" (31). Wanamaker, in Drakakis's view, displayed his true exploitative colors in a "final recourse to that most potent of ideological state apparatuses, the law" (30).

The Globe won the court case in 1986, and in retrospect the outcry at the time from critics like Drakakis seems overblown. Day notes that their position "was essentially based on the argument that the people of Southwark were against the Globe" but asks, "How true was this?" (178). Several of the evicted sanitation engineers met Wanamaker to congratulate him on his legal victory, and a photograph of "Sam, champagne bottle in hand, surrounded by back-slapping road sweepers" (Day 179; reproduced here as Figure 16) suggests that these Bankside residents did not feel unduly crushed or exploited.

A shortage of funding prevented work from moving forward in the immediate aftermath of the court victory. If money had been available, the Globe would have been built sooner but would not have had the benefit of several later discoveries. Before 1989, for instance, an authentic thatch roof would have been impossible due to fire regulations. It was only in that year that a new fire-retardant spray was developed which, together with a modern sprinkler system, brought the thatch roof up to code. More significantly, a Globe built in the 1980s could not have incorporated any findings from the

16 Sam Wanamaker with the road sweepers

excavations which began in 1989. As it was, the evaluation of this archaeological data created dissension within the design team. Until this time, Orrell
had posited a twenty-four-sided polygon 100 feet in diameter. He acknowledged that evidence from the digs rendered his twenty-four-sided model "not
only speculative but decidedly open to question" (quoted in Day 219). There
was no agreement, however, as to how many sides the Globe should have
or what its diameter should be. Andrew Gurr published all the available evidence and summoned scholars to an October 1992 seminar in order to reach a
decision.

The two major alternatives proposed at this meeting were Orrell's revised
plan of twenty sides with a 100-foot diameter and an eighteen-sided, 90-foot
model submitted by Franklin J. Hildy. The cases for these schemes are
thoughtful and complex, and were further developed in a series of articles
by both scholars. While considering the archaeological evidence, these arguments focus primarily on the validity of Orrell's painstaking "trigonometric
analysis" of the Hollar drawing, which takes into account the "anamorphosis"
by which "spheres and horizontal discs are distorted in true linear perspective if they are far removed from the central ray." Orrell concluded "that the
theatre was somewhere between 101.37 and 103.32 ft. wide, plus or minus a
further two percent" ("Accuracy" 7). Hildy questioned whether the Hollar
drawing was "ever intended to have the kind of accuracy Orrell's analysis
requires of it." He further noted that Orrell had "used the inked-in lines of
the drawing," while the original "pencil tracings" were "more reliable." Hildy
asserted that when these pencil lines were used the techniques of Orrell's
analysis yield "a Globe 93 ft. across" rather than "one of 100 ft." ("Minority
Report" 10). Orrell countered that the pencil marking on which Hildy made
his case was "not a deliberate line at all, but a scuff mark which continues its
random way through the area of the roof" ("Accuracy" 8).

This may seem an arcane dispute, but it has serious theatrical implications.
The diameter of the building necessarily determines the breadth of the yard,
which directly impacts performance. Hildy notes that "as the size of the yard
increases, the distance between the gallery audience and the stage increases"
resulting in "serious consequences for audibility" ("Minority Report" 9). The
scales were somewhat tilted in favor of Orrell's plan because two bays had
already been constructed to conform to his proposal. The burden of proof
was therefore higher for Hildy's scheme, which would have required the
costly dismantling of these sections. I do not presume to offer an opinion as
to whether a 90-foot or 100-foot diameter is better justified by the evidence.
I would instead suggest that if neither plan is conclusively superior in terms
of historical authenticity, as would seem to be the case when such esteemed
experts as Orrell and Hildy disagree, then the solution adopted should be
the one which best serves the building's theatrical function. Such considerations were rarely a factor in the new Globe's decision-making process. This
was partly due to under-representation of the theatrical community at planning meetings. While Gurr writes that "actors" and "directors" were present
at the "five major seminars" held prior to 1986 (*Rebuilding* 42), there is little
evidence of such participation. For example, a list of attendees from the 1983

and 1986 seminars, published in a supplement to *Renaissance Drama News-letter* ("Shape of the Globe" 2, 31), does not include any of the well-known performers, like Douglas Fairbanks, Jr., Michael York, and Nicol Williamson, who were then participating in Globe fundraising efforts or serving on the Artistic Directorate (Day 156). Nor were any of the cast members from the Globe's 1996 and 1997 seasons present at these meetings (Kiernan 158–61). Hildy, a Professor of Theater, called attention to the performance conse-quences of the 100-foot diameter, but he was outvoted. The presence of more theater practitioners might have swayed the decision in Hildy's favor.

As it is, the Globe has been successful in spite of the acoustic and visual challenges posed by its 100-foot diameter. "If the theatre consistently plays to eighty percent capacity audiences," Hildy wrote in 1992, "the apprehensions of the minority should seem groundless" ("Minority Report" 10). Actual attendance at the new Globe has exceeded this estimate, but touristic audi-ences seduced by London's charms have been particularly forgiving. Other early modern reconstructions currently in development, including a second Globe for the American Shakespeare Center in Staunton, Virginia, will not have the advantage of a historically authentic Bankside location. Their eco-nomic survival will depend on audience satisfaction, and they should there-fore carefully consider those "judgment calls" in design which affect the qual-ity of performance.

Another cautionary tale concerns the placement of onstage pillars, which Pauline Kiernan calls "the most controversial feature of the new Globe" (76). All the evidence, including the Swan drawing, the Fortune contract, and the Hollar and Norden illustrations, points to some kind of stage cover as a standard feature of early modern playhouses. In 1599, such a structure could not have been built without supportive pillars anchored in the stage. Hodges addresses the question of how these pillars would impact sight lines. "The answer must be," he writes, "that the pillars *did* impair visibility; and that was that. To what extent they did so would depend upon their exact placing" (*Globe Restored* 30). The further downstage the pillars are, the greater per-centage of stage action they will obstruct. A roof that covers the entire play-ing area would, by the methods of sixteenth-century construction, require supporting posts very far downstage. The Swan drawing, however, shows a "heavens" which covers only half the stage. A similar partial covering appears in William Poel's Globe, Hodges's 1953 design, and Southern and Hosley's early model for the Wanamaker project.

In 1982 John Orrell, with the support of seminar participants, rejected the Southern-Hosley demi-roof in favor of a "heavens" that would cover the entire stage, as suggested by the Hollar drawing. Of the exact placement of the supporting pillars, Day acknowledges, "For once there really was so little historical evidence to go on that it was anyone's guess. It was agreed to let structural considerations dictate the decision" (226). He does not specify that these "structural considerations" were determined by the notion that the new Globe's roof must shield its entire playing area. This assumption was based principally on the Hollar drawing, even though the amphitheater por-trayed therein is the second Globe which, according to Hodges, could have supported a full stage covering without the aid of pillars (*Shakespeare's Second Globe* 59). The de Witt sketch, by contrast, portrays the interior of an amphitheater built much closer in time to the first Globe and shows "the front of the stage" to be "unprotected by its roof" (Wilson 71).

As in the case of the controversy regarding diameter, my intention is not to suggest that a half-roof is necessarily better justified by contemporary evidence than a full-roof. Rather I assert that, where the historical record is unclear, designers should choose the option which best supports the playhouse's eventual function as a living theater. This was not the path taken by the new Globe's planners. Gurr, for instance, does not mention visual obstruction as a potential challenge in his discussion of the onstage pillars in *Rebuilding Shakespeare's Globe* (166). It was not until the "Workshop Season" of 1995 that the position of these stage posts became a point of contention. On 1 October John Peter reported in the *Sunday Times*, "A polite but ferocious row has blown up between the academic theatre historians who advised on the construction, and the artists who will have to use it" ("Dramatic" 14). The actors and directors of the Workshop Season, led by Peter Hall, complained that the onstage pillars unduly interfered with performance. These posts were too cumbersome, too far downstage, and too far out to each side. They therefore impeded both movement and visibility.

Supporters of the current design accused the theater practitioners of applying anachronistic preconceptions. These actors and directors were, Day writes, "prompted by a desire to adapt the theatre to their hard-learned techniques rather than adapt their techniques to a new and challenging space" (298). For Alan Dessen, the objections from Workshop participants were an example of the essentialist attitude that "theater is theater." These stubborn thespians relied on their "intuitions" in insisting that "no sensible theater person then or now would interpose these obstructions to sightlines where the scholars had placed them." Dessen claims that Hall and company refused to be swayed by "any evidence to the contrary" ("Globe" 196), but he overlooks the fact that there is no "evidence" for the pillars' downstage position. There are only inferences drawn from the Hollar and Norden illustrations. The only direct visual evidence of onstage pillars in an Elizabethan playhouse, from the Swan drawing, indicates that these posts should be placed upstage, roughly half-way to the *frons scenae*. This is not to claim that the Swan drawing is definitive but rather that "the actual scholastic facts," as Peter Hall points out, "are so vague and contradictory that almost anybody can make them mean anything" (quoted in Day 298).

Hall's complaint received the support of the broader theatrical community, including those performers who served in the Globe's "Artistic Directorate." Jon Greenfield, who took over as lead architect following the death of Theo Crosby in 1994, recalls that "actors in a group never agree on anything, and to hear them speaking with one voice was alarming" (94). Greenfield reluctantly agreed to negotiate a compromise. Hall argued that the columns should be positioned at least 12 feet from the front and 9½ feet from the edges of the stage. The construction team rejected Hall's plan as "untenable for designs in which a full stage cover was to be retained" (Nelsen 329), a condition that Greenfield claims is dictated by "historical evidence" (95). The designers countered with a proposal in which the columns would be set 8 feet 3 inches back from both the front edge and the sides. The new Artistic Director, Mark Rylance, agreed to this solution, but he was in an awkward situation. Sam Wanamaker's death in 1993 had left the Globe without artistic leadership. "When Sam died," Rylance notes, "we lost the leadership of a man who guided the Globe from many different perspectives," most importantly "the perspective of an actor" ("Playing" 169). Had Wanamaker been present in 1995, the players' concerns regarding the pillars might have been received more sympathetically.

Greenfield believed that the compromise placement of the stage posts adopted in 1996 had solved the problem. "The mistake of the workshop season of summer 1995," he wrote, "was not repeated" (94). Critics during the new Globe's first few seasons did not agree. 1997's *The Maid's Tragedy* was for Stephen Orgel "largely hidden behind [a] column" ("What's the Globe" 191). The *Independent* this same year identified "the two huge pillars on either side of the stage" as "the biggest problem for the directors and actors (and the audience if you are unlucky enough to be sitting in the wrong place)" ("Open House at the Globe" 3). John Peter noted that the stage posts "can get in the way and clog up the flow" ("Where the Audience" 16); and Michael Coveney complained that these columns "simply deaden the stage and leave only two strong areas for the actors to engage with themselves and the audience" (5). In 1998, Richard Proudfoot featured the pillars prominently in his list of the Globe's "discomforts and discontents" (228); and Lois Potter referred to them in 1999 as "the least-loved and most-discussed features of the Globe" ("Stage" 80).

Rylance acknowledged in 1998 that "there are still those who maintain the pillars are not quite right" and held out hope that "the stage will be changed in time" (quoted in Day 318). A minor adjustment was made to the columns in 1999. They remained in the same position but were mounted on "new slimmer bases" in an effort to make them less obtrusive (Potter, "Roman" 508). This may have done the trick, as published complaints have greatly diminished in recent years. Or perhaps critics and audiences have come to accept the pillars as actors have grown more skilful in minimizing sight-line problems. In any case, future Elizabethan reconstructions might want to avoid this difficulty altogether by adopting a half-stage roof, which is no less historically accurate than the full covering employed at the Bankside Globe. A rebuilt second Globe, such as is currently under consideration in Virginia, could also consider Hodges's model for this later amphitheater, in which a full-roof is supported without pillars. Whatever design a future reconstruction follows, its organizers would do well to solicit, early in the process, the input of those theater practitioners who will eventually work on its stage. "What case has scholarship on its own?" John Peter asks in considering such involvement. "We are, after all, talking about a building in which, pre-eminently, conception will have to serve function. In the theatre, nobody understands this better than actors and directors" ("Dramatic" 14).

Theatrical Production at the New Globe

PERFORMANCE at the new Globe has been, Alan Dessen writes, "driven by several not-always-compatible constituencies and agendas" ("Globe" 195). Authenticity had been the dominant rationale during the long period of planning and construction. After opening, this quest for historical accuracy merged with the demands of theatrical practice. While the Globe's historical construction meant that it could never be "just another theatre" (Gurr, "Rebuilding" 12), the scholars and architects who built the Globe had "to get used to the messier human pragmatics of practical day to day invention" (King 126). The task of balancing the legacy of early modern architecture with the demands of postmodern performance fell to Artistic Director Mark Rylance.

Rylance was an odd choice to head the company. The *Times* described him in 1991 as a new age eccentric who liked "to talk of circles of power, yin and yang and other matters mystical" ("Rubble, rubble" 37). Shortly before assuming his duties at the Globe, Rylance directed an infamous production of *Macbeth* at the Greenwich Theatre, which featured Jane Horrock urinating on stage during the sleepwalking scene. This Scottish tragedy did not inspire confidence in the director's ability. "The Globe is already in trouble," warned the *Daily Telegraph*. "If Rylance offers work like this, we can look forward to a fiasco of monumental proportions" (quoted in Hoggard 5). Against such expectations, the new Artistic Director adopted a level-headed approach to the challenges facing him. Rylance said of the Globe's mission, "Authenticity is certainly a purpose but not the *prime* purpose." While he acknowledged that historical accuracy "should have a place" in the playhouse's priorities, Rylance tied its value to a pragmatic agenda. "Authenticity," he believed, "is nothing unless it's authenticity that reveals better methods of doing things." Rylance realized that the Globe offered the possibility "of a closer marriage than other theatres have between actual practitioners and the academic world." But he also cautioned, "If the academic world is going to come in without an open mind, high handedly – as I feel some are – it won't be a happy marriage." At the same time, Rylance set limits to the kind of modernist experimentation he planned to tolerate at the Globe. "I'm all for people trying what they want on that stage, as long as they realize that this is a new kind of stage," he opined. "There's absolutely no point in building sets; they must do it minimally" (quoted in Day 279). Directors would frequently test the boundaries of this proscription.

The new Globe's productions during its first decade reflected the playhouse's distinct missions of historical recovery and postmodern expression. Rylance writes that he "considered two streams of work to be valid experiments, 'original practices' and also 'free-hand' work" ("Research" 105). The first of these was defined as "a disciplined, faithful exploration of as many original playing practices as possible or appropriate," while the second approach meant giving directors "a 'free hand' to explore the space with any and all of their modern theatre instincts, except electric lights and sound" (Rylance, Vazquez, and Chahidi 196). In reality, the distinction between these two schools was sometimes fluid. Alan Dessen, for instance, laments the use of the yard "for entrances, exits, processions or special effects" in productions billed as "original practice," because "no evidence exists" that early modern players employed this custom (" 'Original' " 48). Rylance also notes that " 'Free-hand' play revealed many aspects of how the space might have worked originally" ("Research 105), and that insights gleaned from "free-hand" stagings informed later "original practice" productions. He cites as an example Tim Carroll's successful "original practice" *Twelfth Night* in 2002, which developed largely from discoveries Carroll had made during his 2001 "free-hand" *Macbeth* (110).

Sometimes these two styles appeared in a single season. 1997 featured a *Henry V* that followed early modern precedents in costuming and all-male casting. This same year saw a *Winter's Tale* that employed a "freer, modern approach." It was "played on a carpet of red earth and with a tribal African feel" in its "striking costumes and design" (Taylor, Paul, review of *Henry V* and *The Winter's Tale* 12). The seasons of 1998–2000 continued to employ a mixture of these two staging paradigms, but Rylance notes that "in 2001 it was all 'free-hand' " (Rylance, Vazquez, and Chahidi 196). Lois Potter writes of this season, "the company apparently agreed not to treat the Globe as a set in its own right but to use it as if it were any other theater, apart from the fact that it happened to have a couple of big pillars on its stage." She observes that "all the directors seem to have been encouraged to do whatever they liked to conceal the fact that they were performing on a reconstructed Renaissance stage" (Potter, "2001 Season" 95). Success with Carroll's "original practices" *Twelfth Night* in 2002 led the Globe to pursue this method for its entire 2003 and 2004 seasons. Rylance writes of this period that "original practices" was "what audiences wanted and they continued to come with us as we demanded more and more of their imaginations." The approach was never purely historical, however, as the company was always, in Rylance's phrase, "mixing things up a bit" by integrating anachronistic techniques (Rylance, Vazquez, and Chahidi 197). In 2005, Rylance's final season, an "original practice" *Winter's Tale* shared the season with a "three-actor *Tempest*" and "a very 'free-hand' flying *Pericles*" (197). Since taking over as Artistic Director in 2006, Dominic Dromgoole has pursued a consistently "presentist position" on matters of staging, emphasizing original works written for the Globe space; "hybrid" costuming; and an "extensive (and some argue) 'inauthentic' use of the yard" (Carson and Cooper 180).

Paradoxically, an Elizabethan approach at the new Globe has sometimes seemed more modern. Georgina Brown identifies 2002's *Twelfth Night* as "the most historically authentic yet" of the company's efforts. But she also writes, "For the first time, a Globe production is not a dreary exercise in heritage Shakespeare but a valuable and hugely entertaining celebration." (76). More contemporary approaches, by contrast, have often appeared stale and lifeless. Richard Proudfoot writes of 1998's *The Honest Whore* by Dekker and Middleton that "twentieth-century tables and chairs, even a bulky sofa, were overused, robbing scenes of their physical energy by making characters sit down, and reducing the mobility needed if an in-the-round audience is to be fully engaged with the action" (216). 2001's high-concept *Macbeth* used for its design a "basic metaphor" which "seemed to be that of a New Year's or Halloween party, with the entire cast in tuxedos and long dresses" (Potter, "2001 Season" 102). According to Lyn Gardner, this production aspired to be "smoky and spellbinding" but was instead "just camp" (22). Nicholas De Jongh wrote that 2005's *Tempest* was "inspired by Carl Jung's psychological interpretation of alchemy" and used "five pages in the programme" to explain this approach. "I have never been so flummoxed by a Shakespeare production in my life," De Jongh proclaimed in his *Evening Standard* review (wittily subtitled "Shakespeare for the Jung"). This *Tempest* tried to "integrate analytical psychology, Renaissance Philosophy and pantomime knockabout" but "these elements mix about as well as chalk and beer" (29).

Just as modern notions regarding design and directorial concepts fall flat on the Globe stage, twentieth-century approaches to acting also appear out of place. Michael Cordner observes of Ade Sapara's performance as Camillo in 1997's *Winter's Tale* that the actor "was allowed to cling to old-style proscenium arch technique, his soliloquies and extended asides numbly addressed to some unpeopled spot in the middle distance. This fearful refusal to acknowledge our presence disabled his entire performance" (207). Proudfoot similarly writes that Jack Shepherd's 1998 Antonio in *The Merchant of Venice* "seemed to belong in a different production from the rest of the cast. His inward, underplayed and vocally strained performance turned the enigma of Antonio's sadness from the focal point of the scene into a gap at its center" (217). These and other criticisms suggest that the modern style of "Method Acting," which Hugh Richmond defines as "subjective, even solipsistic" ("Techniques" 161) in "its excessive self-centeredness" (175), does not work at the Globe. Instead, a more interactive approach that emphasizes "no physical or psychological dividing line between the playgoers and the players" (Kiernan 18) has proven more successful in this venue. As Matthew Scurfield, a veteran of several playhouse productions, notes, performance at the Globe "has to be shared with the audience ... As an actor, you realize you can't deliver soliloquies to yourself" (quoted in Kiernan 116).

Sensing a disconnect between Renaissance plays and postmodern performance styles, W. B. Worthen in 1989 defined Stanislavskian attempts to "to create character before – not with, not for, not among – a silent majority of disembodied spectators" as "undesirable – even unimaginable – on Shakespeare's more open, public, and interactive stage" ("Deeper" 454–5). Yet while Worthen here identifies the Method as inappropriate for Shakespearean interpretation, he does not in his 1999 article on the new Globe acknowledge the advances Rylance and company have made toward developing a more presentational approach ("Reconstructing" 33–45). Worthen's unwillingness to recognize the Globe's contribution to the development of an alternative performance style adheres to a larger pattern of ambivalence regarding the Bankside project. In 2003, Worthen comes close to acknowledging the Globe's achievements when he cites the playhouse's role in calling the "modern proscenium" model "very much into question as a paradigm for the 'classical ontology' of theatre" (*Force* 6). He continues, however, to see the Globe as an artistically regressive "monument to a writerly understanding of theatre" (25), which is obsessed with revealing "original Shakespearean meanings" (28). While Worthen seems open to some of the amphitheater's possibilities, he has apparently not yet, as Richard Paul Knowles recently paraphrased Stanley Kubrick, "Learned to Stop Worrying and Love" the Globe.

The new Globe possesses attributes not found in earlier Elizabethan-style theaters like Nugent Monck's Maddermarket or Tyrone Guthrie's Stratford Festival Stage. The steeply stacked galleries mean that the furthest distance between any spectator and the center of the stage is just 50 feet, closer even than in Guthrie's Ontario configuration. A significant portion of the audience, 700 among a total capacity of 1,500, stand in the yard around the stage. These "groundlings" are very close to the platform, and their standing posture encourages participation to an extent not expected by the new Globe's planners. The playhouse is open to the sky, and during daytime performances stage and auditorium are illuminated by the sun. In a radical inversion of twentieth-century practice, the covering over the stage means that audiences are better lit than performers. "It is the playgoers," Pauline Kiernan writes, "who are highly visible – to the actors on stage and, most significantly, to one another" (5). Floodlights are used for evening performances, but the intent of this "discreet background lighting" is to "simulate daylight conditions" (Gurr, *Rebuilding* 22). This means that the playhouse consistently employs the concept of "universal lighting" with which Guthrie flirted at various points in his career. Rylance claims that while "darkness divides and isolates an audience" shared illumination unites spectators with each other and with the actors, encouraging the public to "play along" (quoted in Kiernan 132). William Russell, who played the King of France in 1997's *Henry V*, considers the amphitheater unique. "Even when I've worked in the round," Russell says, "I've never had this wall of people so near and yet so far with the sea of groundlings all around." He defines this "living link with the audience" as the "key to the whole experience" (quoted in Kiernan 133).

The presence of playgoers as active participants means that a Globe performance will be, more so than in traditional theaters, what the audience wishes it to be. As Rylance observes, "We have to let go of the idea of controlling the reaction" (quoted in Day 318). Audiences love this sense of empowerment, and it is a major reason for the Globe's financial success. Scholars and journal critics, however, have frequently expressed reservations. One problem is that the participation of the pit (where tickets cost an affordable £5) has sometimes been based not exclusively on an honest and unmediated response to events on stage but also on a preconceived notion of what the behavior of "groundlings" should be. Ros King noted of Globe playgoers in 1997 that "whether or not the descriptions of rowdiness" traditionally attributed to early modern audiences are accurate, "the modern public certainly believes that this is how 'they' behaved." These spectators "regularly exchanged such information amongst themselves and, encouraged by newspaper reports, came prepared to play the part" (King 132).

Critics took particular exception to the public's xenophobic jeering of French characters during the inaugural season's *Henry V*. "They persisted in their cheerfully assumed jingoism throughout," complains David Schalk-wyk. "I found their behavior as an audience irritating, even offensive" (45). Michael Cordner similarly laments "the kind of anti-French laugh the audience was only too willing to provide and the production to encourage" (211). King moralizes, "As an audience member – on three occasions – opposed to gratuitous racial abuse I was deeply angered by feeling that I was being allowed only one option: to join in the booing" (133). But Yu Jin Ko suggests that the audience's behavior at *Henry V* did not reflect a mindless endorsement of yahoo militarism. Instead this vociferousness indicated recognition of the public's authority in enabling the theatrical experience, which in turn mirrors the broader role of the populace in manufacturing political consent. "Part of what the audience becomes conscious of," Ko writes, "is its power as makers of kings and queens" (119). In any event, audience reactions at the Globe have moderated since 1997. Reflecting on the playhouse's first decade, Mark Rylance describes a learning curve shared by spectators and performers. He writes that "the audience was learning how to be in the Globe just as we actors were learning. They were changing and growing and finding their feet with us and over time some of their cruder responses went away." "Eventually," Rylance concludes, "we had no one coming along pretending to be a member of an Elizabethan audience or throwing things" ("Research" 113).

Some observers nevertheless continue to resent those reactions of Globe spectators which do not jibe with conventional expectations. Rylance notes that "there is a lot more humour in a Globe audience than elsewhere" and claims that this added mirth is "something truly revealed in Shakespeare's writing by the reconstruction" ("Research" 109). Patricia Tatspaugh, however, laments of 2004's *Measure for Measure* that the audience "laugh[ed] at rape, deserted mothers, castration, death in several guises, clergy of dubious Christianity, Claudio's incarceration, and the mistreatment of prisoners. The comic reading compromised any attempt to address the[se] issues seriously" (474). Peter J. Smith agrees. "Call me a purist," he writes, "but *Measure for Measure* is not a funny play" (143). These critiques betray preconceptions that are based on twentieth-century interpretations. This problematic comedy is, despite Smith's protestations, in many ways "a funny play." Tatspaugh's comment on *Measure*'s finale, that "in any other production [Isabella] would have remained isolated from the other characters, and the closing image would have been dark or ambiguous" (474), illustrates that she has been influenced by recent theatrical interpretations that emphasize a sinister atmosphere. We can never know how *Measure for Measure* was originally received; but new Globe spectators, many of whom come to Shakespeare for the first time, might with their honest laughter provide a more "authentic" reaction than critics indoctrinated by contemporary readings. Rylance's assertion that Shakespeare "wanted us to laugh much more than we do at his plays" may be presumptive of authorial intent, but his observation that "We are still a bit Victorian in our reverence" ("Research" 109) rings true when considered alongside the comments of Tatspaugh and Smith. Nor does laughter necessarily negate a profound emotional response. As Tim Caroll observes:

> One of the most important lessons I learned at the Globe is that laughter from an audience does not necessarily mean, "We simply found that funny and we do not think anything serious could have happened." This is what some of our critics, in their shallow way, assumed was happening when the audience laughed at the "wrong" things. But … [often] it meant something much more profound. It meant that they had shared … a moment of beautiful revelation. (39–40)

Laughing at the darker moments in *Measure for Measure* is therefore not necessarily, as Smith asserts, an indication of "audience philistinism" (143).

Despite initial concerns, the contemporary Bankside public has readily accepted many Elizabethan conventions. The practice of males playing female roles, for instance, has been highly successful. Andrew Gurr warned against employing this device because it "creates some odd problems" in today's society. He was particularly wary of postmodern notions regarding "the erotic sexual politics of this cross-dressing" ("Staging" 165), which Gurr considers ahistorical. In practice, such casting has proven surprisingly uncontroversial. Toby Cockerell, who played Katherine in *Henry V*, notes that "some people didn't realize it was an all-male cast" (quoted in Kiernan 130). Globe audiences have even suspended their disbelief when women's roles were played not by adolescent boys, as would have been the case in Shakespeare's day, but by the company's middle-aged artistic director. Ian Hislop calls Mark Rylance's 2002 performance as Olivia "a revelation" (3), and Lois Potter uses this same accolade to describe Rylance's 1999 interpretation of Cleopatra ("Roman" 514). Such casting is not strictly authentic, but it illustrates how "original practices" at the Globe have led to new but historically inspired conventions that serve the needs of the twenty-first century. All-female productions exemplify this same trend. In 2003, for example, *Richard III* and *The Taming of the Shrew* were presented traditionally in terms of staging and costumes, but with exclusively distaff casts. Louis Muinzer wrote that this choice "served to underscore an important tenet of Shakespeare's Globe, that Theatre is not Biology, but Art – that it involves the creation of characters who define their own gender in the context of the stage" (66). How well this "important tenet" reflects the sexual dynamics of Shakespeare's own era is an open and probably unanswerable question. What matters is how this freedom of gender identity speaks to today's audiences and performers.

Mark Rylance's title, prior to stepping down in 2005, was "Artistic Director," but he was also a leading actor in the company. Potter likens him to "a great actor-manager in the old tradition" ("Distracted" 128), but this comparison is not completely accurate. Unlike Irving and Beerbohm Tree, Rylance always performed under a director, although this position (redefined as "Master of Play" since 1999) was not as powerful as at most modern theaters. Rylance's decision to lead the Globe from the stage produced mixed results. At times his performer's vanity may have harmed productions, as Michael Billington suggests in his review of 2003's *Richard II*. "One admires Rylance's energy," Billington writes, "but wishes that Tim Carroll, as Master of Play, also showed a bit more mastery of his lead player" (review of *Richard II* 28).

Rylance acknowledged in 2008 that he had not been able to balance the two roles of Artistic Director and actor "effectively enough" for him "to be able to stay" at the playhouse. He also notes, however, the advantages of his uniquely "Shakespearean" position as "someone who was sitting at the highest, most removed and protected level of Boardroom decision-making" while also being "out in the most visceral, rainy, afternoon matinees" (Rylance, Vazquez, and Chahidi 194). Paul Taylor is probably correct that "only one man could have launched Shakespeare's Globe and made it such a thriving theatrical concern. That man is Mark Rylance" (review of *The Tempest* 46).

Rylance's success was based on his ability to blend the historical authenticity of the theater's architecture with the contemporary sensibilities of its audience, as exemplified during his 2005 performance in an adaptation of Plautus titled *The Storm*. Maddy Costa writes that she was struck by an "eerily beautiful" sequence in which "Rylance conjure[d] up a lightning storm by encouraging the crowd to take pictures with their mobile phones." While this intrusion of modern gadgetry could not be less "authentic," it nevertheless captured the spirit of actor–audience engagement in an outdoor setting which is the essence of the Globe experience. This particularly postmodern incident of spectator participation also exemplifies Christie Carson's link between Elizabethan staging and shifting theatrical expectations in the digital age ("Democratising" 117). It was a moment, Costa writes, which "surely even cynics couldn't resist" (20).

SCHOLARLY advocates of Elizabethan reconstructions traditionally discounted the theatrical potential of such ventures. C. Walter Hodges wrote that the notion of a rebuilt early modern playhouse as "a commercially viable *theatre*" was "ill-judged, unpractical, and doomed to failure from the start." Audiences would, according to Hodges, "when they had had it once, have had it for good." Such spectators "would like it and they would recommend it to others, but they would not themselves feel any urgent compulsion to go back. Thereafter, they would go as before to more comfortable modern theatres" (Hodges, *Shakespeare's Second Globe* 95). The new Globe has disproved this logic. Against Andrew Gurr's prediction, the Bankside amphitheater has become "a rival to the National Theatre or the Royal Shakespeare Company" (*Rebuilding* 163). Mark Rylance's replacement, the second Artistic Director Dominic Dromgoole, initially dismissed Wanamaker's project. "It had all the chutzpah, energy and passion of Americans," he told *The New York Times* in May 2006. "As an English person, I sneered at it from afar." Dromgoole now admits that "theaters are constantly being built everywhere, but incredibly few work as well as this" (quoted in Riding 23). He calls the Globe's popular and economic achievements "unprecedented for a theatre" and "little short of a phenomenon" (quoted in "Shakespeare's Globe Makes £1.5 Million" 9).

The precise attraction of the Globe remains difficult to define. "The trouble is," says Rory Edwards, who played Orleans in 1997's *Henry V*, "if you start to try to analyze it you have to start talking about things like 'a higher consciousness' which can sound crap [*sic*]" (quoted in Kiernan 138). The Globe's magic may relate to the "tingle factor" of the playhouse's nearly authentic location (Schmitz 89); to Rylance's theory that the playhouse is geographically located "on a very powerful magnetic line [which] links us to the past" (Rylance quoted in "Rubble, rubble" 37); and perhaps even to the fact that, as Barry Day notes, the amphitheater stands in relation to the sun at "the same orientation as Stonehenge" (98). These imprecise and unscientific notions help explain why the Globe so "troubles the cultural materialists, and encourages their special condescension" (Wood 22). These postmodern scholars have also been piqued by the unreconstructed essentialism of the new Globe's founders.

Mark Rylance sees Shakespearean drama as "universal in application" ("Playing" 175), and Sam Wanamaker likewise believed that these plays "express the human condition in a form recognizable to all people" (Wanamaker quoted in Holderness, "Interview" 19). Terry Eagleton dismisses this view as "dismally regressive" (206) and "gullibly" humanist (204) because it denies the historical uniqueness of each artistic moment. Raphael Samuel, for similar reasons, condemns the Bankside playhouse as a "reactionary folly" (233). Critics are rightly suspicious that the desire to "provide theatrical experiences that reflect and enrich human nature" (Rylance, "Playing" 175) might mask a more sinister ideological project. Yet if they analyze too empirically the performance experience, scholars may overlook its fundamentally irrational origins. "The Globe," as James Wood writes, "is a triumph of excessive love" (22). Commenting on the company's tradition of concluding productions of Shakespeare with a spirited jig, Paul Taylor observes of 2004's *Romeo and Juliet*:

> It's a piercing sight here when, in a fresh twist, the bodies of the hero and heroine are tenderly taken down from the tomb and propped up facing each other for a long moment of eye-to-eye suspension. Then, as the music kicks in, those bodies, as it were, magically defrost, take each other by the hand and embark on the joyous, disciplined abandon of a dance that shifts from a poignant what-might-have-been to a what-is, in this strange alternative reality of the postscript jig. (review of *Romeo and Juliet* 11)

This extra-textual sequence recalls another Shakespearean resurrection, the coming to life of Hermione's statue at the end of *The Winter's Tale*, which similarly celebrates the healing power of art. This theme is not accessible from a theoretical perspective. Instead, "It is required," as Paulina tells us, "You do awake your faith" (*Winter's Tale* 5. 3. 115–16).

The new Globe has proven that the plays of Shakespeare (and theater in general) still have the power to affect a broad segment of the population. The success of the Bankside amphitheater combines with the earlier achievements of Guthrie, Monck, and Poel to point toward a continued revival of early modern staging in the twenty-first century.

Conclusion

ELIZABETHANISM has always been "old and new in the same breath" (Womack 79). As was often the case with the twentieth-century avant-garde, from Antonin Artaud's fascination with traditional Balinese dance to William Butler Yeats's emulation of Japanese Noh Theater, a progressive desire to create new forms in response to the pressures of modernity motivated the Elizabethanists' embrace of historical practices. Despite the claims of its detractors, the movement has never primarily pursued the fetishistic objective of freezing Shakespeare's plays in a distant and unobtainable era. From William Poel's *Troilus and Cressida*, which critiqued growing militarism on the eve of World War I, to Mark Rylance's 2005 *Tempest*, which deconstructed this play in a three-man production based on the philosophy of Carl Jung, Elizabethanists have frequently sought to connect their efforts to the zeitgeist of contemporary audiences. Nor are early modern practices inherently tied, as W. B. Worthen claimed in 1997, to an agenda of literary hegemony which minimizes the creative contributions of theater practitioners while revering the authorial intent of long-dead playwrights (*Authority* 33). While critics like Muriel St Clare Byrne sought to enlist the movement in the cause of textual fidelity, Elizabethanists from Poel onward consistently cut and adapted Renaissance plays to suit the needs of twentieth-century productions.

Even when initially drawn to early modern staging from a sense of literary duty, some practitioners have come to value the Elizabethan approach primarily for its impact on a contemporary public. Ralph Alan Cohen, the Professor of English who founded the American Shakespeare Center in Staunton, Virginia, writes of his company's early efforts, "we thought – rather grandly – that we were saving the plays, saving them from over-production and too-reverent treatment. What we discovered was that we were saving the audiences, too" ("Our Mission" 1). The expansion of Cohen's mission from "saving the plays" to also "saving the audiences" recalls performance scholar Diana Taylor's distinction between an "*archive* of supposedly enduring materials (i.e., texts, documents, buildings, bones)" and a more "ephemeral *repertoire* of embodied practice/knowledge (i.e., spoken language, dance, sports, ritual)" (19). Worthen suggests that, for scholars like Taylor, "the oppressive character of the *archive* of text-based drama" (Worthen, "Reading" 80) engages what we traditionally think of as "theater" – actors performing a predetermined script – as "a means of reinforcing dominant culture" (*Hamlet* 305).

While Taylor's stated goal of studying "the many ways in which the archive and the repertoire work to constitute and transmit social knowledge" (33) suggests a more dialectical approach than the simple "antitextualism" described by Worthen (*Hamlet* 305), she acknowledges that scholars in her discipline see scripted drama as "supposedly resistant to change" (Taylor 19). Very little of Taylor's book, *The Archive and the Repertoire: Performing Cultural*

Memory in the Americas, deals with what Worthen terms "the dramatic the-ater" (*Hamlet* 305), which suggests that she in fact sees little value in this art form. Cohen's formulation of serving, and indeed "saving," both the "audi-ences" and the "plays" hints at a paradigm in which the goals of dramatic theater need not exclude the progressive agenda of Performance Studies. His approach is also consistent with the socially engaged activities of earlier Elizabethanists, from Poel and Monck to Guthrie and Wanamaker. This is not to assert that early modern staging does not emphasize the verbal text. Cohen elsewhere writes of the new Globe and Blackfriars that "one major advantage of such stages is that they minimize the distractions for the words at the heart of these plays" ("Directing" 213). But this attention to language need not preclude societal engagement. Instead, the interpersonal delivery of dramatic text in a form unmediated by electronic technology serves a vital healing function in the new millennium.

Cohen describes the role of Elizabethan staging in combating alienation in twenty-first-century America. He asserts that "de Tocqueville's conviv-ial nation of citizens joined in countless fraternal, religious, political, and social groups" has been replaced by "a nation of individuals, suspicious of one another, more comfortable with IM'ing than with front porch social-izing, listening to iPods instead of attending concerts, withdrawing from all that is the life of a community." This high-tech isolation is a postmodern descendant of the industrial anomie against which William Morris rebelled, and Cohen thus reinforces the Elizabethan movement's status as the heir of Pre-Raphaelitism. He also follows Guthrie in championing early modern methods as an alternative to the soporific medium of cinema. "At a movie," Cohen writes, "the audience sits in the dark – individual and anonymous – and passively watches what a director, with the help of Industrial Light and Magic, has created." He contrasts this with his company's mission of "Theatre as Civic Engagement" ("Our Mission" 1), in which the public becomes an active participant in performance.

This echoes Christie Carson's assertion that the work of the new Globe fits "within the movement in the theatre more generally towards a more par-ticipatory model" ("Introduction" 33). Carson also notes how Elizabethan staging takes advantage of "the profound shift that has taken place in the perceptions and expectations of our current theatre audiences in response to a digital communications world" ("Democratising" 117). She cites the work of Philip Auslander to support the notion that postmodern culture has moved beyond a "televisual" paradigm (related to the cinematic dis-course described by Cohen) toward "a new digital aesthetic" that, because of the interactive quality of much new media, "demands at least a sense of democracy and fuller individual participation." The irony of this is not lost on Carson, who acknowledges that "the intimacy of the live theatrical experi-ence at Shakespeare's Globe, stripped of technological intervention" seems at first to have little connection to digital media. She nevertheless insists that, because of the high degree of participation that they afford their audi-ences, Globe performances "present an interesting and complex example of the way the new digitally dominant world has influenced audience expectations" (121). Although Carson's observations are novel, they conform to the long-established recognition that, as Cohen writes, Elizabethan staging "look[s] backward to an understanding of how the text and the stage worked together when the plays were first performed" while at the same time "look[ing] forward to a theatre freed of the nineteenth- and twentieth-century developments that in many ways have fettered it and its audiences" ("Directing" 212). Such staging gives us, as Shaw noted over a century ago, a "picture of the past" which is "really a picture of the future" (review of *Doctor Faustus* 37).

I hope that if scholars and critics come to see Elizabethan methods in this more progressive light they may become more sympathetic. Theater practitioners, however, have the greatest opportunity to impact the future of the movement. In the few remaining pages, I will therefore suggest ways in which they can utilize early modern conventions. The three principal features to consider are a permanent architectural set, universal lighting, and the placement of the audience in a deep-thrust configuration. The first two conditions are relatively easy to create. The third is more difficult, but is also the most important. One can place an architectural set on the stage of a proscenium theater, but such an arrangement offers a "pictur[e] of an Elizabethan stage rather than the thing itself" (Kennedy, *Looking* 157). This was the fate of William Poel's experiments with his Fortune fit-up at the Royalty Theatre, as well as of Ben Iden Payne's efforts at Stratford-on-Avon in the early 1930s and Tanya Moiseiwitsch's 1951 design for the Henriad at the Shakespeare Memorial Theatre. Recent attempts by the North Carolina Shakespeare Festival to employ an Elizabethan set within the proscenium confines of the High Point Theatre have been similarly unsatisfactory. Universal lighting is also easily achieved in a picture-frame configuration. All one need do is flood the playing area and leave the house lights up. The great distance between the back row and the stage of a typical proscenium theater, however, negates the connection between actors and audience that shared illumination can create. A deep-thrust configuration, on the other hand, achieves much of early modern staging's potential for immediacy, even without universal lighting. Illumination naturally spills from the stage onto the surrounding public so that "spectators can see one another around, and beyond, the more brightly lighted stage" (Guthrie, *New Theatre* 69), and performers become more aware of the audience.

This intimate and inclusive atmosphere creates a three-dimensional perspective that cannot be replicated by film and television. Besides the evidence provided by Tyrone Guthrie's successes and the triumphs of the new Globe, I have been convinced of the superiority of thrust staging by my own personal experience. As an actor on tour with the Shenandoah Shakespeare Express in 1993, I performed three Shakespearean plays in repertory for a full year. These stagings took place in a wide variety of venues. Sometimes we were able to use an existing thrust configuration or create one in an otherwise empty space (like a school gymnasium). Often, however, we were forced to play on stage in a proscenium house. We consistently found that audience configuration was the single biggest factor impacting the success of a given performance. When the audience was placed on three sides, the show almost inevitably went better, even when other elements (such as acoustics) had to be compromised.

Most theaters are still proscenium houses, however, and the average practitioner cannot afford to custom-build an Elizabethan space. For university directors, one solution is to use a smaller theater rather than a department's main stage. These "black-box" spaces can usually be configured in thrust. If performances are successful and demand grows, a Theater Department might consider permanently dedicating its black-box to an Elizabethan model. Assuming the ceiling is high enough, a second tier of seating could be built over the first. This would recreate the critical "stacked gallery" effect while simultaneously increasing public capacity and potential revenue. If the seated audience can be lifted sufficiently, the playing area could also be raised to create room for the kind of standing patrons who have been such a boon to the new Globe.

While historically authentic, a raised stage and the presence of "understanders" make it more difficult to use the auditorium for entrances and exits. Such vomitorium-style staging has been a constant hallmark of the Elizabethan movement. William Poel "blocked some entrances through the two aisles which divided the audience" in his 1895 *Comedy of Errors* at Gray's Inn and his 1896 *Two Gentlemen* at Merchant Taylors' Hall (O'Connor, *William Poel* 48). Guthrie used a similar approach in his Edinburgh productions of *The Thrie Estaits* and in his Stratford Festival configuration. Directors at the new Globe have also employed this tactic. Only five of the first thirteen productions staged at the amphitheatre did not feature "actors entering and exiting thought the yard." While Andrew Gurr claims that this practice has "no precedent" in early modern theatrical history (Gurr, "Enter" 32), it was proposed as historically accurate by Allardyce Nicoll in 1959, and Franklin J. Hildy considers Nicoll's theory to be a "legitimate alternative" (Review of *Dictionary* 92). In any case, twentieth-century Elizabethanists consistently used entrances through the house to increase the number of avenues onto and off of their stages.

This same desire to expand access to the playing area explains the removable stairway at Nugent Monck's Maddermarket Theatre and the multiple staircases in Guthrie's designs for Edinburgh and the two Stratfords. Using only the doors and discovery space in the *frons scenae* poses an interesting challenge, but most modern directors, including Poel, Monck, and Guthrie, have required more variety. Practitioners might therefore consider entrances through the house and/or staircases connecting the onstage balcony to the main playing area as acceptable contemporary adjuncts to Elizabethan staging. Early productions at the reconstructed Blackfriars, for instance, chafed at the natural restrictions of the playhouse's architecture, frequently bringing actors onstage through the house and sometimes repelling performers down from the balcony by means of ropes. It should be noted however that more recent stagings, such as a 2006 *Tempest* directed by Giles Block and Jim Warren's 2008 *King Lear*, have worked harmoniously within the limitations of the *frons scenae*. The desire for scenic variety regarding points of entry to the stage may therefore be more a function of presentist assumptions than essential need.

Many educational and professional directors do not have a black-box that can be configured in thrust. For them the only options are a proscenium theater or a non-theatrical space. The second alternative is generally preferable. The early modern convention of universal lighting means that companies do not have to transport bulky and complex electrical equipment in order to stage Shakespeare in a non-traditional venue. Most gymnasiums have moveable bleacher-style seating, which can be arranged in a three-quarter model. Acoustics in such spaces, however, are often dreadful because of echoes which limit intelligibility. Another option is to look for a "natural" configuration consisting of a balcony above one or more doorways, such as Poel found at Gray's Inn and Middle Temple Hall. Performances can be staged against this kind of backdrop with minimal set-up time, allowing for flexibility in scheduling.

Whether they choose to perform against an existing architectural backdrop or to construct their own set, practitioners interested in Elizabethan staging should consider working in the open air. Al fresco performance provides something of the connection to the natural world experienced in early modern amphitheaters. The glow of sunset on the face of young lovers at the conclusion of a romantic comedy, or the gathering gloom in the fifth act of a tragedy played at twilight, are effects not easily reproduced by the most elaborate stage technology. Universal lighting in such conditions means coordinating show times to coincide with daylight. Many outdoor Shakespeare festivals, such as those in Utah and Kentucky, give performances on long summer days when the sun still shines at curtain time. They often spend thousands of dollars for lighting effects that can only be appreciated after intermission, when darkness has descended. By beginning their performances an hour earlier, such companies could save a huge production expense while simultaneously experiencing the benefits of universal lighting.

Elizabethanism has come a long way since Herbert Beerbohm Tree derided William Poel as "an absolute crank – and an unsuccessful crank to boot" (quoted in Glick 16). Yet directors pursuing this style still meet resistance. Set and lighting designers are sometimes hostile to an approach that challenges the importance of their craft. Administrators often cannot understand why an alternative performance venue is necessary if a proscenium theater sits unused. Journal critics encountering early modern staging for the first time may not know what to make of it, and their reviews sometimes reflect incomprehension. But each passing year provides more successful examples of the Elizabethan approach. The movement has the logic of the marketplace on its side. It is less expensive to stage Shakespeare in this manner, and audiences often prefer it to the traditional proscenium format because of the increased opportunity for active participation. During the twentieth century, the paradigm shifted from an actor-manager's theater to a director's theater to a designer's theater. In the new millennium, Elizabethan staging may finally help create what Mark Rylance calls "an audience's theatre" ("Research" 108).

Works Cited

"100,000 at Chicago Greet Balbo Fleet." *New York Times* 16 July 1933: 1.

Appleyard, Bryan. "All the World's a Globe." *Sunday Times* 15 Jan. 2006: 8.

Archer, William. "The Elizabethan Stage." *Quarterly Review* 108 (1908): 442–71.

—— "The Elizabethan Stage Society." *Theatrical World of 1895*: 219–26.

—— Review of *Doctor Faustus*, dir. William Poel. *Theatrical World of 1896*: 204–12.

Atkinson, Brooks. "Bard in Canada." *New York Times* 3 July 1955: X1.

—— "Canada's Stratford." *New York Times* 19 July 1953: X1.

—— "Critic at Large." *New York Times* 20 Sept. 1963: 29.

—— Review of *All's Well That Ends Well*, dir. Tyrone Guthrie. *New York Times* 16 July 1953: 18.

—— Review of *Merchant of Venice*, dir. Tyrone Guthrie. *New York Times* 1 July 1955: 13.

—— Review of *Richard III*, dir. Tyrone Guthrie. *New York Times* 15 July 1953: 22.

—— Review of *Tamburlaine the Great*, dir. Tyrone Guthrie. *New York Times* 29 Jan. 1956: 97.

—— Review of *Taming of the Shrew*, dir. Tyrone Guthrie. *New York Times* 1 July 1954: 22.

—— Review of *Twelfth Night*, dir. Tyrone Guthrie. *New York Times* 4 July 1957: 16.

—— "Shakespeare and his Stage." *New York Times* 23 Aug. 1953: X1.

Auslander, Philip. "Is there Life after Liveness?" In *Performance and Technology: Practices of Virtual Embodiment and Interactivity*, edited by Sudan Broadhurst and Josephine Machon. Houndmills: Palgrave Macmillan, 2007: 194–7.

Aylmer, Felix. "The One That Got Away." *Drama* n.s. 86 (1967): 31–3.

Banham, Reyner. "How I learnt to live with the Norwich Union." *New Statesman* 6 March 1964: 372.

Barker, Harley Granville. "Alas, Poor Will!" *Listener* 17 (1937): 387–9; 425–6.

—— *Associating with Shakespeare*. London: Oxford University Press, 1932.

—— *The Exemplary Theatre*. New York: Benjamin Bloom, 1969 (originally published 1922).

—— "The Golden Thoughts of Granville Barker." *Play Pictorial* 21.126 (1912): 4.

—— *More Prefaces to Shakespeare*. Edited by Edward M. Moore. Princeton: Princeton University Press, 1974.

—— "A Note on Chapters xx and xxi of *the Elizabethan Stage*." *Review of English Studies* 1.1 (1925): 60–71.

—— *On Dramatic Method*. New York: Hill & Wang, 1956 (originally published 1931).

—— Preface. *Shakespeare's The Tragedie of King Lear*. The Players' Shakespeare [series]. London: E. Benn, 1927: ix–xcix.

—— *Prefaces to Shakespeare*. Edited by M. St Clare Byrne. 4 vols. Princeton: Princeton University Press, 1963 (originally published 1946).

—— "Reconstruction in the Theatre." *Times* 20 Feb. 1919: 11.

—— Review of *Physical Conditions of the Elizabethan Stage*, by W. J. Lawrence. *Review of English Studies* 4.14 (1928): 229–37.

—— "Shakespeare and Modern Stagecraft." *Yale Review* 15 (1926): 703–24.

—— "Shakespeare's Dramatic Art." In *A Companion to Shakespeare Studies*, edited by H. Granville-Barker and G. B. Harrison. New York: Doubleday, 1960: 44–87 (originally published 1934).

—— "Some Tasks for Dramatic Scholarship." *Essays by Divers Hands*. n.s. 3 (1923): 17–38.

—— "Souls on Fifth." In *"Richard Goes to Prison" and Other Stories*, edited by Eric Salmon. Madison, NJ: Farleigh Dickinson University Press, 2004: 57–78.

—— *The Study of Drama*. Cambridge: Cambridge University Press, 1934.

—— "The Theatre in Berlin." *Times* 19 Nov. 1910: 6 and 21 Nov. 1910: 12.

—— *The Use of the Drama*. Princeton: Princeton University Press, 1945.

Bartholomeusz, Dennis. *The Winter's Tale in Performance in England and America, 1611–1976*. Cambridge: Cambridge University Press, 1982.

Bassett, Kate. Review of *Romeo and Juliet*. *Independent on Sunday* 23 May 2004: 18.

Bate, Jonathan, and Russell Jackson. *Shakespeare: An Illustrated History*. Oxford: Oxford University Press, 1996.

Bauerlein, Mark. *The Dumbest Generation*. New York: Penguin, 2008.

Beerbohm, Max. *Around Theatres*. London: Rupert Hart-Davis, 1953.

—— *More Theatres, 1898–1903*. New York: Taplinger Publishing, 1969.

Bennett, Arnold. *The Journals of Arnold Bennett*. Edited by Frank Swinne. London: Penguin, 1954.

Bentley, Eric. "Theatre." *The New Republic* 13 Feb. 1956: 20.

Berry, Ralph. "The Reviewer as Historian." *Shakespeare Quarterly* 36.5 (1985): 594–7.

—— "Two Great Originals." *Shakespeare Quarterly* 35.3 (1984): 374–8.

Billington, Michael. Review of *Pericles*, dir. Kathryn Hunter. *Guardian* 6 June 2005: 24.

—— Review of *Richard II*, dir. Tim Carroll. *Guardian* 16 May 2003: 28.

Binnie, Eric. "Getting Richard Down: The Descent of Richard II into the Base Court: Reflections on a Lesson Plan for a Shakespeare, Theater, or Research Methods Class." In *Staging Shakespeare: Essays in Honor of Alan C. Dessen*, edited by Lena Cowen Orlin and Miranda Johnson-Haddad. Newark: University of Delaware Press, 2007: 81–98.

Blatherwick, Simon, and Andrew Gurr. "Shakespeare's Factory: Archeological Evaluations on the Site of the Globe Theatre at 1/15 Anchor Terrace, Southwark Bridge Broad, Southwark." *Antiquity* 66 (1992): 315–28.

Booth, John. "Shakespeare in the English Theatre." *Times Literary Supplement* 17 April 1919: 212.

Bridges-Adams, W. *The Lost Leader*. London: Sidgwick & Jackson, 1954.

—— *A Bridges Adams Letter Book*. Edited by Robert Speaight. London: Society for Theatre Research, 1971.

—— "Proscenium, Forestage and O." *Drama* 62 (1961): 24–8.

Bristol, Michael, and Kathleen McLuskie. "Introduction." In *Shakespeare and Modern Theatre: The Performance of Modernity*. London: Routledge, 2001: 1–19.

Brown, Georgina. Review of *Twelfth Night*, dir. Tim Carroll. *Mail on Sunday* 15 June 2002: 76.

Brown, Ivor. "*Ane Satyre of the Thrie Estates* at the Edinburgh Festival." In *Ane Satyre of the Thrie Estates* by Sir David Lindsay, edited by James Kinsley. London: Cassell & Co., 1954: 27–33.

—— "Salute to William Poel." *Saturday Review* 16 July 1927: 90–1.

—— "The Very Spot." *Theatre Arts Monthly* Nov. 1937: 873–80.

Brown, Ivor *et al.* Letter. *Times* 15 Oct. 1953: 9.

Brown, John Russell. "Modern Uses for a Globe Theatre." In *The Third Globe*, edited by C. Walter Hodges, S, Schoenbaum, and Leonard Leone. Detroit: Wayne State University Press, 1981: 14–28.

Bulman, James C. "Introduction." In *Shakespeare, Theory, and Performance*, edited by James C. Bulman. London: Routledge, 1996.

Burnett, Mark Thornton. *Filming Shakespeare in the Global Marketplace*. Houndmills: Palgrave Macmillan, 2007.

Butler, Martin. *The Stuart Court Masque and Political Culture*. Cambridge: Cambridge University Press, 2008.

Byrne, M. St Clare. "Fifty Years of Shakespearean Production, 1898–1948." *Shakespeare Survey* 2 (1949): 1–20.

—— "Foreword." In *Prefaces to Shakespeare*, by Harley Granville Barker. Vol. 1. Princeton: Princeton University Press, 1963: ix–xxiii.

—— "Introduction" to the Illustrations. In *Prefaces to Shakespeare*, by Harley Granville Barker. Vol. 2. Princeton: Princeton University Press, 1963: xii–xlvi.

—— "The Shakespeare Season at The Old Vic, 1958–9 and Stratford-Upon-Avon, 1959." *Shakespeare Quarterly* 10.4 (1959): 545–67.

—— "A Stratford Production: *Henry VIII.*" *Shakespeare Survey* 3 (1950): 120–9.

Calthrop, Dion Clayton, and Harley Granville Barker. *The Harlequinade: An Excursion*. Boston: Little, Brown & Company, 1918.

Carroll, Tim. " 'Practising Behaviour To His Own Shadow.' " In *Shakespeare's Globe: A Theatrical Experiment*, edited by Christie Carson and Farah Karim-Cooper. Cambridge: Cambridge University Press, 2008: 37–44.

Carson, Christie. "Democratising the Audience?" In *Shakespeare's Globe: A Theatrical Experiment*, edited by Christie Carson and Farah Karim-Cooper. Cambridge: Cambridge University Press, 2008: 115–26.

—— "Introduction" to Part I. In *Shakespeare's Globe: A Theatrical Experiment*, edited by Christie Carson and Farah Karim-Cooper. Cambridge: Cambridge University Press, 2008: 29–34.

Carson, Christie and Farah Karim-Cooper. "Introduction" to Part III. In *Shakespeare's Globe: A Theatrical Experiment*, edited by Christie Carson and Farah Karim-Cooper. Cambridge: Cambridge University Press, 2008: 177–82.

Carson, Neil. "Some Textual Implications of Tyrone Guthrie's 1953 Production of *All's Well That Ends Well.*" *Shakespeare Quarterly* 25.1 (1974): 52–60.

Casson, Lewis. "Foreword." In *Harley Granville Barker: Man of the Theatre, Dramatist and Scholar*, by C. B. Purdom. London: Salisbury Square, 1955: vii–viii.

—— "William Poel and the Modern Theatre." *Listener* 58 (1952): 56–8.

Chambers, E. K. *The Disintegration of Shakespeare*. London: Annual Shakespeare Lecture, 1924.

"Chicago to Mark Italo Balbo Day." *New York Times* 15 July 1933: 3.

"Chichester Festival Theatre Proposed." *Times* 4 Feb. 1960: 3.

Clarke, Cecil. "Stratford Ontario (Canada)." *World Theatre* 5 (1955–6): 42–50.

Clout, Martin. "Hester Thrale and the Globe Theatre." *New Rambler* 1993–4: 34–50.

Clurman, Harold. Review of *Tamburlaine*, dir. Tyrone Guthrie. *Nation* 4 Feb. 1956: 99.

Cohen, Nathan. "That Great First Night at Stratford." *Toronto Daily Star* 4 June 1966: 25.

—— "Stratford After Fifteen Years." In *Canadian Theatre History: Selected Readings*, edited by Don Rubin. Toronto: Copp Clark, 1996: 259–77.

—— "Theatre Today: English Canada." In *Canadian Theatre History: Selected Readings*, edited by Don Rubin. Toronto: Copp Clark, 1996: 228–37.

—— "Tyrone Guthrie – a Minority Report." *Queen's Quarterly* 62 (1955): 423–6.

Cohen, Ralph Alan. "Directing at the Globe and Blackfriars: Six Big Rules for Contemporary Directors." In *Shakespeare's Globe: A Theatrical Experiment*, edited by Christie Carson and Farah Karim-Cooper. Cambridge: Cambridge University Press, 2008: 211–25.

—— "Keeping the Promise in Compromise: Matching Mission and Money at Shakespeare Companies/Festival." *Shakespeare Association of America* Seminar Paper, 2006.

—— "Our Mission: Theatre as Civic Engagement." Unpublished statement of purpose for the American Shakespeare Center, distributed to auditioning actors in the 2005 and 2006 seasons.

Cook, R. W. "The Norwich Players." *John O'London's Weekly* 20 May, 1922: 212.

Cordner, Michael. "Repeopling the Globe: The Opening Season at Shakespeare's Globe, London 1997." *Shakespeare Survey* 52 (1999): 205–17.

Costa, Maddy. Review of *The Storm*, dir. Tim Carroll. *Guardian* 16 Aug. 2005: 20.

Coveney, Michael. Review of *The Winter's Tale*, dir. David Freeman. *Daily Mail* 6 June 1997: 5.

Craig, Edward. *Gordon Craig: The Story of his Life*. New York: Alfred A. Knopf, 1968.

Craig, Edward Gordon. *The Theatre – Advancing*. Boston: Little, Brown & Co., 1923 (originally published 1919).

—— *On the Art of the Theatre*. New York: Theatre Arts Books: 1960 (originally published 1911).

Crosby, Theo. *The Necessary Monument: Its Future in the Civilized City*. Greenwich, CT: New York Graphic Society, 1970.

Cushman, Robert. *Fifty Seasons at Stratford.* Toronto: McLellan & Stewart, 2002.

Darlington, W. A. "Visit to Scotland." *New York Times* 12 Sept. 1948: X3.

——"The Life and Times of Old Vic." *New York Times* 28 Apr. 1946: X1.

David, Richard. "Actors and Scholars: A View of Shakespeare in the Modern Theatre." *Shakespeare Survey* 12 (1959): 76–87.

Davies, Robertson. "The Director." In *Renown at Stratford* by Tyrone Guthrie, Robertson Davies, and Grant MacDonald. Toronto: Clarke, Irwin & Co., 1953: 35–40.

——"Foreword." In *Stratford: The First Thirty Years* by John Pettigrew and Jamie Portman. Toronto: Macmillan of Canada, 1985: xiii–xv.

——"The Genius of Dr. Guthrie." *Theatre Arts* 6.3 (1956): 28–30; 90.

——"The Merchant of Venice." In *Thrice the Brinded Cat Hath Mewed* by Robertson Davies, Tyrone Guthrie, Boyd Neel, Tanya Moiseiwitsch. Toronto: Clark, Irwin & Co., 1955: 46–80.

——"Through Ritual to Romance." *Saturday Night* 1 Aug. 1953: 7–8.

——"The Taming of the Shrew." In *Twice Have the Trumpets Sounded: A Record of the Stratford Shakespearean Festival in Canada 1954* by Tyrone Guthrie, Robertson Davies, and Grant MacDonald. Toronto: Clark, Irwin & Co., 1954: 19–60.

Day, Barry. *This Wooden O: Shakespeare's Globe Reborn.* New York: Limelight, 1998.

De Jongh, Nicholas. Review of *The Tempest*, dir. Tim Carroll. *Evening Standard* 19 May 2005: 29.

De Marinis, Marco. "The Dramaturgy of the Spectator." Trans. Paul Dwyer. *Drama Review.* 31:2 (1987): 100–14.

Dessen, Alan C. "Globe Matters." *Shakespeare Quarterly* 49.2 (1998): 195–203.

——" 'Original Practices': A Theatre Historian's View." In *Shakespeare's Globe: A Theatrical Experiment*, edited by Christie Carson and Farah Karim-Cooper. Cambridge: Cambridge University Press, 2008: 45–53.

"Dinner to Mr. William Poel." *Times* 9 Nov. 1912: 11.

Drakakis, John. "Theatre, Ideology, and Institution: Shakespeare and the Roadsweepers." In *The Shakespeare Myth*, edited by Graham Holderness. Manchester: Manchester University Press, 1988: 24–41.

The Drama in Adult Education. A Report by the Adult Education Committee of the Board of Education, being Paper No. 6 of the Committee. London: His Majesty's Stationery Office, 1926.

Duffus, R. L. "The Fair: A World of Tomorrow." *New York Times* 28 May 1933: SM1.

Duncan-Clark, S. J. "1934 World's Fair Bigger and Better." *New York Times* 20 May 1934: E7.

Dymkowski, Christine. *Harley Granville Barker: A Preface to Modern Shakespeare.* Washington, DC: Folger Shakespeare Library, 1986.

Eagleton, Terry. "Afterword." In *The Shakespeare Myth*, edited by Graham Holderness. Manchester: Manchester University Press, 1988: 203–8.

Edinborough, Arnold. "Canada's Permanent Elizabethan Theatre." *Shakespeare Quarterly* 8.4 (1957): 511–14.

Egan, Gabriel. "Reconstructions of the Globe: A Retrospective." *Shakespeare Survey* 52 (1999): 1–16.

"Elizabethan Tourney at Shakespeare's England." *Times* 3 July 1912: 11.

Elliot, Michael. "Cathleen Nesbitt talks to Michael Elliot about Harley Granville Barker." *Listener* 13 (1972): 52.

Farjeon, Herbert. *The Shakespearean Scene.* London: Hutchinson & Co., 1949.

Forsyth, James. *Tyrone Guthrie: A Biography.* London: Hamish Hamilton, 1976.

Fowler, Eric. "A Maddermarket Centenary." *East Anglian Magazine* 37 (1978): 348–50.

Freeman, Neil. "Introduction to *The Tragedie of Macbeth.*" In *The Tragedie of Macbeth* by William Shakespeare, prepared and annotated by Neil Freeman. New York: Applause Books, 1998: xxix–lvii.

French, William W. "A Kind of Courage: *King Lear* at the Old Vic, London, 1940." *Theatre Topics* 3.1 (1993): 45–55.

Garber, Marjorie. "Shakespeare as Fetish." *Shakespeare Quarterly* 41.2 (1990): 242–50.

Gardner, Lyn. Review of *Macbeth,* dir. Tim Carroll. *Guardian* 8 June 2001: 22.

Garnett, Edward. "Mr. Poel and the Theatre." *English Review* July 1913: 589–95.

——"*Troilus and Cressida* and the Critics." *Contemporary Review* 103 Jan.–June 1913: 184–90.

Gaunt, William. *The Pre-Raphaelite Dream.* New York: Schocken Books, 1966.

"Germany and Shakespeare." *Times* 4 March 1915: 5.

Gielgud, John. *Early Stages.* London: Falcon Press, 1948.

——*Stage Directions.* New York: Random House, 1963.

Gilbert, Sandra M., and Susan Gubar. *No Man's Land*: New Haven: Yale University Press, 1988.

Glick, Claris. "William Poel: His Theories and Influence." *Shakespeare Quarterly* 23.1 (1964): 15–25.

Granville Barker and his Correspondents. Edited by Eric Salmon. Detroit: Wayne State University Press, 1986.

Greenfield, Jon. "Design as Reconstruction: Reconstruction as Design." In *Shakespeare's Globe Rebuilt*, edited by J. R. Mulryne and Margaret Shewring. Cambridge: Cambridge University Press, 1997: 81–96.

Greif, Karen. " 'If This Were Played Upon a Stage': Harley Granville Barker's Shakespeare Productions at the Savoy Theatre, 1912–1914." *Harvard Library Bulletin* 28 (1980): 117–45.

Grein, J. T. Review of *The Winter's Tale*, dir. Harley Granville Barker. *Sunday Times* 22 Sept. 1912: 7.

Griffiths, Trevor. "Tradition and Innovation in Harley Granville Barker's *A Midsummer Night's Dream*." *Theatre Notebook* 30 (1976): 78–87.

Groome, Margaret. "Stratford and the Aspirations for a Canadian National Theatre." In *Shakespeare in Canada: "a world elsewhere"?*, edited by Diana Brydon and Irena R. Makaryk. Toronto: University of Toronto Press, 2002: 108–36.

——"Affirmative Shakespeare at Canada's Stratford Festival." *Essays in Theatre* 17.2 (1999): 139–63.

Grotowski, Jerzy. *Towards a Poor Theatre.* New York: Simon & Schuster, 1968.

Guest, L. Haden. "An Orgy of Frohman and the Bijou Theatre." *New Age* 16 May 1907: 49.

Gurr, Andrew. "Enter through the Yard." *Around the Globe* 11 (1999): 32–3.

——"The First Plays at the New Globe." *Theatre Notebook* 51.1 (1997): 4–7.

——"Preface." In *Shakespeare's Globe: A Theatrical Experiment*, edited by Christie Carson and Farah Karim-Cooper. Cambridge: Cambridge University Press, 2008: 29–36.

——"Rebuilding the Globe with the Arts of Compromise." *Shakespeare Jahrbuch* 126 (1990): 11–23.

——*The Shakespearean Stage, 1574–1642.* 2nd edition. Cambridge: Cambridge University Press, 1980.

——"Shakespeare's Globe: A History of Reconstructions and Some Reasons For Trying." In *Shakespeare's Globe Rebuilt*, edited by J. R. Mulryne and Margaret Shewring. Cambridge: Cambridge University Press, 1997: 26–47.

——"Staging at the Globe." In *Shakespeare's Globe Rebuilt*, edited by J. R. Mulryne and Margaret Shewring. Cambridge: Cambridge University Press, 1997: 159–68.

Gurr, Andrew, with John Orrell. *Rebuilding Shakespeare's Globe.* New York: Routledge, 1989.

"Guthrie Inspects his New Theatre." *New York Times* 11 Sept. 1962: 28.

"Guthrie Theater: Celebrating the Shared Act of Imagining." *Guthrie Theatre.* Guthrie Theatre. Web. 1 April 2006.

Guthrie, Tyrone. "10 Favorites from Shakespeare." *New York Times* 15 May 1964: 18.

——"An Audience of One." In *Directors on Directing*, edited by Toby Cole and Helen Krich Chinoy. New York: Bobbs-Merrill, 1963: 245–56.

——"The Case for 'Live' Theatre." *New York Times* 29 April 1962: 210.

——"Dominant Director." *New York Times* 21 Aug. 1960: X1.

——"Do We Go to the Theater for Illusion?" *New York Times* 16 Jan. 1966: X3.

—— "First Shakespeare Festival at Stratford, Ontario." In *Renown at Stratford* by Tyrone Guthrie, Robertson Davies, and Grant MacDonald. Toronto: Clarke, Irwin & Co., 1953: 1–33.

—— "*Hamlet* in Modern Dress." *Drama Survey* 3 (1963): 73–7.

—— "Introduction to *The Tempest*." In *Shakespeare's Ten Great Plays* by William Shakespeare. New York: Golden Press, 1962: 443–52.

—— *In Various Directions: A View of Theatre.* New York: Macmillan, 1965.

—— *A Life in the Theatre.* New York: McGraw Hill, 1959.

—— "A Long View of the Stratford Festival." In *Twice Have the Trumpets Sounded: A Record of the Stratford Shakespearean Festival in Canada in 1954*, by Tyrone Guthrie, Robertson Davies, and Grant MacDonald. Toronto: Clark, Irwin & Co., 1954: 143–93.

—— "A Modern Producer and the Plays." In *The Living Shakespeare*, edited by Robert Gittings. New York: Barnes & Noble, 1968: 85–92.

—— *A New Theatre.* New York: McGraw-Hill, 1964.

—— "Shakespeare at Stratford, Ontario." *Shakespeare Survey* 8 (1955): 127–31.

—— "Theatre at Minneapolis." In *Actor and Architect*, edited by Stephen Joseph Toronto: University of Toronto Press, 1964: 30–47.

—— *Theatre Prospect.* London: Wishart & Co., 1932.

—— "Why I Refuse Invitations to Direct on Broadway." *New York Times* 20 Dec. 1964: X5.

"*Hamlet* at Elsinore." *Times* 2 June 1937: 14.

Hansen, Niels B. "Gentlemen You Are Welcome to Elsinore: *Hamlet* in Performance at Kronborg Castle, Elsinore." In *Shakespeare and his Contemporaries in Performance*, edited by Edward J. Esche. Burlington, VT: Ashgate, 2000: 109–119.

Harrison, G. B. Review of *Harley Granville Barker: Man of the Theatre, Dramatist and Scholar*, by C. B. Purdom. *Shakespeare Quarterly* 8.2 (1957): 229–31.

Hawkes, Terence. "Bardbiz." In *Meaning by Shakespeare*. London: 1992: 141–53.

Hewes, Henry. "Astringency in Ontario." *Saturday Review of Literature.* 4 June 1955: 26.

Hildy, Franklin J. "A Minority Report on the Decisions of the Pentagram Conference." *Shakespeare Bulletin* 10.4 (1992): 9–12.

—— "Playing Spaces for Shakespeare: The Maddermarket Theatre, Norwich." *Shakespeare Survey* 47 (1994): 81–90.

—— "Reconstructing Shakespeare's Theatre." In *New Issues in the Reconstruction of Shakespeare's Theatre*, edited by Franklin J. Hildy. New York: Peter Long, 1990: 1–37.

—— Review of *A Dictionary of Stage Directions in English Drama, 1580–1642*, by Alan C. Dessen. *Theatre Survey* 42 (2001) 91–3.

—— "Reviving Shakespeare's Stagecraft." PhD diss. Northwestern University, 1980.

—— *Shakespeare at the Maddermarket: Nugent Monck and the Norwich Players.* Ann Arbor: UMI Research Press, 1986.

—— "Why Elizabethan Spaces?" *Theatre Symposium* 12 (2004): 98–120.

Hills, Ross. "The Maddermarket Theatre, Norwich." *Tabs* 19 (1961): 17–24.

Hislop, Ian. Review of *Twelfth Night*, dir. Tim Carroll. *Sunday Telegraph* 16 June 2002: 3.

Hodges, C. Walter. *The Globe Restored.* London: Ernest Benn, 1953.

—— *Shakespeare's Second Globe: The Missing Monument.* London: Oxford University Press, 1973.

—— "What is Possible: The Art and Science of Mistakes." In *New Issues in the Reconstruction of Shakespeare's Theatre*, edited by Franklin J. Hildy. New York: Peter Long, 1990: 39–53.

Hoggard, Liz. "The Will of the People." *Observer* 2 Feb. 2003: 5.

Holbrook, David. *A Play of Passion.* London: W. H. Allen, 1978.

Holderness, Graham. "Bardolatry: Or, the Cultural Materialist's Guide to Stratford-upon-Avon." In *The Shakespeare Myth*, edited by Graham Holderness. Manchester: Manchester University Press, 1988: 2–15.

—— "Interview with Sam Wanamaker." In *The Shakespeare Myth*, edited by G. Graham Holderness. Manchester: Manchester University Press, 1988: 16–23.

Hotspur (pseud.). "Pericles at Norwich." *Shakespeare Pictorial* Jan. 1930: 15.

House, A. W. "The Miracle of Stratford." *Industrial Canada* 54.5 (1953): 60–5.

Howard, Tony. "Blood on the Bright Young Things: Shakespeare in the 1930s." In *British Theatre Between the Wars, 1918–1939*, edited by Clive Barker and Maggie B. Gale. Cambridge: Cambridge University Press, 2000: 135–61.

Hunt, Hugh. "Granville-Barker's Shakespearean Productions." *Theatre Research* 10 (1969): 44–9.

—— *The Live Theatre*. London: Oxford University Press, 1962.

—— "The Maddermarket Theatre, Norwich." *Theatre World* Jan. 1934: 48.

"Improvements at the Old Vic." *Times* 6 Sept. 1937: 10.

Innes, Christopher. *Edward Gordon Craig: A Vision of the Theatre*. Singapore: Harwood Academic Publishers, 1998.

Jackson, Barry. Review of *William Poel and the Elizabethan Revival*, by Robert Speaight. *Shakespeare Quarterly* 6.1 (1955): 89–90.

Jacoby, Susan. *The Age of American Unreason*. New York: Vintage, 2009.

Kennedy, Dennis. *Granville Barker and the Dream of Theatre*. Cambridge: Cambridge University Press, 1985.

—— *Looking at Shakespeare*. Cambridge: Cambridge University Press, 1993.

—— "Shakespeare and the Global Spectator." *Shakespeare Jahrbuch* 131 (1996): 50–64.

Kiernan, Pauline. *Staging Shakespeare at the New Globe*. New York: St Martin's Press, 1999.

"*King Lear* for the Stage." *Times Literary Supplement* 23 June 1927: 437.

King, Ros. "Staging the Globe." In *Where Are We Now in Shakespearean Studies?*, edited by W. R. Elton and John M. Mucciolo. Aldershot: Ashgate, 1999: 121–41.

Knight, G. Wilson. *Shakespearian Production*. London: Faber & Faber, 1964.

—— "The Producer as Hamlet." Review of *Prefaces to Shakespeare Volume VI*, by Harley Granville Barker. *Times Literary Supplement* 26 July 1974: 794–5.

—— Review of *A Companion to Shakespeare Studies*, edited by Harley Granville Barker and G. B. Harrison. *Scrutiny* 3 (1934): 306–14.

Knowles, Richard Paul. "*The Death of a Chief*: Watching for Adaptation; or, How I Learned to Stop Worrying and Love the Bard." *Shakespeare Bulletin* 25.3 (2007): 53–65.

—— "From Nationalist to Multinational: The Stratford Festival, Free Trade, and the Discourses of Intercultural Trade." *Theatre Journal* 47.1 (1995): 19–41.

—— "The Legacy of the Festival Stage." *Canadian Theatre Review* 54 (1988): 39–45.

—— "Shakespeare, 1993 and the Discourses of the Stratford Festival, Ontario." *Shakespeare Quarterly* 45.2 (1994): 211–25.

—— "Shakespeare, Voice, and Ideology: Interrogating the Natural Voice." In *Shakespeare, Theory, and Performance*, edited by James C. Bulman. London: Routledge, 1996: 92–112.

Ko, Yu Jin. "A Little Touch of Harry in the Light: *Henry V* at the New Globe." *Shakespeare Survey* 52 (1999): 107–19.

Lanier, Douglas. "Drowning the Book: *Prospero's Books* and the Textual Shakespeare." In *Shakespeare, Theory, and Performance*, edited by James C. Bulman. London: Routledge, 1996: 187–209.

Lee, Sidney L. "The Topical Side of the Elizabethan Drama." *Transactions of the New Shakespeare Society* ser. 1 no. 11 (1887): 1–35.

Leiter, Samuel L. *From Belasco to Brook: Representative Directors of the English-Speaking Stage*. New York: Greenwood Press, 1991.

Lewalski, Barbara K. "Milton's *Comus* and the Politics of Masquing." In *The Politics of the Stuart Court Masque*, edited by David Bevington and Peter Holbrook. Cambridge: Cambridge University Press, 1998: 301–25.

Long, Tania. "Around the Globe with Guthrie." *New York Times* 15 Jan. 1956: X1.

Loper, Robert Bruce. "Shakespeare 'All of a Breath.'" *Quarterly Journal of Speech* 39.2 (1953): 193–7.

Lundstrom, Rinda F. *William Poel's Hamlet's: The Director as Critic*. Ann Arbor: UMI Research Press, 1984.

MacCarthy, Desmond. *Drama*. New York: Benjamin Bloom, 1971.

—— Review of *Love's Labour's Lost*, dir. Nugent Monck. *Speaker* 28 April 1906: 91.

MacDonald, Jan. " 'An Unholy Alliance': William Poel, Martin Harvey, and *The Taming of the Shrew*." In *The Taming of the Shrew: Critical Essays*, edited by Dana E. Aspinall. New York: Routledge, 2002: 307–15.

"Maddermarket Theatre, Norwich: Twenty-fifth Anniversary." *Times* 18 Sept. 1946: 8.

Maloon, James. "From Beast to Mad Beast: A Further Look at Tyrone Guthrie's *Tamburlaine*." *Theatre Survey* 18.1 (1977): 1–29.

Marshall Norman. "Guthrie Here, There and Everywhere." *Drama Survey* 3 (1963): 96–103.

—— *The Other Theatre*. London: John Lehman, 1947.

—— *The Producer and the Play*. London: Macdonald & Co., 1967.

Martin, John. "The Dance: In Chicago." *New York Times* 9 Sept. 1934: X2.

Mazer, Cary M. "Historicizing Alan Dessen: Scholarship, Stagecraft, and the 'Shakespeare Revolution.' " In *Shakespeare, Theory, and Performance*, edited by James C. Bulman. London: Routledge, 1996: 149–67.

—— *Shakespeare Refashioned: Elizabethan Plays on Edwardian Stages*. Ann Arbor: University of Michigan Press, 1981.

McCarthy, Lillah. *Myself and My Friends*. New York: E. P. Dutton & Co., 1933.

McCormack, Helen. "Exit the Man who Turned Shakespeare on its Head." *Independent* 19 May 2005: 3.

McDonald, Jan. " 'The Promised Land of the London Stage' – Acting Style at the Court Theatre London 1904–7." In *The Role of the Actor in the Theatrical Reform of the Late 19th and Early 20th Centuries*, edited by Milan Lukes. Seventh International Congress on Theatre Research, 3–8 September, 1973. Prague: Univerzita Karlova, 1976: 75–89.

McVicar, Leonard H. "From Little Acorns … Stratford's Shakespearean Festival." *Recreation* 48 (1955): 110–11.

Menzer, Paul. "Afterward: Discovery Spaces? Research at the Globe and Blackfriars." In *Inside Shakespeare: Essays on the Blackfriars Stage*, edited by Paul Menzer. Selinsgrove: Susquehanna University Press, 2006: 223–30.

Miller, Burgoyne. "Theatre to Remember: The Maddermarket, Norwich." *Bookman* 79 (1931): 326.

"Miscasting Handicaps Robeson's Othello." *Times* 8 April 1959: 14.

Moiseiwitsch, Tanya. "Problems in Design." *Drama Survey* 3 (1963): 113–16.

Monck, Nugent. "The Maddermarket Theatre." *Drama* n.s. 12 (1949): 19–21.

—— "The Maddermarket Theatre." *War-Time Drama* (Oct. 1944): 3–4.

—— "The Maddermarket Theatre and the Playing of Shakespeare." *Shakespeare Survey* 12 (1959): 71–5.

—— "The Maddermarket Theatre." *Theatre Arts Monthly* 15.7 (1931): 581–2.

—— "Shakespeare and the Amateur." *Listener* 17 Feb. 1937: 321–4.

Montreux, V. V. "Short Thoughts about 'The Glorious Moment.' " *Shakespeare Bulletin* 26.4 (2008): 65–75.

Moore, Edward M. "Introduction." In *More Prefaces to Shakespeare*, by Harley Granville Barker. Princeton: Princeton University Press, 1974: 8–18.

—— "William Poel." *Shakespeare Quarterly* 23.1 (1972): 21–36.

Morgan, Charles. "Underneath Big Ben." *New York Times* 4 Feb. 1934: X3.

Morris, William. "Art and the People." In *An Anthology of Pre-Raphaelite Writings*, edited by Carolyn Hares-Stryker. New York: New York University Press, 1997: 285–8.

Mottram, Ralph Hale. *The Maddermarket Theatre*. Norwich: A. E. Soman Co., 1936.

"Mr. Nugent Monck." Obituary. *Times* 23 Oct. 1958: 17.

"Mr. William Poel: A Tribute on his 80th Birthday." Letter. *Times* 22 July 1932: 10.

Muinzer, Louis. "The 2003 Season at Shakespeare's Globe." *Western European Stages* 15.3 (2003): 65–70.

Nelsen, Paul. "Positing Pillars at the Globe." *Shakespeare Quarterly* 48.3 (1997): 324–5.

Nesbitt, Cathleen. *A Little Love and Good Company*. Owings Mills, MD: Stemmer House, 1977.

"The Norwich Players: Amateurs in Shaw and Shakespeare." *Times* 20 Aug. 1920: 8.

"The Norwich Players' New Theatre." *Times* 27 Sept. 1921: 8.

"The Norwich Players: Maddermarket Theatre to be Enlarged." *Times* 6 Sept. 1949: 8.

"Nugent Monck of Norwich." *Times* 9 Dec. 1952: 9.

O'Connor, Marion F. "Theatre of Empire: 'Shakespeare's England' at Earl's Court, 1912." In *Shakespeare Reproduced: The Text in History and Ideology*, edited by Jean E. Howard and Marion F. O'Connor. New York: Methuen, 1987: 68–98.

—— " 'Useful in the Year 1999': William Poel and Shakespeare's 'Build of Stage.' " *Shakespeare Survey* 52 (1999): 17–32.

—— *William Poel and the Elizabethan Stage Society*. Cambridge: Chadwyck-Healey, 1987.

Odell, George C. D. *Shakespeare from Betterton to Irving*. Vol. 2. New York: Charles Scribner's Sons, 1920.

Olivier, Laurence. *On Acting*. New York: Simon & Schuster, 1986.

"Open House at the Globe but Glyndebourne it's Not." *Independent* 7 June 1997: 3.

Orgel, Stephen. *The Illusion of Power: Political Theater in the English Renaissance*. Berkeley: University of California Press, 1975.

—— "What's the Globe Good For?" *Shakespeare Quarterly* 49.2 (Summer 1998): 191–4.

Orrell, John. "The Accuracy of Hollar's Sketch of the Globe." *Shakespeare Bulletin* 11.2 (1993): 5–9.

—— "Designing the Globe." In *Shakespeare's Globe Rebuilt*, edited by J. R. Mulryne and Margaret Shewring. Cambridge: Cambridge University Press, 1997: 51–65.

—— "The Original Globe." In *Rebuilding Shakespeare's Globe*, by Andrew Gurr with John Orrell. New York: Routledge, 1989: 93–123.

Palmer, John. Review of *Hamlet*, dir. William Poel. *Saturday Review* 31 Jan. 1914: 139–40.

—— Review of *A Midsummer Night's Dream*, dir. Harley Granville Barker. *Saturday Review* 14 Feb. 1914: 202–3.

—— Review of *Twelfth Night*, dir. Harley Granville Barker. *Saturday Review* 23 Nov. 1912: 637–9.

—— Review of *The Winter's Tale*, dir. Harley Granville Barker. *Saturday Review* 28 Sept. 1912: 391–2.

Payne, Ben Iden. *A Life in a Wooden O*. New Haven: Yale University Press, 1977.

Pearce, Brian. "Granville Barker's Production of *The Winter's Tale* (1912)." *Comparative Drama* 30, 3 (Fall 1996): 395–411.

Peck, Seymour. "Tyrone Guthrie's Three-Ring Circus." *New York Times* 23 Dec. 1956: 105.

Peter, John. "Dramatic Conflict." *Sunday Times* 1 Oct. 1995:14.

—— "Where the Audience is King." *Sunday Times* 15 June 1997: 16.

Peters, Sally. *Bernard Shaw: The Ascent of the Superman*. New Haven: Yale University Press, 1996.

Pettigrew, John, and Jamie Portman. *Stratford: The First Thirty Years*. Toronto: Macmillan of Canada, 1985.

Poel, William. *An Account of the Elizabethan Stage Society: Printed for the Society*. London: Elizabethan Stage Society, 1898.

—— "An Elizabethan Playhouse: The Norwich Enterprise." *Manchester Guardian* 1 Oct. 1921: 7.

—— "*Hamlet* Retold." *Saturday Review*. 27 Jan. 1914: 73.

—— "Hindu Drama on the English Stage." *Asiatic Quarterly Review* n.s. 1 (April 1913): 319–31.

—— "History in Drama." *Manchester Guardian* 30 Sept. 1925: 5.

—— "Incompetent Actors." *Times* 13 Oct. 1930: 8.

—— "The King in 'Hamlet.'" *Pall Mall Gazette* 3 May 1913:5; 5 May 1913: 7.

—— *Monthly Letters*. London: T. Werner Laurie, 1929.

—— "Mr. Gordon Craig." *Westminster Gazette* 19 Dec. 1921: 12.

—— *The Playhouse of the Sixteenth Century*: London: Elizabethan Stage Society, 1905.

—— "Picture Pedantry." *Manchester Playgoer* 1 (1912): 60–2.

—— "Reply to Mr. Archer." *Daily Chronicle* 11 July 1908: 8.

—— "The Responsibilities of Playgoers." *Playgoers' Review* 15 April 1891: 109–12.

—— "The Right to Kill." Letter to the Editor. *Times* 6 Nov. 1929: 15.

—— *Shakespeare in the Theatre*. New York: Benjamin Bloom, 1913.

—— "Shakespeare Memorial Theatre." Points from Letters. *Times* 7 Nov. 1927: 10.

—— "Shakespeare on the Stage in the Elizabethan Manner." *Times Literary Supplement* 2 June 1905: 178.

—— "Shakespeare's 'Prompt Copies.' " *Times Literary Supplement* 3 Feb. 1921: 75.

—— "The Staging of Shakespeare" *Fortnightly Review* n.s. 68 (July 1900): 355–6.

—— "Trade in Drama." *Contemporary Review* 106 (July/Dec. 1914): 209–14.

—— "The Truth about the Stage." *Contemporary Review* 115 (Jan./June 1919): 563–7.

—— *What's Wrong with the Stage*. London: George Allen & Unwin, 1920.

Potter, Lois. "The 2001 Globe Season: Celts and Greenery." *Shakespeare Quarterly* 53.1 (2002): 95–105.

—— "This Distracted Globe: Summer 2000." *Shakespeare Quarterly* 52.1: 124–34.

—— "Roman Actors and Egyptian Transvestites." *Shakespeare Quarterly* 50.4 (1999): 508–17.

—— "A Stage Where Every Man Must Play a Part?" *Shakespeare Quarterly* 50.1 (1999): 74–86.

Price, Joseph G. *The Unfortunate Comedy: A Study of "All's Well That Ends Well" and its Critics*. Toronto: University of Toronto Press, 1968.

"Protection for Dramatists" (Letter). *Saturday Review* 21 Feb. 1914: 236–7.

Proudfoot, Richard. "The 1998 Globe Season." *Shakespeare Survey* 52 (1999): 215–28.

Purdom, C. B. *Harley Granville Barker: Man of the Theatre, Dramatist and Scholar*. London: Salisbury Square, 1955.

"A Regisseur Reflects" (interview with Tyrone Guthrie). *Times* 10 April 1959: 14.

Review of *The Alchemist*, dir. Tyrone Guthrie. *Times* 29 Nov. 1962: 16.

Review of *All's Well That Ends Well*, dir. Tyrone Guthrie. *Times* 22 April 1959: 16.

Review of As *You Like It*, dir. Nugent Monck. *Times* 27 Sept. 1921:8.

Review of *Hamlet*, dir. Martin Harvey. *Saturday Review* 3 Jan. 1920: 4.

Review of *Hamlet*, dir. Tyrone Guthrie. *Times* 6 Jan. 1937: 10.

Review of *Hamlet*, dir. William Poel. *Athenaeum* 31 Jan. 1914: 171–2.

Review of *Hamlet*, dir. William Poel. *Era* 3 March 1900: 7.

Review of *Hamlet*, dir. William Poel. *Times* 22 Feb. 1900: 7.

Review of *Hamlet*, dir. William Poel. *Times* 28 Jan. 1914: 9.

Review of *Henry V*, dir. Tyrone Guthrie. *Times* 7 April 1937: 14.

Review of *Henry VIII*, dir. Tyrone Guthrie. *Times* 25 July 1949: 7.

Review of *Henry VIII*, dir. Tyrone Guthrie. *Times* 30 March 1950: 8.

Review of *Henry VIII*, dir. Tyrone Guthrie. *Times* 7 May 1953: 12.

Review of *King John*, dir. Tyrone Guthrie. *Times* 9 July 1941: 6.

Review of *King Lear*, dirs. Harley Granville Barker and Lewis Casson. *Manchester Guardian* 17 April 1940: 6.

Review of *King Lear*, dirs. Harley Granville Barker and Lewis Casson. *Times* 16 April 1940: 4.

Review of *A Midsummer Night's Dream*, dir. Harley Granville Barker. *Era* 11 Feb. 1914: 13.

Review of *A Midsummer Night's Dream*, dir. Harley Granville Barker. *Illustrated London News* 144 (14 Feb. 1914): 252.

Review of *A Midsummer Night's Dream*, dir. Harley Granville Barker. *Times* 7 Feb. 1914: 8.

Review of *A Midsummer Night's Dream*, dir. Tyrone Guthrie. *Times* 28 Dec. 1937: 10.

Review of *A Midsummer Night's Dream*, dir. Tyrone Guthrie. *New Statesman and Nation*. 1 Jan. 1938: 148.

Review of *A Midsummer Night's Dream*, dir. Tyrone Guthrie. *Times* 27 Dec. 1951: 2.

Review of *Richard II*, dir. Tyrone Guthrie. *Times* 22 April 1933: 8.

Review of *Richard II*, dir. William Poel. *Times* 13 Nov. 1899: 5.

Review of *Richard III*, dir. Tyrone Guthrie. *Times* 14 Sept. 1944: 6.

Review of *Richard III* and *All's Well That Ends Well*, dir. Tyrone Guthrie. *Time* (magazine) 27 July 1953: 32.

Review of *Tamburlaine the Great*, dir. Tyrone Guthrie. *Times* 25 Sept. 1951: 8.

Review of Taming *of the Shrew*, dir. Nugent Monck. *Times* 27 Sept. 1927: 12.

Review of *The Three Estates*, dir. Tyrone Guthrie. *Times* 26 Aug. 1948: 6.

Review of *Troilus and Cressida*, dir. Tyrone Guthrie. *New York Times* 27 Dec. 1956: 21.

Review of *Troilus and Cressida*, dir. William Poel. *Times* 11 Dec. 1912: 10.

Review of *Twelfth Night*, dir. Harley Granville Barker. *Times* 16 Nov. 1912: 10.

Review of *Twelfth Night*, dir. Harley Granville Barker. *Illustrated London News* 141 (23 Nov. 1912): 780.

Review of *Twelfth Night*, dir. Tyrone Guthrie. *Times* 19 Sept. 1933: 10.

Review of *Twelfth Night*, dir. Tyrone Guthrie. *Times* 24 Feb. 1937: 12.

Review of *Two Gentlemen of Verona*, dir. Harley Granville Barker. *Era* 16 April 1904: 12.

Review of *Two Gentlemen of Verona*, dir. William Poel. *Times* 21 April 1910:12.

Review of *The Winter's Tale*, dir. Harley Granville Barker. *Athenaeum* 28 Sept. 1912: 351.

Review of *The Winter's Tale*, dir. Harley Granville Barker. *Times* 23 Sept. 1912: 7.

Richmond, Hugh. *King Henry VIII*. Manchester: Manchester University Press, 1994.

—— "Techniques for Reconstructing Elizabethan Staging." In *New Issues in the Reconstruction of Shakespeare's Theatre*, edited by Franklin J. Hildy. New York: Peter Long, 1990: 159–84.

Riding, Alan. "Shakespeare's Globe is an American's Experiment Thriving in London." *New York Times* 10 May 2006: 23.

Rigby, Charles. *Maddermarket Mondays: Press Articles Dealing with the Famous Norwich Players*. Norwich: Roberts & Co., 1933.

Rossi, Albert. *Astonish Us in the Morning: Tyrone Guthrie Remembered*. London: Hutchinson & Co., 1977.

—— *Minneapolis Rehearsals: Tyrone Guthrie Directs "Hamlet"*. Berkeley: University of California Press, 1970.

Rowell, George. *The Old Vic Theatre: A History*. Cambridge: Cambridge University Press, 1993.

"Rubble, Rubble." *Times* 17 May 1991: 37.

Rutherston, Albert. "Decoration in the Art of the Theatre." *Monthly Chapbook* 1.2 (Aug. 1919): 1–33.

Rylance, Mark. "Playing the Globe: Artistic Policy and Practice." In *Shakespeare's Globe Rebuilt*, edited by J. R. Mulryne and Margaret Shewring. Cambridge: Cambridge University Press, 1997: 169–76.

—— "Research, Materials, Craft: Principles of Performance at Shakespeare's Globe." In *Shakespeare's Globe: A Theatrical Experiment*, edited by Christie Carson and Farah Karim-Cooper. Cambridge: Cambridge University Press, 2008: 103–14.

Rylance, Mark, Yolanda Vazquez, and Paul Chahidi. "Discoveries from the Globe Stage." In *Shakespeare's Globe: A Theatrical Experiment*, edited by Christie Carson and Farah Karim-Cooper. Cambridge: Cambridge University Press, 2008: 194–210.

Salenius, Elmer W. *Harley Granville Barker*. Boston: Twayne Publishers, 1982.

Salmon, Eric. *Granville Barker: A Secret Life*. Rutherford, NJ: Fairleigh Dickinson University Press, 1984.

Salter, Denis. "Acting Shakespeare in Postcolonial Space." In *Shakespeare, Theory, and Performance*, edited by James C. Bulman. London: Routledge, 1996: 113–32.

Samuel, Raphael. *Theatres of Memory*. Vol. I. New York: Verso, 1994.

Schafer, Elizabeth. *Lilian Baylis: A Biography*. Hatfield: University of Hertfordshire Press, 2006.

Schalkwyk, David. "From Globe to Globalization: Shakespeare and Disney in the Postmodern World." *Journal of Literary Studies* 15.1 (1999): 33–65.

Schmitz, Johanna. "Location as a Monumentalizing Factor at Original and Reconstructed Shakespearean Theatres." *Theatre Symposium* 12 (2004): 86–97.

Shakespeare, William. *Hamlet*. Edited by Edward Hubler. New York: Signet Classic, 1963.

——*Macbeth*. Edited by G. K. Hunter. New York: Penguin Books, 1967.

——*The Winter's Tale*. Edited by Frank Kermode. New York: Signet Classic, 1963.

"Shakespeare at the Maddermarket: Mr. Nugent Monck on his Productions." *Times* 8 Jan. 1953: 9.

"Shakespeare on the Modern Stage." *Times* 25 Oct. 1905: 8.

"Shakespeare at Norwich: Mr. Nugent Monck's Experience." *Times* 6 Sept. 1957: 5.

"Shakespeare as the Sleeping Beauty." *Times Literary Supplement* 2 June 1905: 178.

"Shakespeare under Shakespearean Conditions." *Times* 11 Nov. 1893: 4.

"Shakespeare's Globe Makes £1.5 Million Profit without any Subsidy." *Daily Telegraph* 12 Jan. 2006: 9.

"Shakespeare's Plays at Norwich." *Times* 18 March 1925: 12.

"The Shape of the Globe." *Renaissance Drama Newsletter* Supplement 8 (Autumn 1987) [entire supplement devoted to this article].

Shapiro, I. A. "The Bankside Theatres: Early Engravings." *Shakespeare Survey* 1 (1948): 25–37.

Shaughnessy, Robert. "Dreams of England." In *World-wide Shakespeares: Local Appropriations in Film and Performance*, edited by Sonia Massai. London: Routledge, 2005: 112–21.

——*The Shakespeare Effect: A History of Twentieth-Century Performance*. New York: Palgrave Macmillan, 2002.

Shaw, George Bernard. "Aside." In *Myself and My Friends*, by Lillah McCarthy. New York: E. P. Dutton & Co., 1933: 1–8.

——*Collected Letters, 1911–1925*. Edited by Dan Lawrence. New York: Viking, 1985.

——"John Bull's Other Island." In *Modern Irish Drama*, edited by John P. Harrington. New York: W. W. Norton & Co., 1991: 119–203.

——*Letters to Granville Barker*. Edited by C. B. Purdom. New York: Theatre Arts Books, 1957.

——*Shaw On Shakespeare*. Edited by Edwin Wilson. New York: Applause, 1961.

——Review of *Doctor Faustus*, dir. William Poel. *Saturday Review* 11 July 1896: 36–7.

——Review of *The Spanish Gypsy*, dir. William Poel. *Saturday Review* 16 April 1898: 521.

Shepard, Richard F. "Guthrie to Leave Minneapolis." *New York Times* 28 July 1964: 19.

Shepherd, Simon, and Peter Womack. *English Drama: A Cultural History*. Oxford: Blackwell Publishers, 1996.

Shumlin, Herman. "Give my Regards to Sir Tyrone." *New York Times* 24 Jan. 1965: X3.

"Sir Tyrone Guthrie." Obituary. *Times* 17 May 1971:14.

Smith, Peter J. Review of *Measure for Measure*, dir. John Dove. *Shakespeare Bulletin* 22.4 (2004): 143–6.

Soman, Mariette. *The Norwich Players: A History, an Appreciation and a Criticism*. Norwich: Mariette Soman at the Book House, St Andrews, 1920.

Somerset, J. Alan. *The Stratford Festival Story*. New York: Greenwood Press, 1991.

"Southern Route Safer, Says Balbo." *New York Times* 17 July 1933: 15.

Speaight, Robert. *William Poel and the Elizabethan Revival*. Cambridge, MA: Harvard University Press, 1954.

——*Shakespeare on the Stage*. Boston: Little, Brown & Co., 1973.

Stasio, Marilyn. "Wanamaker's Wild Idea Takes Wing." *American Theatre* 14.7 (1997): 54–5.

Stephenson, Andrew. "The Maddermarket Theatre." *Theatre Arts Magazine* 7.3 (1923): 203–12.

——"The Maddermarket Theatre." *Theatre Arts Monthly* 12.4 (1928): 288–90.

——*The Maddermarket Theatre Norwich*. Norwich: Soman-Wherry Press, 1971.

Stern, Tiffany. *Rehearsal from Shakespeare to Sheridan*. Oxford: Clarendon Press, 2000.

——" 'You that walk i'th Galleries': Standing and Walking in the Galleries of the Globe Theatre." *Shakespeare Quarterly* 51.2 (2000): 211–16.

Styan, J. L. "Elizabethan Open Staging: William Poel to Tyrone Guthrie." *Modern Language Quarterly* 37 (1976): 211–20.

——*The Shakespeare Revolution*. Cambridge: Cambridge University Press, 1977.

"A Talk about the Stage with Granville Barker." *New York Times* 26 July 1914: SM9.

Tatspaugh, Patricia. "Shakespeare Onstage in England, 2004–2005. *Shakespeare Quarterly* 56.4 (2005): 448–78.

Taylor, Diana. *The Archive and the Repertoire: Performing Cultural Memory in the Americas*. Durham, NC: Duke University Press, 2003.

Taylor, Gary. *Reinventing Shakespeare: A Cultural History from the Restoration to the Present*. New York: Weidenfeld & Nicolson, 1989.

Taylor, Paul. Review of *Henry V*, dir. Richard Olivier, and *The Winter's Tale*, dir. David Freeman. *Independent* 9 June 1997: 12.

—— Review of *Romeo and Juliet*, dir. Tim Carroll. *Independent* 27 May 2004: 11.

—— Review of *The Tempest*, dir. Tim Carroll. *Independent* 20 May 2005: 46.

"The Theatres." *Times* 28 April 1952:9.

Tree, Herbert Beerbohm. "The Staging of Shakespeare: A Defense of Public Taste." *Fortnightly Review* n.s. 68 (July 1900): 53–66.

Trewin, J. C. *Shakespeare on the English Stage, 1900–1964*. London: Barrie & Rockliff, 1964.

Truman, Nevill. "Norwich Maddermarket Theatre: An Account of its History and Activities." *Amateur Stage* (May 1929): 144.

"Weather Unkind to British Players." *Time* 3 June 1937: 12.

White, Martin. "William Poel's Globe." *Theatre Notebook* 53.3 (1999): 146–62.

Whittaker, Herbert. *The Stratford Festival, 1953–1957*. Toronto: Clarke, Irwin & Co., 1958.

"William Poel." *Times Literary Supplement* 11 July 1952: 453.

Williamson, Audrey. *Old Vic Drama: A Twelve Years' Study of Plays and Players*. New York: Macmillan, 1949.

—— *Old Vic Drama 2: 1947–1957*. London: Salisbury Square, 1957.

Wilson, Jean. *The Archaeology of Shakespeare*. Stroud: Alan Sutton Publishing, 1995.

Winter, William. *Shakespeare on the Stage*. Third Series. New York: Benjamin Bloom, 1969.

Wolfe, William. *From Radicalism to Socialism*. New Haven: Yale University Press, 1975.

Womack, Peter. "Notes on the 'Elizabethan' Avant-Garde." In *Shakespeare and the Twentieth Century*, edited by Jonathan Bate, Jill L. Levenson, and Dieter Mehl. Newark: University of Delaware Press, 1996: 75–84.

Wood, James. "Do We Love the Bard Not Wisely but Too Well?" *Observer* 25 Aug. 1996: 22.

Worsley, T. C. "The Stratford Lear." *New Statesman and Nation*. 25 July 1953: 100.

Worthen, W. B. (William). "Deeper Meanings and Theatrical Technique: The Rhetoric of Performance Criticism." *Shakespeare Quarterly* 40.4 (1989): 441–5.

—— "*Hamlet* at Ground Zero: The Wooster Group and the Archive of Performance." *Shakespeare Quarterly* 59.3 (2008): 303–22.

—— "Reading the Stage." *Shakespeare Bulletin* 25.4 (2007): 69–83.

—— "Reconstructing the Globe Constructing Ourselves." *Shakespeare Survey* 53 (1999): 33–45.

—— *Shakespeare and the Authority of Performance*. Cambridge: Cambridge University Press, 1997.

—— *Shakespeare and the Force of Modern Performance*. Cambridge: Cambridge University Press, 2003.

—— "Shakespearean Performativity." In *Shakespeare and Modern Theatre: The Performance of Modernity*, edited by Michael Bristol, Kathleen McLuskie and Christopher Holmes. London: Routledge, 2001: 117–41.

—— "Staging 'Shakespeare': Acting, Authority, and the Rhetoric of Performance." In *Shakespeare, Theory, and Performance*, edited by James C. Bulman. London: Routledge, 1996: 12–28.

Wright, Louis B., and Virginia A. LaMar. "Introduction." In *Troilus and Cressida*, edited by Louis B. Wright and Virginia A. LaMar. The Folger Library General Reader's Shakespeare. New York: Washington Square Press, 1966: vii–xx.

Index

Note: While individual directors of new Globe and reconstructed Black-friars Playhouse (American Shakespeare Center) productions are listed in the index, their productions are catalogued under the "New Globe" and "Black-friars Playhouse (reconstruction)" headings.